KT-582-806

Olympic Event Organization

Olympic Event Organization

Eleni Theodoraki

ELSEVIER

AMSTERDAM BOSTON HEIDELBERG LONDON NEW YORK OXFORD
PARIS SAN DIEGO SAN FRANCISCO SINGAPORE SYDNEY TOKYO
Butterworth-Heinemann is an imprint of Elsevier

Butterworth-Heinemann is an imprint of Elsevier
Linacre House, Jordan Hill, Oxford OX2 8DP, UK
30 Corporate Drive, Suite 400, Burlington, MA 01803, USA

First edition 2007

British Library Cataloguing in Publication Data
A catalogue record for this book is available from the British Library

Library of Congress Cataloging-in-Publication Data
A catalog record for this book is available from the Library of Congress

ISBN: 978-0-7506-8476-7

For information on all Butterworth-Heinemann publications
visit our web site at books.elsevier.com

Typeset by Charon Tec Ltd (A Macmillan Company), Chennai, India
www.charontec.com

Printed and bound in Hungary
07 08 09 10   10 9 8 7 6 5 4 3 2 1

Working together to grow
libraries in developing countries

www.elsevier.com | www.bookaid.org | www.sabre.org

ELSEVIER   BOOK AID
International   Sabre Foundation

Contents

Contents

List of figures

List of tables

Acronyms

ANOC	Association of National Olympic Committees
ANOCA	Association of National Olympic Committees of Africa
AOB	Athens Olympic Broadcasting
AOC	Australian Olympic Committee
AOF	Australian Olympic Foundation
ATHOC	Athens Organising Committee for the 2004 Olympic Games
BINGO	Business INGO
BOA	British Olympic Association
BOB	Beijing Olympic Broadcasting Co., Ltd
BOBICO	Beijing Olympic Games Bid Committee
BOC	Brazilian Olympic Committee
BOCOG	Beijing Organising Committees for the Olympic Games
BPC	Brazilian Paralympic Committee
CAS	Court of Arbitration for Sport
CO-RIO	Rio Organizing Committee of the 2007 Pan American Games
COC	Canadian Olympic Committee
CONI	Comitato Olimpico Nazionale Italiano
CPC	Canadian Paralympic Committee
CPC	Communist Party of China
DCMS	Department of Culture Media and Sport
DDS	Directorate for the Development of Sochi
EOC	European Olympic Committees
EU	European Union
EYOD	European Youth Olympic Days
EYOF	European Youth Olympic Festival
FIFA	Fédération Internationale de Football Association
GLA	Greater London Authority
GSSE	Games of the Small States of Europe
HMT	Her Majesty's Treasury
IBC	International Broadcasting Centre
IF	International Federation
ILO	International Labour Organization
INGO	International Non-Governmental Organization
IOC	International Olympic Committee
IOC T & MS	IOC Television and Marketing Services SA

IOSD	International Organization of Sport for the Disabled
IPC	International Paralympic Committee
IPSF	International Paralympic Sports Federation
IT	Information Technology
ITVR	International Television and Radio
MSI	La Maison du Sport International SA
LDA	London Development Agency
LOCOG	London Organizing Committee for the 2012 Olympic Games
MOC	Main Operations Centre
NFS	National Sport Federation
NOC	National Olympic Committee
NPC	National Paralympic Committees
NSW	New South Wales
OBO	Olympic Broadcasting Organization
OBS	Olympic Broadcasting Services SA
OBSG	Olympic Board Steering Group
OCA	Olympic Council of Asia
OCOG	Organising Committee of the Olympic Games
ODA	Olympic Delivery Authority
OF	Olympic Foundation
OGG	Olympic Games Group
OGKS	Olympic Games Knowledge Services SA
OM	Olympic Museum
ONOC	Oceania National Olympic Committees
OPAB	Olympic Photographic Archive Bureau
OSO	Olympic Sport Organization
OTAB	Olympic Television Archive Bureau
PASO	Pan American Sports Organization
RHB	Right holder broadcaster
RF	Russian Federation
ROC	Russian Olympic Committee
SINGO	Sporting INGO
SLOC	Salt Lake City Organizing Committee for the 2002 Olympic Games
SOCOG	Sydney Organizing Committee for the 2000 Olympic Games
SOOC	Sochi Olympic Organizing Committee for the 2012 Olympic Games
SPE	Specific Purpose Society
TfL	Transport for London
TOP	The Olympic Partners
TOROG	Turin Organizing Committee for the 2010 Olympic Games
UNEP	United Nations Environment Programme
USOC	United States of America Olympic Committee
VANOG	Vancouver Organizing Committee for the 2010 Olympic Games
VMD	Venue Management Department
WADA	World Anti-Doping Agency
WFSGI	World Federation for Sporting Goods Industry

Acknowledgements

In line with this book's focus on organizations involved with the organization of the Olympic event I feel that my acknowledgements ought to refer to organizations where I received help and support in the process of my investigations on the topic.

Colleagues at the following organizations allowed me opportunities that were invaluable in the development of my understanding. I am grateful for their generosity.

Athens Organizing Committee for the 2004 Olympic Games, Greece.
Barcelona Organizing Committee for the 1992 Olympic Games, Spain.
Beijing 2008 Olympic Games Bid Committee, China.
Beijing Organizing Committee for the 2008 Olympic Games, China.
British Olympic Association, UK.
British Olympic Foundation, UK.
British Paralympic Association, UK.
Centre d'Estudis Olímpics, Spain.
Centre for Olympic Studies and Research, UK.
Centre for Olympic Studies, Beijing University of Physical Education, China.
China Sports Museum, China.
Comitato Olimpico Nazionale Italiano, Italy.
Department of Physical Education and Sport Science, Aristotelion University, Greece.
Event Knowledge Services, Switzerland.
Fédération Internationale de Football Association, Switzerland.
Housing Centre of City of Vancouver, Canada.
Hellenic Olympic Committee, Greece.
International Olympic Academy, Greece.
International Olympic Academy Participant's Association, worldwide.
International Olympic Committee, Switzerland.
London Organizing Committee for the 2012 Olympic Games, UK.
Master Exécutif en Management des Organisations Sportives, MEMOS team, worldwide.
Olympic Studies Centre, Switzerland.

Research Team Olympia, Johannes Gutenberg- Universität Mainz, Germany.
School of Sport and Exercise Sciences, Loughborough University, UK.
Shanghai Institute of Physical Education, China.
Sydney Organizing Committee for the 2000 Olympic Games, Australia.
Turin Organizing Committee for the 2006 Olympic Games, Italy.
Vancouver Organizing Committee for the 2010 Olympic Games, Canada.

Introduction

Sporting events provide wonderful opportunities for communities to social-
ize and in the long history of mankind numerous forms of such events have
evolved to serve particular purposes. In ancient Egypt small-scale archery
events were held in the presence of the Pharaohs and ancient Olympia
flooded with people every four years as pilgrims and athletes gathered to
honour their gods and celebrate excellence in sporting competitions.
Centuries later, Pierre de Coubertin used the revival of the ancient Olympic
Games to instil a sense of purpose among the French youth and help improve
the nation's performance in and outside the sports fields. As the event gained
popularity and grew in size more elaborate management structures were
required to deliver it.

Planning for and hosting a sports event includes, as one would expect, a
number of steps from bidding to post-games evaluation and the Olympic
Games are no exception in that event planning principles apply overall.
There are, however, certain particularities created by the complexities of the
scale of the Olympic Games and by the ideological foundations of the
Olympic Movement that shape its cultural expression. The modern winter
and summer Olympic Games are big and complex enough in scale to be
named mega-events using tremendous aggregate resources (human, physical, financial as well as intangible) for their timely execution and the effects
of such investments are long lived and significant even for host countries
with strong national economies. Their organization has always been
demanding of skills and expertise and when Pierre de Coubertin revived the
Games he also led the formation of a body to lead them and guide their
organization by the host city – Athens being the first one in 1896. This body
of no-paid volunteers was the International Olympic Committee (IOC) and
it was established in 1894, two years prior to the 1896 Athens Games under the
presidency of Greek Dimitrios Vikelas. The Olympic Games grew gradually
in the decades and have also been affected by world events like the two
world wars, decolonization in Africa and Asia, the growth of Nazism and
Fascism in Europe, the cold war and, more recently, the collapse of communism and the growth in fear of terrorist activity around the globe. Although

early leaders in the revival of the ancient games focussed on the noble aspects of human endeavour through sporting competition, the notion of amateurism and gentlemanship, since antiquity, the Olympic Games have been affected by scandals of corruption, unethical competition, bribery as well as extreme competition between cities (that were sending competitors and officials to Ancient Olympia). Such phenomena continued in the history of the Olympic Games till their demise in 393 BC when Roman Emperor Theodosious forbade the holding of the Games, and are well documented in the literature (Palaeologos, 1962).

It was not until after 1980 when President Samaranch took leadership of the IOC and the 1984 Los Angeles Games met with financial success, that commercial interest in the Olympic Games catapulted and the IOC became the custodian of a multibillion US dollar business.

With the advent of television coverage spectatorship also grew along with an increased interest in the accumulation of medals by nations as they fought for sporting supremacy and kudos. The games have since diversified into winter and summer editions whilst before both editions were hosted in the fourth year of the Olympiad. As the Olympic Games had grown in size and complexity the IOC session decided to alter the Olympic Calendar so that the winter Olympic Games of 1992 in Albertville France were the last ones to coincide with the summer Olympic Games of the same year in Barcelona and the next winter games took place just two years later in Lillehammer in Norway in 1994. Sponsors were rather pleased with this development and the IOC was also able to streamline its activities better.

It would be erroneous to suggest that the IOC is singly responsible for the management of these mega-events. After the relative financial benefits from hosting the Olympic Games cities started to bid for the right to host the summer or winter editions of the event, with increasing revenues from commercial activity, it became evident that various agents were affected by (a) the organization of the Olympic Games and (b) the processes taking place during bidding as well as after the conclusion of the event. Such agents include politicians, private sector entrepreneurs, civil society representatives much like their equivalent in antiquity when the organization of the Olympic Games also include city officials, representatives of the sports establishments (e.g., trainers), and religious leaders.

Although the modern Olympic Games belong to the IOC the Olympic Games are delivered predominantly by other organizations, namely (a) the host city/nation that undertakes to deliver all the infrastructure and management services and (b) the International Federations (IFs) representing the summer and winter Olympic events in the programme of the Olympic Games, who actually carry out the competitions in the field of play, be it the track, the rowing lake, or the shooting range for example. Notwithstanding the fundamental role played by the public sector in the host country, the private sector also gets involved in the delivery of the Olympic Games by providing sponsorship, other value in kind, and/or contracted services. Furthermore, thousands of volunteers contribute to the running of the event in a number of roles and the staging of the Olympic Games would arguably be prohibitively expensive without their non-paid labour of the volunteers.

The Olympic Games have gained popularity because of their international and later universal appeal and some argue that it is the coming together of the talented sports men and women of all those recognized nations that has led to the increasing popularity of the Olympic Games for spectators, as well as, very important, the sponsors and the broadcasters who finance them. When Pierre de Coubertin and his contemporaries at the IOC decided on the members of their committee and their modus operandi, they created a governance framework that would allow them to operate in a variety of nations, through national branches, but seeking to avoid excessive intervention from individual governments. Although the IOC was influenced by Anglo-Saxons and other Western Europeans it also included representatives from more peripheral states; and as more nations were created following decolonization, the number of members of the IOC based in these newly independent states also rose. The Olympic Games in Athens on 1896 involved 14 countries whilst the same city hosted 201 national teams at the 2004 games. Before a country can participate it must have established, with the permission of the IOC, a National Olympic Committee (NOC) that undertakes to gather the team of athletes that are eligible to compete and bring them to the Olympic Games where they will compete in the Olympic events. Such recognition by the IOC has not always been a right and international politics have often in the past meant that some countries were excluded while others that did not have a recognized status of a nation were allowed to have a NOC and compete in the Olympic Games. These committees also handle the financial transactions behind the country's representation/participation in the Olympic Games through the athletes' participation and where necessary, raise funds for that purpose.

But the growth of the Olympic Games is not just due to the efficiency of the organization of the Olympic Games. It is the Olympic brand that makes the Olympic Games so popular with media, sponsors, spectators, and the athletes. When Pierre de Coubertin worked tirelessly to find solutions for the lack of physical activities of the French youth he searched for a set of ideas that he could 'sell' to people for his dreams to come true. These sets of ideas still 'sell' today and, although numerous threats to the brand have come and gone, the financial might of the IOC and the political stakes involved with hosting the Olympic Games and topping the medals table are considerable and still growing.

The five interlocking rings that represent the Olympic Games are one of the most widely recognized symbols in the world and one that represents humankind in sporting competition. Market research reveals the power of the symbol and the preparedness of multinationals to pay handsomely for the privileged use of the rings is additional testament to this. To understand the Olympic brand today one must try to understand Olympic ideology, what it stands for, and what it means to consumers of sponsors' goods, athletes, and various world audiences. Arguably, the notion of excellence is central to the ideology and the emphasis on gold medal accumulation (instead of silver or bronze) showcases this regardless of claims that it is the 'taking part, not necessarily the winning' that counts. The idea of excellence finds fertile soil in the minds of politicians who cherish the idea of bathing in the reflected glory of a nation that outperforms others or its own past performance in the Olympic Games. Olympism, as Olympic ideology is termed, is claimed by the IOC to be a philosophy of life that seeks to combine sporting performance with spiritual endeavour in an environment of fair play where there is respect of individuality, the environment, and the educational needs of the young and the athletes at large. The Olympic brand, therefore, is also supported by an ideology that claims to seek to improve men and women in their continuous attempts at achieving excellence and the spectacle of the Olympic Games provides expressions of this ideology in the ways in which all those involved with the Olympic Games choose to experience and/or utilize them.

The IOC identifies the aggregate of agents it works with to deliver the Olympic Games as the Olympic Family and its works more broadly as the Olympic Movement. In its long history the Olympic Movement has been linked to or affected by elitism, colonialism and neo-colonialism, nationalism, Nazism, communism, capitalism, and of late, terrorism. Given the visibility of the Olympic Games and their increasing popularity, it is understandable that socio-political movements and ideologies would seek to link up to the Olympic message to promote the interests of their proponents. Being a product of its time, each Olympic Games influences, and is influenced by societal structures, human agency, and its broader context. To understand the creation of each one of these mega-events one needs to unpack the layers and clusters of interests of the component parts of the Olympic Movement. Such consideration can constitute an analysis of the events' organization, which can then inform the choices available to organizers and the paths for implementation available. The approaches to organizational analyses reviewed here allow a variety of ways of viewing context, structures, and co-ordinating processes taking place whilst hosting a mega-event like the Olympic Games and conceptual frameworks from organization theory help deliver in this book theoretically informed accounts of responses to challenges in the Olympic Games' event organization. These evolve, as one would expect, within the timescale of the set of activities involved with bidding, planning for, and staging the Olympic Games. Such activities are carried out by various agents in organizations, be it the local organizing committee, the Ministry of public works, the IOC, contractors, or numerous others. Considering the life cycles of temporary or episodic organizations involved with the Olympic Games, it is possible to understand processes in the event's organization better. To this end the organization theory literature offers insights into what constitutes the parts of the Olympic Movement in general and the event organization group in the host city in particular;

what triggers change; and what type of change one can expect in the respective organizations. The idea that some organizational structural features are better in certain contexts than others has led to the expression of configuration theory and the associated notion that in pursuit of efficiency, ideal types of configuration can be utilized as a diagnostic tool. As the organizations involved with the Olympic Movement and the staging of the Olympic Games evolve in the life cycle of the movement and the event, respectively, considerations of examples of what configurations have appeared so far can reveal tensions (in configurational terms). It is important to note that the governance of the Olympic Movement, the Olympic Games management model, and the actual processes involved do not develop independently. Guidance from the IOC, consultants as well as national institutional frameworks, predispose towards or, in some cases, even dictate organizational behaviour. Knowledge management mechanisms of the IOC and of other private companies also facilitate mimesis, adoption of norms, and acceptance of rules. Given the various levels of interorganizational relationships that exist between all the agents involved in the movement and in the organization of the Olympic Games and for clarity and focus in the discussion this book adopts a macro-level analysis framework; taking the parts of the movement and the roles they play in the production of the summer and winter Olympic event as the main units of analysis.

The Organising Committee of the Olympic Games (OCOG) plays a primary role in the event's production which is a temporary organization that is created shortly after the award of the Olympic Games to a city and ceases to exist normally one to two years after the events finish. Given the centrality of the roles this organization holds – along with the IOC and the NOCs – in the web of 'Olympic' interactions, the organizational analysis of the three set of bodies form the foundational axis of the narrative. In addition, the use of case studies from past and current Olympic Games editions allows the use of details that illuminate the arguments made in light of the adopted conceptual frameworks. This book addresses a number of important questions in contemporary mega-event management:

Which organizations are involved in the Olympic Movement and in what capacity? What are the interorganizational flows of authority and finance between them? How is work grouped, in what unit sizes, how specialized and formalized are work processes? How complex, dynamic, diversified, or friendly is their environment? What are the power issues and how do the technological processes affect these organizations? How do the OCOGs evolve in their life cycle, what pressures shape their structures and management processes and how is work co-ordinated? The examination of the Olympic Games event organization in the 10-year period, from bidding to post-games closing down, draws material from host cities to explore the types of interorganizational flows that take place at various stages for the Olympic Games to be delivered.

Knowledge transfer from one host city to the next and an established organizational field also mean that management practises sometimes follow some externally imposed organizing logics. The challenges faced by organizers are discussed and the tensions that a strong management template from the IOC creates are also examined. Finally, the issue of sustainability of the Olympic Games is identified along with an analysis of the ways in which the concepts of impact are appropriated by the various stakeholders involved with the Olympic Games as they attempt to influence public opinion.

Part One identifies the methodological underpinnings of the work reported and explains the ways in which examples are examined in light of the various conceptual frameworks that inform the analysis. Developments in the organization theory literature are briefly reviewed and Mintzberg's work on the structuring of organizations is presented along with his main ideas on configuration theory.

The event and mega project planning literature is also grouped along the criteria of whether it is analytic and prescriptive in nature. Prescriptive work concerns itself with providing guidance on how best to host a mega sporting event whilst more analytic work centres attention on what processes surface in various contexts and seeks to understand the reasons for such actions and explore their impacts on overall organizational behaviour.

Part Two sketches the political economy of the Olympic Movement identifying its parts, their respective roles as well as the authority and financial flows within.

Considering where the money that finances the movement originates from and how it is spent and who decides on these issues, the discussion centres on an analysis of the fundamental issues which arise from the accumulation and distribution of the surplus product of the Olympic Movement.

Henry Mintzberg's ideas on the structuring of organization are employed to identify which parts of the movement represent senior and middle management, which are the operating core and so forth. Other structural design parameters like specialization of work and formalization of procedures are also explored in various parts of the movement and their respective environment, age, size, power, and technical system are discussed. Having carefully guarded its autonomy throughout its history, the Olympic Movement now faces increasing challenges from the commercialization powers that it itself successfully attracted. The breaking away of sports leagues in many sports is a reminder of how powerful private interests become when administration does not allow them to fully develop as they wish. Similarly, EU legislation is challenging IOC autonomy and monopoly through insistence on the fair competition in borderless Europe. Related to the growing commodification of the Olympics as a mega-event is the priority of sustainable development which has become pertinent in light of widespread concern over project overruns, cost escalations and negative environmental, social and even economic impact. This also highlights power issues in the organization of the Olympic Movement and facilitates discussions on the various interests involved, for example, who gains or looses from developments linked to the event.

As urban regeneration motives are often used to rally support for an Olympic bid, this part also explores the literature that connects the two and, where appropriate provides evidence behind the claims of regeneration through mega-sports-events like the Olympic Games.

Part Three focuses on the organizations involved with the actual delivery of the Olympic events. Arguably, the IOC and the IFs are always involved in that process but OCOGs co-ordinate the activities between them and the host country/city whilst another temporary organization that emerges in the host city, often called the Olympic Delivery Authority (ODA), delivers all the infrastructure needed (including urban landscaping, transport, etc). Following the identification of the key partners in the delivery of the event, the life cycle of the preparations for the event is explored during the bidding, planning, and games time phases. The various structural design parameters employed in these organizations such as specialization and formalization along with the situational features of size, environment, and power are also analysed in the main parts of the movement that are primarily involved with the event's production and delivery.

Finally, the book reviews the ways in which host city agendas have been hijacking event preparations and how the existence of models or templates of games management (that have proved successful so far) may stifle the formation of alternative models that could potentially evolve.

Part One: Perspectives

The aim of this part is to discuss methodological issues surrounding the analysis of organizations in general and Olympic organizations in particular, review developments in the organization theory literature with a focus on structural formations and types and finally discuss approaches to event management in the context of mega project planning.

Defining the Scope of the Analysis

The approach adopted here is to conceptualize the organizational analyses presented in this book as a series of conversations (Clegg & Hardy, 1996) that relate to the (Olympic) organizations as empirical objects and organizing as a social process. In line with Clegg (1990) we start with the premise that organizations are empirical objects. By this we mean that we see something when we see an organization, but each of us may see something different.

As researchers, we participate in enactment and interpretation processes. We choose what empirical sense we wish to make of organizations by deciding how we wish to represent them in our work. How aspects of Olympic organizations are represented, the means of representation, the features deemed salient, those features glossed and those features ignored, are not attributes of the organization. They are an effect of the reciprocal interaction of multiple conversations: those that are professionally organized, through journals, research agendas, citations, and networks; those that take place in the empirical world of these organizations. The dynamics of reciprocity in this mutual interaction can vary: some conversations of practice inform those of the profession; some professionals talk dominated practice; some practical and professional conversations sustain each other; others talk past, miss, and ignore each other (p. 4).

With this conceptualization of analyses of (Olympic) organizations one can strive for reflexivity, by which we allude to ways of seeing which act back on and reflect existing ways of seeing. None is a more 'correct' analysis than any other: there are different possibilities. Like any good conversation, the dialectic is reflexive and oriented not to ultimate agreement, but to the possibilities of understanding of and action within the contested terrains (p. 5).

Plenty of homogenized textbooks exist which offer certainties enough for those who require them and converting the anxieties of their readers into easy recipes and conventions. For students reading this book who endeavour to understand the Olympic events' organization and grasp the complexity of the interactions between the various agents and agencies involved the book provides a starting point. For those aiming to engage theory to understand practise there are conceptual frameworks that aid theorizing. For managers in Olympic organizations there is the opportunity to see the broader organizational picture, the interdependencies of the Olympic business setup and the challenges presented by the contexts within which this array of organizations is operating.

For Smith and Peterson (1988: pp. 47–48) definition of events of any kind have certain amount of elasticity in both space and time. Tentative boundaries defining an event could be placed around an exchange between individuals and organizations. The context, which would be an implicit but integral part of this event, would include things like the previous relationships between them, other occurrences in their respective work and personal lives, and the physical characteristics of the setting. Alternatively, an event could be defined as the entire history of the relationship between these two parties. If we choose the second perspective, the organization's history as well as occurrences within the industry or the nation must be considered as the implicit context of the event. Thus, an 'event' comprised of various 'occasions' is constructed out of the information available to an observer, whether that observer is an actor or an 'objective' outsider. However, the imposition of boundaries around an event is not arbitrary, and it derives from what is actually done by the parties involved. The involved parties are seen as actually constructing 'Gestalts' or unified sets of perceptions, which may parallel the events constructed by observers. Similarly, Olympic events can be defined as the history of relationships between the Olympic Movement and the host city country.

Positivist and constructivist research paradigms are important in the sense that they can provide particular sets of lenses for seeing the social world.

The theoretical approach of the organizational analyses reported in this book is founded on the realization that the ability to analyse phenomena of various kinds in organizations depends on the adequacy of the theoretical schemes employed. Such theoretical schemes not only guided the search for significant relationships that exist in the organizational settings of Olympic organizations but also assisted in establishing the difference in the researcher's eyes, between simply knowing of a phenomenon and understanding its meaning. As a consequence, the research efforts were aided by the substantive bodies of theories that are discussed in this part. Bedeian (1980) claims that theory serves both as a tool and as a goal. The tool function being evident in the proposition that theories guide research by generating new predictions not otherwise likely to occur. As a goal, theory is often an end in itself, providing an economical and efficient means of abstracting, codifying, summarizing, integrating, and storing information.

Before reviewing the emerging theoretical perspectives available to organizational analysts an attempt can be made to investigate how such perspectives can be mediated for purposes of inclusion and application. Morgan (1997) argues that the research possibilities raised by different theoretical perspectives need to be harnessed in order to yield the rich and varied explanations offered by multiple paradigm analysis. Like Morgan, Willmott (1990) is also concerned with paradigm plurality. Both examine Burrell's (1996) scheme of competing paradigms, according to which social science can be conceptualized in terms of four sets of assumptions related to ontology, epistemology, human nature, and methodology (Figure 1.1).

Willmott (1990) explores the possibilities for reconciling what Burrell (1996) regard as the irreconcilable features of these paradigms. He argues that the assumption of paradigmatic closure should be challenged by examining the attempts of Giddens (1979; 1982) to integrate subjective and objective paradigms.

The organizational analyses presented in this book have been concerned to move away from approaches based upon the dualism between action and structure, whereby a contrast is drawn between a structural perspective which specifies abstract dimensions and abstract constraints, to an interactionist perspective which attends to symbolic mediation and negotiated processes. Willmott (1990) argues that these procedures and perspectives which, used to be regarded as incompatible, must be incorporated in a more unified methodological framework.

It is important to note that the aim of the research undertaken within the organization theories perspectives was to provide a better understanding of the organizational characteristics and dynamics found in Olympic organizations. This was to be achieved through the development of analytically

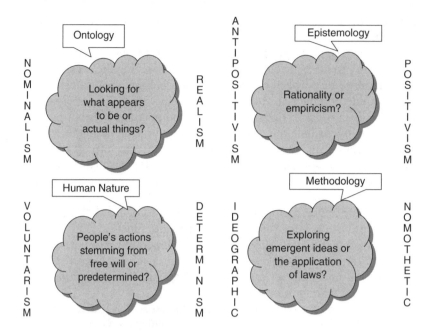

Figure 1.1 Variety of assumptions about the nature of social sciences (*Source:* Adapted from Burrell (1996))

structured narratives which, as Hassard and Pym (1990) argue, link agents' actions, structure, and context as they interweave within structural inertia, random events, contextual discontinuities, and significant changes in the environment.

> Theoreticians have attempted to 'fix' the organizational world and by reducing its dynamics to a static classificatory system, imprison it. In this they have forced organizational analysis onto a procrustean bed on which it groans and squirms because it is not the right size to fit the cramping framework into which it is being pressed. Yet the forcing goes on. Each of the terms to be addressed below forces the subject into an understandable and simplifying framework. This after all is what science does. But we must realize that what every concept does is to exclude as well as include, ignore as well as concentrate upon, to consign to obscurity as well as bring into the limelight. Concepts stretch the point and nowhere more than in the concept of paradigm (Burrell, 1996: p. 646).

Morgan (1997) argues that by using different metaphors to understand the complex and paradoxical character of organizational life, we are able to manage and design ways that we may not have thought possible. His use of different metaphors can also aid identification of issues and areas of friction in organizations. The political metaphor for example, allows researchers to focus on the different sets of interests, conflicts, and power plays that shape organizational activities. Using it one can explore organizations as systems of government drawing on various political principles to legitimize different kinds of rule, as well as the detailed factors shaping the politics of organizational life. As regards the organizations as instruments of domination metaphor, the focus is on the potentially exploitative aspects of organization. The ways in which organizations often use their employees, their host communities, and the world economy to achieve their own ends, and how the essence of organization rests in a process of domination where certain people impose their will on others. An extension of the political metaphor, the image of domination helps understand the aspects of modern organization that have radicalized labour–management relations in may parts of the world. This metaphor is particularly useful for understanding organizations from the perspective of exploited groups, and for understanding how actions that are rational from one point can prove exploitative from another. Images of organizations can generate ideas and concepts that we can use for diagnosis and evaluation to understand organizations in specific settings.

This aspect of organization has been made a special focus of study by radical organization theorists inspired by the insights of Karl Marx and sociologists Max Weber and Robert Michels.

The negative impact that organizations often have on their employees or their environment, or which multinationals have on patterns of inequality and world economic development, are not necessarily intended impacts. They are usually consequences of rational actions through which a group of individuals seek to advance a particular set of aims, such as increased profitability or corporate growth. 'The overwhelming strength of the domination metaphor is that it draws our attention to this double-edged nature of rational action illustrating how talking about rationality one is always speaking from a partial point of view. Actions that are rational for increasing profitability may have a damaging effect on employees' health. Actions designed to spread an organization's portfolio of risks, for example by divesting interests in a particular industry, may spell economic and urban decay for whole communities of people who have built their lives around that industry. What is rational from one organizational standpoint may be catastrophic from another. Viewing organization as a mode of domination that advances certain interest at the expense of others forces this important aspect of organizational reality into the centre of attention. It leads to an appreciation of Max Weber's insight that the pursuit of rationality can itself be a mode of domination, and to remember that in talking about rationality one should always be asking the question "rational for whom?" ' (pp. 315–316). The real thrust of the domination metaphor should be to critique the values that guide organization and the focus of analysis should be to distinguish between exploitative and non-exploitative forms, rather than to engage in critique in a broader sense.

It is argued (Bryman, 1988; 1989) that doing research in organizations poses particular challenges to researchers. There is a wealth of academic gossip about the false starts that are part of the everyday world of the social researcher. Researchers make mistakes and change their minds. The lack of guidance to some of the realities of social research that textbooks offer can be held partially responsible for these tendencies. In addition, one needs to consider the influence of funding bodies and gatekeepers.

There is a tendency to present research as though its origin and course are largely uninfluenced by external institutions. But such research may be funded and commissioned by external bodies and where research is conducted within organizations, gatekeepers have to allow the researcher access. Those who fund and those who provide access may seek to influence research very directly. Luck and serendipity in research also play an important role; being at the right place at the right time for picking up a number of important leads. The role of resources often surfaces in relation to very specific issues, such as the impact on sample size or the relative savings through the use of certain instruments in comparison to others. But they can also influence the climate in which research is done. The presence and absence of resources may constitute a key determinant of what is and is not studied not to mention how research is done. As regards the human resources involved in research it is important to note that there is often great fragility in research teams. They can easily deteriorate into hotbeds of discontent over the distribution of work, the decision-making process, the authority structure, and the appointment of credit. Researchers are attuned to a number of ethical issues like the ethics of covert observation and deception in experiments and the need for informed consent. Research in organizations can also be seen as something of a political minefield as is the case when the researcher is placed between opposite groups/parts of the industry under investigation.

There are certain recurring themes in organizational research: gaining entry to organizations and then getting on with people who work in them. While the field of organization studies has been heavily influenced by quantitative research, there is a growing recognition of the role of qualitative methods. Here we observe the associated difficulty of knowing how far generalizations from single cases can be stretched.

What we know or think we know about organizations is based on samples providing little external validity. Researchers sample organizations or subunits of organizations in opportunistic ways. When they do achieve a modicum of generalizability, the populations from which samples are selected often are themselves defined arbitrarily. . . They rarely work with samples that are representative of even the restricted types of organizations they choose to study. This has often led them to develop bodies of theory that do not apply generally.

Studies into Olympic organizations, including the present one are not immune to the above challenges. Games impact studies are mostly carried out ex ante rather than ex post, are funded by government agencies and produced by global consultants (KPMG for the Sydney and London Games). Other pressures are felt by researchers considering mismanagement or corruption in global sports organizations like Fédération Internationale de Football Association (FIFA) and the International Olympic Committee (IOC). Such pressures may stem from the epistemic community as well as public culture when it becomes antipatriotic to report on negative aspects of the organization of the Olympic Games. Having been contractually bound to ensure the protection of the image of Olympism, Organising Committees for the Olympic Games (OCOGs) are particularly eager to avoid scandal or defamation at home as well as abroad and this has implications on the level of support they offer to researchers.

Furthermore, there is the problem of access to respondents from such organizations. Considering the fact that OCOGs are temporary organizations, it is possible to see that managers are quite busy before the games and immediately after the Olympic Games are over people leave the organization. Access to them is therefore often problematic and in addition to this the IOC has an embargo on recent corporate material. Even when access to OCOG interviewees prior to the Olympic Games is secured the issue of maintaining a positive image often surfaces as there are overwhelming pressures on staff not to compromise the company's public image or risk raising issues prior to the IOC co-ordination commission visit.

Numerous studies have highlighted the complexity of doing research in another country. Issues and challenges may be interpreted differently there. Some issues are unique to that setting while some others become redundant. Hofstede (1980; 1984) studies on value differences highlight how these have implications on behaviour at work. Such values including power distance, uncertainty avoidance, individualism versus collectivism, and masculinity versus femininity. The literature contains ample reminders of the challenges of doing research in foreign country, on culture's consequences, on language and meaning (what Wittgenstein meant when he argued that: 'Meaning is use. If you do not use a language on a regular basis then you cannot understand how it is used by the natives' (Burrell, 1996)). Furthermore the challenge of generalizability is acentuated by the fact that as the Olympic Games are always held in a new country researchers need to be able to travel to the host city, maybe understand the language spoken there, and be able to add to their generic framework the particularities of the host city organizational environment. The Olympic Movement operates via a number of interconnected parts/units and to understand the movement, researchers and managers need to understand the component parts, the National Olympic Committees (NOCs), the International Federations (IFs), and the OCOGs. These straddle the spectrum of organizational activity. Some being limited companies, other charities, associations, or public companies. Having control over the Olympic trademark, and deriving its funds from the sale of exclusive rights, the IOC is eager to protect its monopoly business power. Current funding distribution arrangements create dependencies and conformity whilst ensuring the non-disturbance of the status quo. Research that exposes the profit-making beneficiaries has the potential to be received as damaging to the image of Olympism, of fair play and the joy found in effort. If such bodies are funding the research they may pressure exercised to clear material with them before it is made public and this may be felt as a form of censorship. Similar pressures can sometimes be felt on the broader epistemic community by political imperatives for growth of national identity and pride. Under such conditions it may be seen as antipatriotic to critique Olympics-related efforts or processes.

There are also issues with respecting any anonymity requests by respondents and the help of the gatekeepers that allow access to the organizations under investigation and reporting research findings without exposing them to others in the community.

1

Structures in context

Organization theory is the sociological and multi-disciplinary analysis of organizational structure and the dynamics of social relationships in organizations. It is concerned with how organizations are created and maintained and how they function internally. The unit of analysis, therefore, is the whole organization (Banner & Gagne, 1995). The focus of this specialist area is upon all types of organization (including non-profit, voluntary organizations) in an attempt to arrive at a general theory of organizations, develop typologies of organizations, and explain similarities and differences in organizational structure. In practice, the boundaries between the multi-disciplinary study of organization theory and the sociology of organizations are difficult to discern, since writers in these fields often publish in the same journals, and many organizational issues (such as managerial strategy, decision making, and innovation) draw upon a multi-disciplinary framework.

Over the past half century, researchers from a wide variety of disciplines have developed various strategies for studying organizations. Historically an interdisciplinary field, organization theory has been particularly influenced by its constituent disciplines especially sociology, psychology, anthropology, and economics. As a consequence, diversity has long been a dominant feature of research on organizations. Such a diversity has contributed to the dynamic and pluralistic growth of organizational research, and assisted in avoiding academic isolation and conceptual stagnation. However, it has also produced differences in concepts, terminologies, and methods which have led to disagreements.

The growth of an interest in organization paralleled the growing economic and industrial development of the United States of America and Western Europe. The forces of expanding technology, paired with new advances in transportation and communication, dramatically increased the scope and complexity of organizational undertakings. These changes necessitated the formulation and investigation of new concepts for the design and function of organizations (Bedeian, 1980). Since the 1970s much sociological writing on organizations has adopted a more critical stance towards managerially defined applied issues and 'problems' in organizations, such as worker motivation and efficiency, in an attempt to re-establish the study of organizations in historical context and in relation to the wider society, to include, for example, studies of the way in which class and gender inequalities are reproduced in organizational contexts.

Reed (1996: p. 46) structures sub-themes in organization theory under the themes: agency–structure, constructivism–positivism, and local–global. Those who emphasize agency, focus on an understanding of social order that stresses the social practices through which human beings create and reproduce institutions. Those located on the structures' side highlight the importance of external relations and patterns that determine and constrain social interaction within specific institutional forms.

Agency–structure debates are concerned with how creativity and constraint are related through social activity; with whether one is observing the social practices of human beings or patterns and institutional forms of social interaction.

Constructivism–positivism are radically opposed epistemologies that legitimate very different procedures and protocols for assessing the knowledge claims which organization researchers make. Positivistic epistemology severely restricts the range of knowledge claims allowable in organization studies to those who pass a rigorous trial by methods and the law-like generalizations that it sanctions. Constructivism takes a much more liberal, not to say relativistic stance. Rational-integrationalist and market narratives developed on the basis of a realist ontology and positivist epistemology. Power, knowledge, and justice traditions were more disposed towards a nominalist constructionist ontology and anti-positivist conventionalist epistemology.

The local–global debate emerges from the narratives focused on questions relating to the level of analysis at which organizational research and analysis should be pitched. Power, knowledge, and justice focus local microprocesses and practices. Rational-integrationalist and market global macroconception of organization.

As regards individualism–collectivism, if individualism offers a vision of organization as the unintended creation of individual actors following the dictates of their particular instrumental and political objectives, then, collect-ivism treats organizations as an objective entity that imposes itself on actors with such force that they have little or no choice but to obey its commands (Reed, 1996).

Classic School of Organization Theory

Weber's ideal type of bureaucracy provided the point of departure for the post-war development of a sociology of organizations that concerned itself with rationality and order. His work has been a key resource for mainstream perspectives, especially on questions of rationality and efficiency. His ideas in this area have to be considered as part of a broader conception of ration-alization which was considered to be the key modernizing characteristic of the development of industrial societies. Gouldner's (1955) distinction between 'punishment-centred' and 'representative' bureaucracy, and Burns and Stalker (1961) comparison of 'mechanistic' and 'organic' forms of organization have been particularly influential for later research. Gouldner (1955) demonstrated how bureaucratic rules can be resisted and suggested that bureaucratization can take different forms with varying levels of participation by its members. The contrast between mechanistic and organic organization was used by Burns and Stalker to suggest that different organizational structures are appropri-ate depending on the degree of stability or uncertainty in the environment. Mechanistic structures are bureaucratic, hierarchical, and rigid in contrast to organic structures which are flexible, decentralized, and more able to cope with innovation and rapidly changing environments. Morgan (1997) suggests that comparisons between organizations were further elaborated in the attempt to develop general organization typologies based on types of goals which lead to different outputs, the criterion of who benefits from the orga-nization's existence, and activities and on structures of compliance in which those who control organizations utilize types of power to secure the involve-ment of other members.

The Human Relations School

The subsequent development of organization theory reflects both the vari-ous theoretical approaches in sociology as a whole and the influence of man-agerial perspectives, particularly scientific management and the human relations school with a focus on integration and consensus. The ideas of Taylor, the founder of scientific management at the turn of the century, com-plement those of Weber. Despite his emphasis on rationality in organizations, Weber did not explicitly deal with the role of management. In developing schemas for the potentially scientific character of management Taylor was building on the themes of rationality and formal control, subsequently advocated by Weber. Emphasis was put on a series of techniques to measure and control work and define clearly the relative tasks of management and worker. It fits clearly in a positivistic framework of belief that there are objective means of measurement which can help discover laws governing work activity. Taylor's ideas were a crucial ingredient in legitimizing the conception of management as a rational, scientific activity, and this has been an enduring feature of mainstream analysis ever since (Clegg & Dunkerley, 1980; Morgan, 1997).

Following Taylor, the sociological analysis of Emile Durkheim had a major impact on approaches to organizational analysis. His contribution centres on the significance of the division of labour in sustaining the social solidarity necessary for the survival of the 'organism' of society, or the enterprise. He recognized that the bureaucratic arrangements and formal structures developing in industrial societies contained sources of social disorganization, conflict, and individualism. It was, therefore, management's role to organize the technical and formal needs of the organization and cater for the social needs of those who worked in it (Durkheim, 1957; 1984). This represents the beginning of the human relations tradition. A prominent figure within this tradition was Elton Mayo who was principally responsible for publishing the Hawthorne experiments. Echoing Durkheim, he felt that scientific and technical developments had outstripped the social skills and social arrangements of man, one consequence of which was widespread anomie (Mayo, 1949). His approach underlined the importance of the social engineering role given to management in maintaining equilibrium and integrating the parts of the organization. This strand of management is clearly related to the humanistic school of psychology of Maslow and reappears in contemporary management writing such as Peters and Waterman (1982).

The main weakness of human relations theory is that it fails to acknowledge the relations of power implied by social engineering. In so doing, it provides a management-centred view of organizational reality, in which theory is used to legitimate the manipulation of the work force to achieve managerial ends.

Systems Theory

The classical and human relations theories tended to have a rather static view of the organization in which structures and practices could be internally regulated, with little reference to the outside world. Organizations were conceived of as closed systems balancing the various human and technical components. To counter this, the notion of organizations as systems was introduced drawing on the basic organic analogy used by Durkheim and others, in which all social systems were described as adapting to the environment in order to survive (Katz, 1966). This became a theme of functionalist social theory which regards social systems as self-regulating bodies, tending towards a state of equilibrium and order. Each part of any system plays a positive functional role in this process. Thus the organization is a system of interrelated parts or sub-units each functioning to mobilize resources towards meeting wider goals. These parts are at the same time differentiated and interdependent, aiding processes of integration and co-ordination (Parsons, 1956).

A crucial development within systems theory was the acceptance of the importance of interaction with the environment which was based on the premise that the survival of an organization depends on its capacity to adapt to markets and technologies. Open systems theory became the mainstream approach explaining how organizations coped with uncertainty through exchange and transaction with the external environment (Parsons, 1956). Functionalism has exerted a powerful influence on organization theory either explicitly, as in the concept of the organization as a system, or implicitly via assumptions about organizational 'survival' and 'adaptation' to the environment.

Following increases in the levels of environmental complexity experienced by organizations, open systems theory has focused on interdependencies with the environment (although the environment is seen as existing separate from and outside of the organization's system). Managing and controlling an environment has become an important managerial goal, especially because the environments in which organizations operate are characterized by increasing turbulence, or rapid change along with increased uncertainty. Open systems theory provides a model for the understanding of organizations in which an 'energetic' input–output system exists. Social organizations are open systems in that the input of energies and the conversion of output into further energetic input consists of transactions between the organization and the environment (Scott, 1992). Open systems theory defines an organization in terms of interrelated subsystems, and attempts to establish congruencies between different systems (e.g. strategic, environmental, technological, managerial, and structural subsystems), and to identify and eliminate potential dysfunctions (Morgan, 1997).

Collectively, these ideas have pointed the way to theories of organization and management that allow a move away from bureaucratic thinking, and the fostering of organizing in a way that meets the requirements of the environment. These insights have been used under contingency theory which is discussed below. The difference between systems and open systems approaches rests in the assumptions of adapting to the environment (systems theory) or modifying it (open systems theory). Both approaches, however, suffer from the weaknesses of functionalist thinking more generally, with the 'function' of organizational changes being explained by the needs of the organization (to adapt, etc.) rather than by reference to the interests and intentions of organizational actors.

Population Ecology Model

The goal of much organizational research is to discover how organizations adapt to change, but one school of thought has as its hypothesis that organizations cannot adapt very much. This is the population ecology model (Freeman, 1989). All ecological perspectives attribute patterns from nature to the action of selection-market-led processes, whereas the bulk of the literature on organization–environment relations focuses on adaptation processes. The crux of the natural selection view of population ecology is that the environment enables particular types of organizations to survive and others to fail based on the fit between structural and environmental characteristics. Proponents of the model argue that because constraints or inertia make it difficult for organizations to adapt their structures to a given set of environmental conditions, an organization must find a niche where its particular structural strengths are useful.

Population ecology theory contradicts the basic premise of the industrial paradigm which refers to the ability to manipulate external circumstances or internal structures to produce results pleasing to the individual or the organization. An argument that being at the right place at the right time is the major factor in determining organizational survival will not be accepted by those who wish to argue that managerial decisions, strategic and tactical, control an organization's destiny. Furthermore, population ecology runs counter to the premises of structuration allowing no room for human agency. Empirical evidence suggests that not only does equifinality occur (i.e. similar outcomes for organizations of very different structures and employing varied strategies) but also different outcomes occur for organizations employing similar structures and strategies operating in the same environment (Whittington, 1989). The 'effects' of the environment therefore, are not uniform across organizations with similar structural and strategic characteristics. Some account of agency is therefore required for explanations to be adequate.

Contingency Theory

The main ideas underlying contingency theory include the notions that organizations are open systems that need careful management to satisfy and balance internal needs and to adapt to environmental circumstances. Furthermore it is recognized that no single formula of structure or strategy will be applicable in all circumstances. Appropriate organizational forms and strategies will depend on the kind of task or environment with which one is dealing. Management thus is to be concerned with achieving good fits. Different approaches to management may be necessary to perform different tasks within the same organization, and quite different types or species of organization are needed in different types of environment. One of the most influential studies establishing the credentials of this approach was that conducted by Burns and Stalker (1961) who identified the distinction between mechanistic and organic approaches to organization and management, and thought that more flexible forms are required to deal with changing environments. Lawrence and Lorsch (1986) refined the contingency approach by showing that styles of organization may need to vary between organizational sub-units because of the detailed characteristics of their sub-environments.

Contingency theory has been widely employed as an empirical, survey-based approach to establish correlations between 'contextual variables' (size, technology, and environment), structural aspects of the organization (degree of formalization, standardization, and centralization), and their effect upon performance. The most influential of these empirical studies were what became known as the 'Aston studies' (Pugh & Hickson, 1976). The contingency approach has been embraced by management theorists because of its potential in relating organizational design to performance, and the implication that earlier prescriptions from scientific management for organizational structure and strategy 'blue-prints' were inappropriate. Interestingly, contingency approaches have been criticized by some management theorists with a renewed emphasis on universal principles such as the need for a 'power organizational culture' (Peters & Waterman, 1982). Within the organization theory field, contingency theory has been criticized for its deterministic assumptions and untheorized empiricism (Clegg, 1990). The neglect of power relations by contingency theorists has been stressed by Child (1984), who proposes a strategic contingency approach to organizations which concentrates upon the role of managerial choice in actively shaping organizational structures in response to contingencies. Contingent factors, such as the environment, are, in turn, not treated as 'independent variables' but partly chosen or controlled by particularly powerful organizations.

In its prediction of organizational performance or effectiveness, resulting from the congruence between elements of the organization's context – size, technology, or environment – contingency theory specifies an interaction. Pfeffer (1997) suggests that this interaction has seldom been tested. What is needed, he argues, is much more precisely stated and potentially falsifiable hypotheses. These might include more attention to which of the various elements of organizational context was important for understanding which elements of structure, and under what conditions.

Configuration Theory

The configuration approach makes a clear break from the contingency mainstream, which has been preoccupied with abstracting a limited set of structural concepts like centralization and formalization, and measuring their relationships with a limited set of abstracted situational concepts, such as size and technological uncertainty. By synthesizing broad patterns from contingency theory's fragmented concepts, and grounding them in rich, multivariate descriptions, the configurational approach may help consolidate the past gains of contingency theory (Meyer, Tsui, & Hinings, 1993). Configurational enquiry assumes a holistic stance, asserting that the parts of a social entity take their meaning from the whole and cannot be understood in isolation.

Social systems are seen as tightly coupled amalgams entangled in multi-directional causal loops. Non-linearity is acknowledged, so variables found to be causally related in one configuration may be unrelated or even inversely related in another. In acknowledging that there is more than one way to succeed in each type of setting, the configuration approach explicitly accommodates the important concept of equifinality.

Organizational analysis has a research tradition rife with attempts at classifying organizations, as documented by Carper and Snizek (1980). Classification has been at the basis of organizational theorizing, from Weber's notions of charisma, traditionalism, and bureaucracy, through Burn's and Stalker's distinction between mechanistic and organic structures, to Mintzberg (1979) distinctions between simple structure, machine bureaucracy, professional bureaucracy, divisionalized form, adhocracy, and missionary organization. It has been used to support a central tenet of organization theory, namely that there are different kinds of organization and that many (or all) aspects of organizational functioning are related to organization type.

Organizational scholars taking configurational approaches fall into the group of typologists or taxonomists. Conceptually derived sets of configurations are referred to as typologies while empirically derived ones as taxonomies. Typologists generally follow the Weberian logic of ideal types, accentuating key characteristics so as to draw a priori distinctions between organizations. The logic of taxonomy, on the other hand, lies in empirical classification based on multivariate analysis of multiple dimensions that may cover structures, processes, strategies, and contexts (Meyer et al., 1993). So the rationale for the production of theoretically based, empirical taxonomies is the theorized impact of taxonomic position on a wide range of other organizational phenomena. The historical emphasis on classification derives from the idea of generalizable, holistic, structural differences between classes of organization which are central to all aspects of organizational life.

Institutional Theory

Institutional theory first appeared in the mid-1970s and has generated much interest and attention. It has raised provocative questions about the world of organizations, such as why organizations of the same type, such as schools and hospitals, located in widely scattered locales, so closely resemble one another (Scott, 1992). Institutions have been defined as consisting of cognitive, normative, and regulative structures and activities that give stability and meaning to social behaviour (DiMaggio & Powell, 1983). It is argued that various carriers – cultures, structures, and routines – transport institutions and they operate at multiple levels of jurisdiction (Scott, 1992).

The term 'organizational field' is used to describe organizations that in aggregate constitute a recognized area of institutional life: key suppliers, resource and project consumers, regulatory agencies, and other organizations that produce similar services or products (DiMaggio & Powell, 1983). Similarly, Scott (1992) defines fields as a set of diverse organizations attempting to carry on a common enterprise. In the initial stages of their life cycle, organizational fields display diversity in approach and form. Once a field becomes well established, however, there is an inexorable push towards homogenization (DiMaggio & Powell, 1983). The concept used in the literature to capture the process of homogenization is 'isomorphism' and is defined as the constraining process that forces one unit in a population to be like other units that face the same set of environmental conditions (DiMaggio & Powell, 1983).

Institutions, according to Scott (1992) have a regulative, normative and cognitive dimension. Each of the pillars provides a basis for legitimacy, albeit a different one. In the resource dependence or social exchange approach to organization, legitimacy is sometimes treated as simply a different kind of resource. However, from an institutional perspective, legitimacy is not a commodity to be possessed or exchanged but a condition reflecting cultural alignment, normative support, or consonance with relevant rules or laws. In explaining the conditioning of organizations by institutions in their field, new institutionalists provide a framework that allows the investigation of the inter-actions among organizations and forces at play that lead to isomorphic change.

Meyer and Rowan (1977) argue that isomorphism with environmental insti-tutions has some crucial consequences for organizations: (i) they incorporate elements which are legitimated externally, rather than in terms of efficiency; (ii) they employ external or ceremonial assessment criteria to define the value of structured elements, and (iii) dependence on externally fixed institutions reduces turbulence and maintains stability. Incorporating externally legiti-mated formal structures increases the commitment of internal participants and external constituents, and the use of external assessment criteria can enable an organization to remain successful by social definition. However, DiMaggio and Powell (1983) contend that isomorphism occurs as the result of processes that make organizations more similar without necessarily making them more effi-cient. Bureaucratization and other forms of homogenization emerge, they argue, out of the structuration of organizational fields. They identify three mechanisms through which institutional isomorphic change occurs, each with its own antecedents: (i) 'coercive isomorphism' that stems from political influ-ence and the problem of legitimacy, (ii) 'mimetic isomorphism' resulting from standard response to uncertainty, and (iii) 'normative isomorphism' associated with professionalization. However, this list is an analytic one and as Powell and DiMaggio (1991) contend, the types are not always empirically distinct.

Organization Theory Development

Within organization theory modernist thinking is seen to find its clearest expression in the intellectual dominance and ideological power of systems analysis. The latter is aligned with the control needs of large-scale technological systems. 'Post-modernist' writers have argued that the dominance of modernist thought in organizational analysis has been challenged and undermined by movements that have striven to expose the limitation of systems driven theories of formalization. By the late 1970s there was a perceived crisis in organization theory (Reed, 1993). The established rational systems approach was seen to have no answer to issues such as the production of organizational reality, the connection of organizations to the larger set of structural arrangements in society, and the continuously emergent character of organizational patterns. This movement in organizational analysis away from paradigm polarization and towards a renewed search for forms which are flexible enough to accommodate a plurality of divergent views, is reflected in a range of transitions in the field. First, there was an attempt to locate developments within organization theory in their wider socio-historical context. Second, a realization that epistemological uncertainty, theoretical plurality and diversity of methods do not lead to a disordered field of study. Third, there is an attempt to establish the dialectical interaction between intellectual development and changing control practices in organizational forms through which social order is managed in advanced industrial societies. Finally, there is a reaction to relativism and paradigm use. In its place, there is an inclination to discover the nature of the epistemologies in use in organization theory and the social networks through which debates are held between different theory or research groups (Clegg, 1990; Willmott, 1990; Hassard, 1993).

The impact of the shifts in intellectual focus and direction outlined in the above section has been to provide a context in which a different kind of research agenda to that prevailing in the late 1970s and early 1980s has taken shape in the late 1980s and 1990s. While the development of this agenda has been influenced by 'post-modern' thinking (most obviously in regard to the growing interest in organizational cultures), both its content and analytical focus seem to stress the continuity with older traditions of thought and research (Reed, 1993). This is to the extent that paradigm incommensurability and closure invoked by post-modernist writers has given way to a much more relativistic assessment of the need for mediation between conflicting paradigms. Underpinning the themes of a 'new' organization theory, lies the debate as regards the extent to which modern organizations can be seen as the primary institutional carriers for the diffusion of technical and instrumental rationality in western industrialized societies (Clegg, 1990). However, the tendency exhibited by recent organizational studies has been seen as entailing a retreat from rationality as the defining feature of discourse and analysis. The proliferation of alternative perspectives that reject the rationalistic bias of mainstream writing seem to have left the field in a state of dissolution and the theory of rational analysis, has given way to a 'cacophony' of multiple and contested rationalities (Reed, 1993).

The trajectory of changes in organization theorizing indicated above, highlights the managerialist limitations of theories such as scientific management and human relations, the functionalist weaknesses of systems theory approaches, and the similar structuralist limitations of population ecology. In essence, the two managerialist schools of thought are flawed 'agency' accounts providing 'objective' rules of thumb for maximizing efficiency by legitimating managerial control. The latter theories, systems, and population ecology, focus on structure, failing to account for the actions of agents or interests groups within organizations.

The Weberian tradition, as seen in Weber's analysis of bureaucracy in the political and cultural hegemony in which it was developed and operationalized, has been sustained in organization studies and is seen as presenting, a more fruitful basis for exploring the dynamics of organizational change and institutional transition. What this implies is not that organizations should be seen to be constituted of single, rational accounts of reality. Rather it implies that the domain assumptions on which this theory is based have been (and continue to be) the dominant ones in both organizational analysis and management prescription. Thus it is this theoretical tradition which provides a useful focus for evaluation. Mintzberg's configuration theory provides a theoretical approach closely related to Weber's analysis of bureaucracy, in that structural and contextual characteristics are explored which constitute an organization's micro- and macro-environment.

Clegg and Hardy (1996) review/gather organizational theory literature in terms of its chronological development along a number of themes. They identify particular perspectives that have been developed in the last three decades to capture aspects or organizational reality. Morgan (1997) also gathered this work in his book *On the Images of Organisations*, arguing that all these perspectives complement each other and offer important insights that are necessary for an analysis to have a well-rounded view. Each school of thought has particular epistemological and ontological assumptions and is predisposed towards a certain mode of analysis and each of these schools can be utilized to illuminate the Olympic Games event organization.

Types of Structures

A simple structure can be thought of as no structure at all. In a simple structure the organization is run by the personal control of the individual. There is little division of management responsibility and little clear definition if there is more than one person involved (Johnson & Scholes, 1999: p. 402). A functional structure is based on the primary activities that have to be carried out such as production, finance and accounting, marketing and personnel. This structure is typically found in smaller companies, or those with narrow rather than diverse product ranges. However, within a multidivisional structure the divisions themselves are likely to be split up into functional management areas. In organizations of any size there is likely to be a diversity of product service and market client groups which may lead to a diversity of positioning decisions for the different strategic business units (SBUs).

For example, an airline or a hotel wishing to differentiate between its business and family customers.

A functional structure can be very problematic in coping with this diversity since the structure is built around business processes which cut across the various SBUs and there is often an attempt to impose an unhelpful uniformity of approach between the SBUs. 'So the lead times in production, debt control in finance, advertising expenditure in marketing, bonus systems in personnel, are too rigid to reflect the diversity which the organization faces. The work of individuals is planned around a specialist business process and no one (other than the most senior managers) has any real ownership of the whole product or client group' (p. 403). 'Ways of minimizing these problems are first improving co-ordination between functions and second creation of substructures within business functions to bring ownership of product or client group. For example, within sales and marketing there might be roles such as product managers or key account sales staff' (p. 404).

A holding company is an investment company consisting of shareholdings in a variety of separate business operations over which the corporate centre exercises simple control. Although part of a parent company these business units operate independently and probably retain their original company names. 'The advantages that a holding company can offer are based on the idea that the constituent businesses will operate their product market strategy to their best potential if left alone, particularly as business environments become more turbulent' (p. 408).

A matrix structure is a combination of structures which often takes the form of product and geographical divisions or functional and divisional structures operating in tandem. Matrix structures do not occur only in large, complex organizations; they are sometimes found in quite small organizations and are very common in professional service organizations in the public and private sector.

In reality few organizations operate entirely like one of the pure structural types as the skill is in blending structure to the organization's circumstances.

A drive for flatter structures/de-layering improvements in speed and quality of management information allows for spans of control wider than was hitherto regarded as desirable and work becomes less dependent on one place of work. Many organizations debating and implementing concepts of virtual organizations which are organizations held together by partnership, networking, and collaboration. Networks can be one-stop shop with a single point of contact and delivery or a one-start shop with one initial contact who then directs work further and finally the service network where there is no single point for clients in the network.

A basic form of structure for a multinational is the retention of the home structure and the creation of overseas subsidiaries which are managed through direct contact between the top manager of the subsidiary and the chief executive of the parent company. 'How co-ordination is achieved will vary with circumstances and over time. International division interests are often managed through division along geographically based international subsidiaries. According to Johnson and Scholes (1999) many of the multinationals founded in colonial days operated this way. The control of the parent company is likely to be dependent on some form of planning and reporting system and perhaps the ultimate veto over national strategies' (pp. 417–418).

Another form of structure is around a global product or integrated structure. Here the multinational is split into product divisions which are then managed across the world whereby following the logic of cost efficiency there is an enhanced transfer of resources and competences.

Transnational corporations sometimes combine the local responsiveness of the international subsidiary with the advantages available from co-ordination found in global product companies by creating an integrated network of interdependent resources and competences. Under such setups each national unit operates independently but is a source of ideas and capabilities for the whole corporation and national units may achieve global scale through specialization on behalf of the whole corporation. Then the challenge for the corporate centre is in managing a global network by first establishing the role of each subsidiary and then sustaining the culture and systems to make the network operate effectively. The success of such a transnational corporation is dependent on the ability simultaneously to achieve global competences, local responsiveness, and organization-wide innovation and learning. This then requires some degree of clarity as to the roles which the various global managers need to perform.

Those in charge of global products or businesses have the overriding responsibility to further the company's global competitiveness which will cross both national and functional boundaries. They must be the product/market strategist the architect of the business resources and competencies, the driver of product innovation, and the co-ordinator of transnational transactions. Managers of countries or territories must also act as a sensor of local needs. They must be able to build unique competences; that is, become a centre of excellence which allows them to be a contributor to the company as a whole.

Managers of functions such as finance and Information Technology (IT) have a major responsibility for ensuring worldwide innovation and learning across the various parts of the organization. This requires the skill to recognize and spread best practise across the organization – a form of internal benchmarking. So they must be able to scan the organization for best practice, cross-pollinate this best practice and be the champion of innovations, for example, in re-engineering business processes. The critical issue is the role played by the corporate managers which is vital in the transnational corporation in integrating these roles and responsibilities. Not only are they the leaders, but they are also the talent spotters among business, country, and functional managers, facilitating the interplay between them, for example they must foster the processes of innovation and knowledge creation. They are responsible for the development of a strong management centre in the organization.

Johnson and Scholes (1999) also refer to the differences between countries in the way that global strategies have tended to develop. Companies originating from Europe (e.g. Unilever) needed to internationalize their activities at an early stage owing to small size of home countries. This took the form of international subsidiary and their challenge is to reduce local autonomy and increase global integration. US companies, with large domestic market, on the contrary favour international divisions. In both contexts organizations now face two issues in globalization: local autonomy and barriers between separate strategic views of the domestic and international business.

Mintzberg's Configurational Analysis

The structure of an organization can be defined simply as the sum total of the ways in which it divides its labour into distinct tasks and then achieves co-ordination among them (Mintzberg, 1979). Before structure is discussed, reference will be made to Mintzberg's account of the basic parts of organizations, the processes of co-ordination of activities, the parameters used to design their structures, and the situational factors as these are defined by Mintzberg (Mintzberg, 1979; 1981; Mintzberg & Queen, 1992). What follows therefore is an adapted account of Mintzberg's scheme that starts by defining the parts of the organization.

This section considers the importance of structural design, the parts which constitute the organization, and the variety of structural types which Mintzberg identifies. He found that many organizations fall close to one of five natural types, each a combination of structure and situation. When managers and organizational designers try to mix and match the elements of different ones, they may end up with a misfit that, like an ill-cut piece of clothing, will not wear very well (Mintzberg, 1979; 1981). The key to organizational design is consistency and coherence. What in fact are these structural types? Are they abstract ideals, real-life structures, or building blocks for more complex structures? In some sense Mintzberg argues, that the answer is yes in all three cases.

Management that grabs at every structural innovation that comes along may be doing its organization a great harm. It risks going off in all directions. In the fashionable world of organizational design, fit remains an important characteristic.

An organization may achieve its own internal consistency and then have it disturbed by the intervention of external controls. Some organizations do indeed achieve and maintain an internal consistency. But then they find that it is designed for an environment the organization is no longer in. Structure is no more designed to fit the situation than the situation to fit the structure, but in industries it is often far easier to shift and retreat to a suitable niche than to undo a cohesive structure.

To conclude, consistency, coherence, and fit – harmony – are critical factors in organization design, but they come at a price. An organization cannot be all things to all people. It should do what it does well and suffer the consequences. Be an efficient machine bureaucracy where that is appropriate and do not pretend to be highly adaptive. Or create some new type of structure to suit the needs. The point is not really which type of structure the organization has; it is that its structure is internally consistent and suitable for the environment of the organization.

Configuration theory supports a central assumption of organization theory, namely that there are different kinds of organizations and that many (or all) aspects of organizational functioning are related to organization type.

As Mintzberg (1994: p. 400) argues, configuration implies system in a most integrated sense. There are no dependent and independent variables in a system; everything influences and is influenced by everything else. Mintzberg (1979; 1983) presented both a typology and a theory. As a typology, his work provides a rich descriptive tool that identifies six potentially effective configurations of structural, contextual, and process factors. As a theory, it presents a series of logical arguments that result in specific predictions about organizational effectiveness as a function of the degree of similarity between a real organization and one or more of the ideal types (Doty, Glick, & Huber, 1993). Mintzberg's typology of configurations was subsequently used to consider various postures that planning, plans, and planners might take under different circumstances. The strategy process is viewed by Mintzberg and Queen (1992) as an interplay of the forces of power, sometimes highly politicized. Rather than assuming that organizations are consistent, coherent, and cooperative systems, tightly integrated to pursue certain traditional ends, Mintzberg exhibits different premises. He shares the views of Quinn (1977) that organizations' goals and directions are determined primarily by the power needs of those who populate them. His analysis raises the question: for whom does the organization really exist? For what purposes? If the organization is truly a political entity, how does one manage effectively within it?

To understand the structural configurations, their planning activities, and power contexts, one must first understand each of the elements that make them up. Accordingly, before the typology of structural configurations is discussed, reference is given to Mintzberg's account of the basic parts of organizations, the processes of co-ordination of activities, the parameters used to design their structures, and the contingency or situational factors as these are defined by Mintzberg (Mintzberg, 1979; 1981; Mintzberg & Queen, 1992). What follows therefore is a fairly detailed account of Mintzberg's scheme.

Parts of the organization
These consist of:

(a) The operating core where the operators, those who perform the basic work of producing products or rendering services are found.
(b) The strategic apex of managers who oversee the systems operation.

(c) The technostructure of analysts or technical staff.
(d) The support staff.
(e) The ideology or culture of the organization which encompasses the traditions and beliefs of an organization.

Co-ordinating mechanisms

The structure of an organization can be defined as the total of the ways in which its labour is divided into distinct tasks and then its co-ordination achieved among those tasks. These are:

(a) Mutual adjustment whereby co-ordination is achieved by the process of informal communication.
(b) Direct supervision as co-ordination is achieved through orders.
(c) Standardization of work processes.
(d) Standardization of outputs.
(e) Standardization of skills.
(f) Standardization of norms (common beliefs).

Parameters of design

The essence of organizational design is the manipulation of a series of parameters that determine the division of labour and the achievement of co-ordination. These include:

(a) Job specialization, performed horizontally and vertically, of unskilled and professional jobs. Complex jobs specialized horizontally but not vertically are generally referred to as professional. Managerial jobs are typically the least specialized in the organization.
(b) Behaviour formalization through the imposition of operating instructions, job descriptions, rules and regulations. This is linked to standardization of processes with the aim of regulation and predictability. Behaviour formalization is most common in the operating core of the organization. At the strategic apex, which typically comes face to face with the most fluid boundary, the environment at large, the work is the least programmes and so we should expect to find highly organic conditions.
(c) Training through use of formal instructional programmes to transfer skills and knowledge and indoctrination which refers to programmes and techniques by which norms of the members of an organization are standardized. Such parameters are linked to formalization professionalization as well as to standardization of skills:
    – Unit grouping.
    – Knowledge or skills.
    – Work processes and function.
(d) Unit grouping which refers to the choice of the bases by which positions are grouped together into units, and those units into higher order units (typically shown on the organization chart).

(e) Unit size as the number of positions contained in a single unit.

(f) Planning and control systems which are used to standardize outputs and are important for performance evaluation and action planning.

(g) Liaison devices which refer to series of mechanisms used to encourage mutual adjustment within and between units. These will include the establishment of liaison positions, task force standing committees, and integrating managers.

(h) Decentralization which refers to the diffusion of decision-making power and can be either vertical or horizontal.

Situational factors

The following contingency or situational factors influence the choice of the design parameters and include:

(a) The age and size of the organization which affect particularly the extent to which its behaviour is formalized and its administrative structure elaborated. As they age and grow organizations appear to go through distinct structural transitions, for example, from simple organic to elaborated bureaucratic structure or from functional grouping to market-based grouping.

(b) The technical system of the organization which influences especially the operating core and those staff units most clearly associated with it. When the technical system of the organization regulates the work of the operating core, as is done in mass production, it has the effect of bureaucratizing the organization by virtue of the standards it imposes on lower level workers. Alternatively, when the technical system succeeds in automating the operating work, as is done in process production, it reduces the need for external rules and regulations enabling the structure to be organic. When the technical system is complex, as is often the case in process production, the organization has to create a significant professional support staff to deal with it and then decentralize selectively to that staff many of the decisions concerned with the technical system.

(c) The environment of the organization which can vary in its degree of complexity, in how static or dynamic it is, in the diversity of its markets, and in the hostility it contains for the organization. The more complex the environment, the more difficulty central management has in comprehending it and the greater the need for decentralization. The more dynamic the environment, the greater the difficulty in standardizing work, outputs, or skills and so the less bureaucratic the structure.

(d) The power factors of the organization include external control, personal power needs, and fashion. The more an organization is controlled externally, the more centralized and bureaucratic it tends to become. This can be explained by the fact that the two most effective means to control an organization from the outside are to hold its most powerful decision maker, the chief executive officer (CEO), responsible for his/her actions and to impose clearly defined standards on him/her (performance standards or rules and regulations). Moreover, because the externally controlled organization must be especially careful about its actions, often having to justify these to outsiders, it tends to formalize much of its behaviour and insist that its CEO authorizes key decisions. A second factor, individual power needs (especially by the CEO) tend to generate excessively centralized structures.

Mintzberg on Planning

Following on from the structure, it is pertinent to consider Mintzberg's work on aspects of planning in organizations. "Planning is future thinking, controlling the future, decision making, integrated decision making, a formalized procedure to produce an articulated result, in the form of an integrated system of decisions" (Mintzberg, 1994: pp. 7–13).

"Planning leads planners to formalize and correspondingly decompose, articulate, and rationalize. But organizations must plan to co-ordinate their activities. A major argument in favour of planning, is that decisions made together formally in a single process will ensure that the efforts of the organization are properly co-ordinated. Organizations must also plan to ensure that the future is taken into account. . . . The future can be taken into account in three basic ways: preparing for the inevitable, pre-empting the undesirable, controlling the controllable. Organizations must plan to be 'rational'. The prime reason put forth for engaging in planning is that it is simply a superior form of management; formalized decision making is better than non-formalized decision making. Organizations must plan to control. Control through planning extends itself in all directions. Planning is meant to control others in the organization, namely those whose work is 'co-ordinated'. . . . Planning is also meant to control the future of the organization and, therefore, the environment outside the organization" (Mintzberg, 1994: p. 17).

Mintzberg and Queen (1992) claim that organizations engage in formal planning not to create strategies but to programme the strategies they already have, that is to elaborate and operationalize the consequences of those strategies formally.

We should really say that effective organizations so engage in planning, at least when they require the formalized implementation of their strategies. Thus strategy is not the consequence of planning but its starting point. Planning helps to translate the intended strategies into realized ones, taking the first step that leads ultimately to implementation.

This strategic programming as it might properly be labelled can be considered to involve a series of steps, namely the codification of a given strategy, including its clarification and articulations, the elaboration of that strategy into sub-strategies, ad hoc action programmes, and plans of various kinds, and the translation of those sub-strategies, programmes, and plans into routine budgets and objectives. In these steps we see planning as an analytical process that takes over after the synthesis of strategic formation is completed.

Thus formal planning properly belongs in the implementation of strategy, not in its formulation. But it should be emphasized that strategic programming makes sense when viable intended strategies are available, in other words when the world is expected to hold still while these strategies unfold so that formulation can logically precede implementation and when the organization that does the implementing in fact requires clearly codified and elaborated strategies. In other circumstances, strategic programming can do organizations harm by pre-empting the flexibility that managers and others may need to respond to changes in the environment, or to their own internal processes of learning (p. 275).

Mintzberg rightly warns about the pitfalls of planning. Planning concerns commitment and may be used to introduce change, to serve specific politics and enable control. There is a fallacy of predetermination, detachment, and formalization but plans may be created as means of public relations. 'Because analysis is not synthesis strategic planning is not strategy formation' (p. 321). The role of planning is seen as a role in strategic programming but the roles of plans are as communication media and control devices and the roles of planners are as finders of strategy (or interpreters of action, pattern recognizers) as analysts, catalysts, and strategists.

2

'Mega' organizing

Aristotle's ideas on the relative virtues of episteme, techne, and phronesis to illuminate planning
research and analyses have been used by Flyvbjerg
(2004) and can be characterized as follows:

Episteme: Scientific knowledge – universal,
invariable, context independent. Based on
general analytical rationality. The original concept is known today in the terms 'epistemology' and 'epistemic'. Planning research
practiced as episteme would be concerned
with uncovering universal truths and laws
about planning. Techne: Craft/art – pragmatic,
variable, context dependent. Oriented towards
production. Based on practical instrumental
rationality governed by a conscious goal. The
original concept appears today in terms like
'technique', 'technical', and 'technology'.
Planning research practiced as techne would
be consulting aimed at arriving at better planning by means of instrumental rationality,
where 'better' is defined in terms of the values
and goals of those who employ the consultants, sometimes in negotiation with the latter.
Phronesis: Ethics – deliberation about values
with reference to praxis. Pragmatic, variable,
context-dependent. Oriented toward action.
Based on practical value rationality. The original

concept is not to be found in an analogous contemporary term; it has dis-appeared from modern language. Planning research practiced as phrone-sis would be concerned with deliberation about (including questioning of) values and interests in planning (p. 287).

Flyvbjerg (2004) goes on to argue that the principal objective for planning research with a phronetic approach is to clarify values, interests, and power relations in planning as a basis for praxis; posing value-rational questions:

(1) Where are we going? (2) Who gains and who loses, and by which mech-anisms of power? (3) Is this development desirable? (4) What, if anything, should we do about it? Question (2), the power question, is what distin-guishes, in particular, contemporary from classical phronesis, and phronetic planning research from other types of such research. The phronetic concept of power will be developed further below. The 'we' referred to in questions (1) and (4) consists of those planning researchers asking the questions and those who share the concerns of the researchers, including people in the community or planning organization under study. Thus the 'we' will always be situated in relation to a specific context. Furthermore, when there is a 'we' there is also usually a 'they', especially when issues get constructed in adversarial terms, which often happens in the planning conflicts planning researchers examine. The questions are asked with the realization that there is no general and unified 'we' in relation to which the questions can be given a final, objective answer. What is a 'gain' and a 'loss' often depends on the perspective taken, and in zero-sum games one person's gain may be another's loss. Phronetic planning researchers are highly aware of the importance of perspective, and see no neutral ground, no 'view from nowhere', for their work. What should be expected therefore, are attempts from phronetic researchers to develop their partial answers to the questions. These answers would be input to the ongoing dialogue about the problems, possibilities, and risks that planning face and how things may be done dif-ferently (pp. 289–290).

The goal then is less to examine planning theory and more to debate about the development of the craft of situated, contextualized research about plan-ning practises and the power relations which define such practises.

Getz (1991) comments on the capacity of mega-events as image makers, urban development and renewal, tourism infrastructure, and general busi-ness and economic development.

It is apparent that major events can have the effect of shaping an image of the host community or country, leading to its favourable perception as a potential travel destination. With global media attention focussed on the host city, even for a short duration, the publicity value is enormous and some destinations will use this fact alone to justify great expenditures on attract-ing events (p. 15).

Mega-events, such as world's fairs and the Olympics, argues Getz (1991), are seen by politicians as catalysts in redevelopment programmes and can also help promote real estate development. Invariably, the events have such land and infrastructure development requirements that the boosting of the destination's overall attractiveness and spin off developments can rightly be anticipated. Politicians also view mega events as providing stimulants to the economy via the associated expenditure, with the added advantage of having public support, given the general attitudes of citizens to events like the Olympic Games. Nevertheless, the costs of participating in the mega event business may be very high and public participation in decision making may not be facilitated. Although benefits are often discussed in studies of forecasted impact, the exact cost of bidding and hosting mega events are rarely exposed to public scrutiny.

Flyvbjerg, Bruzelius, and Rothengatter (2003) claim that in many parts of the world, one is confronted with a new political and physical animal: the multi-billion dollar mega infrastructure project.

In Europe we have the Channel tunnel, the Øresund bridge between Denmark and Sweden, the Vasco da Gama bridge in Portugal, the German MAGLEV train between Berlin and Hamburg, the creation of an inter-connected high-speed rail network for all of Europe, cross-national motor-way systems, the Alp tunnels, the fixed link across the Baltic Sea between Germany and Denmark, plans for airports to become gateways to Europe, enormous investments in new freight container harbours, DM 200 billion worth of transport infrastructure projects related to German unification alone, links across the straits of Gibraltar and Messina, the world's longest road tunnel in Norway, not to speak of new and extended telecommunications networks, systems of cross-border pipelines for transport of oil and gas, and cross-national electrical power networks to meet the growing demand in an emerging European energy market.

Bill Gates, founder and chairperson of Microsoft Corporation, has dubbed the phenomenon 'frictionless capitalism' and sees it as a novel stage in capitalist evolution. When Microsoft and Gates single out a concept or a product one is well advised to pay attention. 'Frictionless society' may sound as an advertiser's slogan in their usage. It is not. The term signifies a qualitatively different stage of social and economic development.

In this development 'infrastructure' has become a catchword on par with 'technology'. Infrastructure has rapidly moved from being a simple pre-condition for production and consumption to being at the very core of these activities, with just-in-time delivery and instant Internet access being two spectacular examples of this. Infrastructure is the great space shrinker, and power, wealth, and status increasingly belong to those who know how to shrink space, or know how to benefit from space being shrunk.

There is a paradox here, however. At the same time as many more and much larger infrastructure projects are being proposed and built around the world, it is becoming clear that many such projects have strikingly poor performance records in terms of economy, environment, and public support.

In consequence, the cost–benefit analyses, financial analyses, and environmental and social impact statements that are routinely carried out as part of mega project preparation are called into question, criticized, and denounced more often and more dramatically than analyses in any other professional field we know. Mega project development today is not a field of what has been called 'honest numbers'. It is a field where you will see one group of professionals calling the work of another not only 'biased' and 'seriously flawed' but a 'grave embarrassment' to the profession. And that is when things have not yet turned unfriendly. In more antagonistic situations the words used in the mudslinging accompanying many mega projects are 'deception', 'manipulation', and even 'lies' and 'prostitution'. Whether we like it or not, mega project development is currently a field where little can be trusted, not even – some would say especially not – numbers produced by analysts (p. 1–2).

Such malpractice goes on despite the availability of some technological tools to contemporary planners as described by (Knox, 2004).

The world wide web (www) is used today for the distribution of information to participants, potential attendees, sponsors, organizers, and suppliers. Via the use acronym www organizers have the ability to connect and inform all aspects of the supply chain quickly and efficiently. This is further enhanced by the ability to keep this process updated on a regular, almost hourly, basis. The www and Intranets have allowed a 'pull' process to the distribution of data as opposed to a 'push' approach. That is interested parties have the ability to select what is relevant and pertinent to them making the whole process more efficient. In the past the ability to open, manipulate, and respond to electronic distribution and its attachments was imperative; now recipients need only log on to a website to access relevant information. This can be used to provide maps of the venue, transportation details, and more specific details such as delivery schedules, traffic information, or weather conditions (Knox, 2004: p.99).

Due to the volatility of the event function, with many participants, resources, services, and activities being involved at any one time, there is a requirement for all of the activities to be up-to-date, communicated, and available. It is also important to identify activities or jobs and in what potential order they need to occur for the event to run smoothly and for successfully meeting all of the aims and objectives identified at the start of the event. 'This level of planning could take a number of forms from a progress calendar, charting events and activities over a yearly time period, to the use of some form of project management software tool as used in construction or engineering or a dedicated events management software' (p. 101).

Software for project planning has a number of functions. Initially, it may be the production of some form of flow chart, which identifies activities, resources, timings, and relationships. Secondly, it could be the allocation of resources to actual individuals, through to preparing individual schedules.

Finally, the critical path analysis allows the identification of the tasks and projects that need to be completed before progress can be achieved in the component parts of the project. By incorporating information on the duration and required order of completion of task this type of analysis allows managers and planners to produce a network diagram where they identify the interconnectedness of resources, activities, and timings. Such visual representation allows one to identify the critical path and so create a workable timeframe in which to complete all tasks and operate a successful event (p. 102).

According to Flyvbjerg, Bruzelius, and Rothengatter (2003)

Project promoters often avoid and violate established practices of good governance, transparency, and participation in political and administrative decision making, either out of ignorance or because they see such practices as counterproductive to getting projects started. Civil society does not have the same say in this arena of public life as it does in others; citizens are typically kept at a substantial distance from mega project decision making. In some countries this state of affairs may be slowly changing, but so far mega projects often come draped in a politics of mistrust. People fear that the political inequality in access to decision-making processes will lead to an unequal distribution of risks, burdens, and benefits from projects. The general public is often sceptical or negative towards projects; citizens and interest groups orchestrate hostile protests; and occasionally secret underground groups even encourage or carry out downright sabotage on projects, though this is not much talked about in public for fear of inciting others to similar guerrilla activities (p. 5).

Kanellis (2005) reviews occasions of such political inequality and sought to describe and explain facets of modern national ideology as this was expressed during the Athens 2004 Olympic Games. To this effect he coins the term 'ethnohouliganism' to describe, amongst others, the ways in which the Greek establishment approached the issues that developed over the doping allegations against two of Greece's leading athletes and the Greek-centred behaviour of the spectators that appeared to be endorsed by exponents of the state sports machinery.

Flyvbjerg et al. (2003) agree that risk can be eliminated from risk society but that risk may be acknowledged much more explicitly and managed a great deal better, with more accountability, than is typically the case today.

They argue, nevertheless, that deliberative approaches to risk, based as they are on communicative rationality and the goodwill of participants, can take us only some of the way towards better decisions and will frequently fail for mega projects. This is so because the interests and power relations involved in mega projects are typically very strong, which is easy to understand given the enormous sums of money at stake, the many jobs, the environmental impacts, the national prestige, etc. Communicative and deliberative approaches work well as ideals and evaluative yardsticks for decision making, but they are quite defenceless in the face of power. And power play, instead of commitment to deliberative ideals, is often what characterizes mega project development, in addition to deliberative processes.

Based on this approach to risk, it is a basic notion of the book that good decision making is not only a question of better and more rational inform-ation, but also of institutional arrangements that promote accountability, and especially accountability towards risk. Flyvbjerg, Bruzelius, and Rothengatter (2003) see accountability not just as being a question about periodic elections, but also about a continuing dialogue between civil society and policy makers and about institutions holding each other accountable through appropriate cheques and balances.

> Thus we replace the conventional decisionistic approach to mega project development with a more current institutionalistic one centred on the practices and rules that comprise risk and accountability. We also hold that our approach must be based on actual experience from concrete projects. The purpose is to ensure a realistic understanding of the issues at hand as well as proposals that are practically desirable and possible to implement.

Flyvbjerg (2005: p. 51) concludes that the studies they carried out show that transportation projects, public buildings, power plants, dams, water pro-jects, sports stadiums, oil and gas extraction projects, information technology systems, aerospace projects, and weapons systems follow a general pattern of cost underestimation and overrun.

> The large projects that get built are not the best ones but instead those for which proponents best succeed in designing – deliberately or not – a fantasy world of underestimated costs, overestimated revenues, overvalued local development effects, and underestimated environmental impacts. Project approval in most cases depended on these factors. Many project proponents don't hesitate to use Machiavellian approaches even if it means misleading lawmakers, the public and the media about the true costs and benefits of the projects. The result is an inverted Darwinism – an unhealthy survival of the unfittest – for large public works and other construction projects (p. 50).

What is most disturbing is not deceptive individual project estimates, it is the massive extent to which rent-seeking behaviour by stakeholders has highjacked and replaced the pursuit of public good in this important and expensive policy area and the high costs this behaviour imposes on society. Deceptive cost–benefit analyses keeps critical scrutiny (by lawmakers, the public, and the media), accountability, and good governance at bay until it is too late, that is, until the sunk costs for a project are so high that its point of no return has been reached and construction must be completed. Thus, there are few half-built bridges and tunnels (plus pressure from opposition parties who will be quick to blame) in the world, although there are many that function poorly.

> Public planning – to deserve its name – presupposes a notion of public good. When this notion is highjacked, planning itself is highjacked. Instead we get one of the most undermining misfits of democracy: the public institution used for private gain. Any society that wants to remain one will have to prevent such highjacking and restore the vital distinction between public good and private interest. The same may be said of planning: The public good, as defined by law, is planning's raison d'etre.

> But the whole structure of incentives for planning major projects is geared towards keeping deception going. Each project is multimillion-dollar and often even multibillion-dollar business, and when it goes forward, many people profit – architects, engineers, contractors, consultants, bankers, landowners, construction workers, lawyers, and developers. In addition politicians with a 'monument complex' gain satisfaction and get to cut ribbons, administrators get larger budgets, and cities get investments and infrastructures that might otherwise go elsewhere. Stakeholders may have an interest in letting a project go ahead even if it is not especially useful from a public point of view (p. 57).

Essex and Chalkley (1998) confer that the host city's exposure to enormous numbers of visitors, have intensified the need to improve an extend transport systems and to up-grade at least parts of the city's landscape and environment. The exposure to the world's media has re-enforced the desire to 'show off' the city to best effect. 'The more extensive the publicity, the more compelling the opportunity to enhance the city's image and reputation. In the modern global economy, in which major world cities compete for investment, the Olympics represent a unique publicity platform and opportunity for place marketing. In the context of post-fordism, as cities strive to present themselves as consumer, leisure, and cultural centres, the growth of the games as an international spectacle has offered its hosts increasing opportunities to claim physical attributes and images which attest to its distinction, taste, and eminence' (p. 201).

Flyvbjerg, Bruzelius, and Rothengatter (2003) claim that although progress is slow, democratic governance is gaining a foothold even in major project development. The conventional consensus is also under attack for the practical reason that mega projects are becoming so large in relation to national economies that cost overruns and benefit shortfalls from even a single project may destabilize the finances of a whole country and region. This happened when the billion-dollar cost overrun of the 2004 Athens Olympics affected the credit rating of Greece. It was also the case when Hong Kong's new $200 billion Chek Lap Kok airport opened in 1998. Lawmakers and governments begin to see that national fiscal distress is too high a price to pay for the mega projects lying game and that reform is needed (p. 58).

Masterman (2003) argues that it is essential that any long-term attributable benefits inherent in the planning process should be comprehensively covered by strategies that ensure that long-term success. Firstly, including a cost–benefit forecast at a feasibility stage of the event planning process would enable organizers to not only forecast the extent of the benefits of their events and budget accordingly, but through that forecast gain support for the event at an early and appropriate stage. Secondly, implementation strategies for the use of new facilities and or regeneration projects need to be built-in to ensure their long-term futures. Thirdly, assessing the impact of such an event requires not only an evaluation of short- and medium-term economic and cultural benefits for instance, but also a long-term evaluation, possibly even 10 years on or more, of the sustainability and durability, in other words the success, of the regeneration and the legacies that were created as a result of staging the event. Fourthly, in order for objectives to be met there is a case for the inclusion of mechanisms in the process that will allow continuous alignment with short-, medium-, and long-term plans. The above, Masterman (2003) claims, is a new event planning process that encompasses both short-term requirements for the implementation of the event and the long-term objectives that become the legacies of the event (p. 460). For him, it is clear that events spell out the dangers and the benefits of not implementing and implementing long-term strategies early in the planning of major international sports events. 'The key stages are considering and budgeting for any legacies and preparing for handover and new ownership at the feasibility stage, implementing these strategies prior to the event, continually aligning the process with the event objectives, and evaluating the event against objectives over the long term' (p. 463).

The key weapons in the war on deception is accountability and critical questioning the professional expertise of planners, architects, engineers, economist, and administrators is certainly indispensable to constructing the buildings and infrastructures that make society work. 'Our studies show however that the claims made by these groups usually cannot be trusted and should be carefully examined by independent specialist and organizations. The same holds for claims made by project-promoting politicians and officials. Institutional cheques and balances – including financial, professional, or even criminal penalties for consistent and unjustifiable biases in claims and estimates of costs and benefits – should be developed and employed. . . . The key principle is that the cost of making a wrong forecast should fall on those making the forecast, a principle often violated today' (Flyvbjerg, 2005: p. 59).

Emery's (2001) studied the selection and sanctioning process of a city wishing to host a major sports event through a major survey of sports organizers and found that there existed a formal process of internal selection and sanctioning but this did not include absolute and immutable selection criteria, nor was it based entirely upon financial information.

Having asked the question: What planning techniques are utilized in the pre-event management process? Emery (2001) found that complacency and vague terms of reference provide evidence of under planning characteristics with no respondent confirming the use of techniques such as capital investment appraisals, and risk/sensitivity analyses. The evidence provided from this study appears to support the notion that the present bidding process is characterized by personal ambition rather than rational management. One explanation may be attributed to the fact that major sports events are characterized by a complex interdependency of national and international organizational relationships that have evolved over many years. Within this context, there exist diverse personal and cultural needs involving opportunities for considerable autonomy and power.

This environment had developed against a background of little professional and/or academic sport management training and or education. In major sports events, those in power are likely to be committed amateurs who possess limited technical and operational knowledge, but considerable political influence and experience. It is little surprise then, that the present formalized antiquated selection process, that typifies most international bidding frameworks, appears to operate more on hidden agendas and informal processes, than on the application of systematic techniques and principles. This seems to occur within and between councils, national governing bodies, and international governing bodies. Is bidding to host a major sports vent seriously becoming a strategic corporate option or does it appear vaguely familiar to a civic leader pursuing his/her dream, and purchasing a national lottery ticket on a Saturday night (p. 106).

Detailed event analysis frameworks are also available in the literature for planners to carry out their tasks. These include practises like checking the detail of the contract, evaluating the employees performance, appraisal as post-event activity and ultimately, an evaluation of the financial success. Rental and lease contracts are very complex in the case of mega events for the size of the Olympic Games. Evaluating liability, and the notification of the insurers on any incident that could possibly lead to a claim are also necessary. Post-event surveys and related research can answer questions like: Did all strategies work? Were employees successful at their assigned tasks? Did the mechanical systems work as expected? Did the marketing campaign bring enough sponsors or ticket sales? Did the event make or lose money? Did the event generate goodwill in the community? What were the levels of customer satisfaction? What are the lessons learnt for marketing for the future? Fried (2005) confers that significant value can come from post-event recognitions and marketing (p. 324).

Such questions are nevertheless rarely answered by planners who move on to the next project. As Gratton, Shibli, and Coleman (2005: p. 998) claim, a sport strategy based around events can deliver significant benefits to cities. Whether such benefits justify the expenditure involved is however a difficult question to answer. There is a need for research to concentrate on the longer-term urban regeneration benefits that sport has the potential to deliver. More often than not, the business elite is spending (or seeking to spend) public money not private money, bidding for grants rather than boosting for growth. As Cochrane, Peck, and Tickell (1996) suggest in British policy discourse, it has become necessary to talk about growth to get grants. It is this which makes it more appropriate in the UK context to think in terms of grant coalitions than growth coalitions. Such coalitions also help to redefine popular understandings of welfare in ways which stress the importance of competitive success rather than service delivery, the possibility of getting bread through the effective promotion of circuses. The politics of elite localism in contemporary Manchester can be seen, then as a response to globalization which involves struggles over the role, and meaning and structure of the state, as well as straightforward attempts to appropriate more public cash. But they are also a relatively unstable and fragile politics which rely on an extensive insulation from processes of public accountability and even from political debate (p. 1333).

Monopoly Power and Organizations

Given the IOC's monopoly over the Olympic trademarks and their authority in recognizing NOCs, awarding games to OCOGs, and accepting sports in the summer and winter Olympic programmes it is relevant to consider the literature on such monopoly organization and their roles in society and economy.

Knights and Willmott (1990) ask how it is possible to make sense of the way work is organized and controlled? To what extent is its design the result of technological demands, the interests of capital or processes of negotiation and struggle? They suggest that labour process analysis, revived by Braverman's Labour and Monopoly Capital, has been most influential in shaping thinking about these questions and contributed to the study of work organization. Providing a fresh response to criticisms of 'Bravermania' and lost momentum, they explore the theoretical foundations of labour process analysis and suggest new directions for its development. Tracing thinking on monopoly power leads to the writing of Braverman and his seminal work on the impacts of monopoly power on the labour process.

Monopoly capital had its beginning, he argues, in the last two or three decades of the nineteenth century. It was then that the concentration and centralization of capital, in the form of the early trusts, cartels, and other forms of combination, began to assert itself; it was consequently then that the modern structure of capitalist industry and finance began to take shape. At the same time, the rapid completion of the colonization of the world and the international rivalries and armed clashes over the division of the globe into spheres of economic influence or dominance opened the modern imperialist era. Monopoly capitalism thus embraced the increase of monopolistic organizations within each capitalist country, the internationalization of capital, the international division of labour, imperialism, the world market and the world movement of capital, and changes in the structure of state power (Braverman, 1998: p. 175).

Associated with the growth of monopoly power over labour is Braverman's thinking on monopoly power on the pursuits of individuals during non-work time which echoes the commodification of free time and the organization of the sports market. He argued that

> in a society where labour power is purchased and sold, working time becomes sharply and antagonistically divided from non-working time, and the worker places an extraordinary value upon this free time, while on the job time is regarded as lost or wasted . . . thus the filling of the time away from the job also becomes dependent upon the market, which develops to an enormous degree those passive amusements, entertainments, and spectacles that suit the restricted circumstances of the city and are offered as substitutes for life itself. Since they become the means of filling all the hours of 'free' time, they flow profusely from corporate institutions which have transformed every means of entertainment and 'sport' into a production process for the enlargement of capital. By their very profusion, they cannot help but tend to a standard of mediocrity and vulgarity which debases popular taste, a result which is further guaranteed by the fact that the mass market has a powerful lowest-common- denominator effect because of the search for maximum profit. So enterprising is capital that even where the effort is made by one or another section of the population to find a way to nature, sport, or art through personal activity and amateur or 'underground' innovation, these activities are rapidly incorporated into the market so far as is possible (Braverman, 1998: p. 193).

The commodification of sport and the sporting experience is well documented (Slack, 2004). The IOC's monopoly power has grown to its current levels due to the exclusive rights over Olympic sport. As Braverman wrote, under monopoly capitalism, the first step in the creation of the universal market is the conquest of all goods production by the commodity form, the second step is the conquest of an increasing range of services and their conversion into commodities, and the third step is a 'product cycle' which invents new products and services, some of which become indispensable as the conditions of modern life change to destroy alternatives (Braverman, 1998: p. 194).

Having established a universal market, the IOC converted the Olympic Games into a commodity and have established a product cycle which brings in new sports and drops others from the Olympic programme whilst the predominance of Olympic sport is inadvertently leading to the demise of some indigenous sport forms which does not get the same state support. The IOC has operated with the Swiss national context in a country where a lot of international organizations base their headquarters and in a city that calls itself Olympic Capital.

As Braverman argues, the use of the power of the state to foster the development of capitalism is not a new phenomenon peculiar to the monopoly stage of the past 100 years. The governments of capitalists countries have played this role from the beginnings of capitalism. In the most elementary sense, the state is guarantor of the conditions, the social relations, of capitalism, and the protector of the ever more unequal distribution of property which this system brings about. But in a further sense state power has everywhere been used by governments to enrich the capitalist class, and by groups or individuals to enrich themselves. With the IOC and so many IF having their headquarters in Lausanne, it is interesting to consider the circumstances and conditions that have made the city such an attractive base. The powers of the state having to do with taxation, the regulation of foreign trade, public lands, commerce and transportation, the maintenance of armed forces, and the discharge of the functions of public administration have served as an engine to siphon wealth into the hands of special groups, by both legal and illegal means (Braverman, 1998: p. 197).

Taylorism was a tool for monopoly capital to strengthen its position and it is prudent to consider whether management processes in the Olympic Movement echo this method to improve productivity. Taylorism can be summarized in the form of three distinct principles: (i) dissociation of the labour process from the skills of the workers, (ii) separation of conception from execution, and (iii) the use of this monopoly over knowledge to control each step of the labour process and its mode of execution (Braverman, 1998: p. xvii).

Aspects of Taylorism can be observed in the ways in which the Olympic Games have been managed. The use of monopoly over Olympic knowledge in particular, give evidence to the fact that the event organization process is provided top down to OCOGs from the IOC and the conception of games management is done by managers whilst delivery takes place predominantly by volunteers. The labour process is dictated by the standardization of outputs expected by stakeholders' and promised in the bid stage. Furthermore, the strict time confines limit the scope for experimentation and often the games labour process conception is formed to predominantely meet IOC priorities and not necessarily those of the country that ultimately delivers the Olympic Games.

Although operating in a monopoly the IOC has to content with a number a significant others in its environment. Chappelet and Bayle (2005: p. 18) claim that the Olympic system is a pyramidal unit of organizations including the IOC, OCOGS, IFs, NOCs, and National Sport Federation (NSF).

Virtually all the organizations within the Olympic system are non-profit ones according to the law of the country where their headquarters are located, including the IOC, in Switzerland. For about 20 years, this associative movement has been increasingly confronted with four other types of actors whose legal nature is different . First come government and intergovernmental organization, public law entities that are becoming increasingly interested in sport because it has become a socio-economic phenomenon that affects an extremely large sector of the population. A second new type of actor is multinational companies that provide international sponsoring and maintain a commercial relationship with the IOC and their continental equivalents. Their equivalents on a national level (sponsors and the national media) are a third type of new actor and have relations with the NOCs and NSFs via sponsoring contracts limited to their national territory. Finally, a fourth type of actor has been emerging strongly for approximately the last 10 years in cooperation with or competing against the NSFs and the IFs. These are leagues of teams of professional athletes. Although these new actors and their legal status vary widely, they have a common objective: achieving profit for their members, owners, or shareholders. At times they cooperate with the Olympic system regarding the participation of their members in the Games (pp. 20–21).

Ferrand and Torrigiani (2005: p. 128) develop four major strategic issues for Olympic Sport Organizations' (OSOs) marketing: Brand equity management, stakeholders' expectations, marketing strategy, and managing sponsorship. According to them, an OSO falls within a competitive framework where it will have a place among other sport organizations competing with each other as well as among commercial entities proposing rival or alternative products and services in various leisure areas.

Attention needs to also turn to the political and business interests served from the games. Urban regimes in the form of political groups and individuals get involved with the bidding for the games having first rallied support for the bid in the host city. Ex ante impact studies that showcase the economic benefit to the host city are often employed by growth regimes and although actual economic impact data does not always reveal benefits to the host city and country the image that the Olympic Games will spur economic, social, sporting, and technological advances is often present in public opinion. As cities embark on a global competition to get on the map by marketing themselves the question of who benefits by hosting the Olympic Games has been posed by Burbank, Andranovich and Heying (2001). They contend that in all three US cities that have hosted recent Olympic Games, Los Angeles, Atlanta, and Salt Lake City, the success of the Olympic mega-event as a mechanism for local development was heavily dependent on non-local actors, ranging form multinational corporate sponsors to non-profit organizations such as the United States of America Olympic Committee (USOC) and the IOC.

The magnitude of the Olympic event required substantial coordination between the host city and other governments in the region that served as hosts for particular venues. Each city was also highly dependent on the state and federal governments either for resources or authority. Thus the appeal on an event such as the Olympic Games is that it can attract non-local resources, such as corporate sponsorship or federal money, to subsidize local development projects. But this approach means that the goals of local development are subject to the decisions and conditions of external actors. One of the outcomes of the Olympics as a vehicle for economic development is that the ability of local leaders to deliver tangible benefits becomes highly dependent on the actions of regime outsiders (Burbank et al., 2001: p. 169).

In this era, cities will undoubtedly continue to be concerned with place marketing, city image, and long-term strategies for subsidizing their development as consumption locations. As such, the allure of hosting a mega-event will remain. The symbolic value of the Olympics will continue to allow the advocates of growth to set the terms of the policy debate in cities. These terms have been narrowly defined around the goals of consumption-oriented economic development – the Olympic dream of a growth regime. As a public policy instrument that has a decade long planning horizon and no broad public-participation requirement, the Olympic mega-event provides an opportunity for development interests to make their vision the local policy agenda. According to Burbank et al., 2001, the experiences of Los Angeles, Atlanta, and Salt Lake City indicate that, despite the rhetoric, the materialization of Olympic dreams serves only narrow purposes. Without change, the long time frame needed for planning, the use of public–private partnerships to design and implement Olympic development, and the absence of meaningful citizen participation add up to an extended business-as-usual theme under the rhetoric and symbolism of Olympic dreams (Burbank et al., 2001: pp. 170–171).

Finally, they argue (p. 170) that questions of access, representation, responsiveness, and accountability must be addressed as well, to better understand under whose rules the game is being played.

Waitt (2004: p. 391) explores the Sydney 2000 Olympic Games as an urban propaganda exercise and argues that for Sydney that was born of mercantile capitalism, the Olympics provided a mechanism to assist the city reposition itself in the world economy.

International sports events are themselves not new. However, they have acquired a renewed significance in the context of globalization. In economic terms the collapse of spatial boundaries has increased the sensitivity of capital to differences between places. Consequently, intensified competition occurs between places in the global market to attract potential investors, employers, and tourists. The successful bidding and hosting of a prestige hallmark event over other cities enables the host city to promote, market, differentiate, and image itself as a winning location (p. 403).

A number of non-elected governing authorities have been responsible for managing the Olympic site, including the New South Wales (NSW) Property Service Group, Homebush Bay Development Corporation, and Sydney Organizing Committee for the Olympic Games (SOCOG). In 1991, Waitt (2004: p. 397) argues that the state effectively gave itself carte blanche over the land remediation processes at Homebush when the NSW Department of Planning exempted all earth works from the mandatory requirement to prepare an Environmental Impact Assessment, extending in 1992 to all designated or significant Olympic Developments; in the absence of these exercises, the planning process exemplifies a series of mechanisms employed by the entrepreneurial state that arguably fast-tracked development in private sector interests.

Chain Operators

Associated to the monopoly of the IOC is its power to control chains of organizations and franchises like the issue franchises to (see figure 2.1) NOCs and OCOGs. Chains represent one of the dominant organizational forms of our time Bradach (1998: p. 3) and franchising constitutes a vital facet of chain operations.(a franchise being an agreement or licence to sell a company's products exclusively in a particular area, or to operate a business that carries that company's name). Franchisees purchase the right to operate a unit under the chain's brand name. Typically, the franchisee agrees to follow certain operating guidelines (to preserve the value of the brand), pays the chain operator a royalty fee based on revenue, and receives the income produced by the unit (Bradach 1998: p. 3). In a company chain such fees are redundant as the chain units are branches of the same organization.

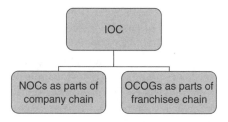

Figure 2.1 The IOC and its company and franchisee chains

Bradach (1998) defines three main characteristics of chain organizations (pp. 16–21), which are also shared by the IOC: (1) there is shared identity in the sense that all organizations serve and believe in Olympic values, (2) there is local production of product/service in the form of the games, the athletes and Olympic ideology, and (3) there is use of small and geographically dispersed units – as in the case of NOCs.

Chain organizations are built on the principle of cloning: replicating a business format with fidelity. This basic organizing principle, the product of the three characteristics of the industry, leads to the four management challenges faced by chain operators (pp. 20–21).

There are four management challenges identified in the literature on chain organizations: adding new units, maintaining uniformity across units, responding locally when appropriate, and adapting the system as a whole when threats or opportunities arise. Like differences between a company

43

chain or a franchise chain so differences in host countries of the Olympic Games present different challenges for games management.

In the chain, employees often have cross-cutting career paths (Figure 2.2) and the franchisee often exhibits similar organizational structures and processes to the franchiser.

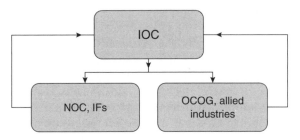

Figure 2.2 Possible career paths in Olympic Games Related Business

For Bradach, adding units to the chain plays a crucial role in its success and management. The direct financial implications of new units are obvious: more revenue and profits from additional company units, and more fees and royalties from new franchise units. Unit growth also produces important indirect effects in the form of leveraging the trademark to the benefit of existing and new units, increasing market presence and identity, and generating more funds for advertising (p. 61). In the case of the IOC the benefits are accrued by the increase in the number of countries participating in the Olympic Games that increases the broadcasting appeal (and consequently rights fees) and the sponsors' exposure to various markets.

Management information systems have the possibility to make the operational detail of local franchisees almost transparent. Superiors are able to view performance, and data may be accompanied with a comparison to a budget, to the previous year's performance or to averages in the company chain. Variances from expected performance could be identified at a glance. Senior managers can then identify projects and numbers that are out of bounds and ask subordinates for explanations and action plans (Bradach, 1998: p. 90). IOC members in various member countries can be seen to be parts of such a reporting process.

By presenting public results (as in the case of the IOC publishing medals, tables, and reports on progress made by host city organizers), the chain operator has the opportunity to force rhetoric to rise or fall in level or intensity by deliberately applying pressure in successive and irreversible stages.

Benchmarking also takes place as one franchise raises the bar (as is the case of OCOGs that seek to outperform previous organizers). Finally, modelling processes take place because if the company arrangement is successful then the franchisees have an incentive to emulate the designs that produced that performance (Bradach, 1998: p. 108). The games management knowledge transfer and the OCOGs' structural modelling is one way in which modelling is achieved and the successful model moves from one host city to the next.

Local responsiveness is instrumental for the success of the chain: issues of pricing, variations of the products, access to key suppliers, knowledgeable labour, and local marketing are very important. Along with being seen as a critical factor in the chain's increasingly competitive environment, systemwide adaptation can be viewed by practitioners as the most complex management challenge that chain organizations face. The particularities of diverse local markets, the difficulty of implementing a new activity in hundreds of units, the potential conflicts of interest between franchisers and chain operators, and the absence of authority in the franchise arrangements were but a few of the problems that make systemwide adaptation a major challenge. The process of adaptation may involve: generating of ideas, testing and evaluating them, decision making, and implementation (Bradach, 1998: p. 133). 'We tell company people we sell to franchisees' (Bradach, 1998: p. 157).

It is possible that not all franchisees will be as enthusiastic about systemwide adaptation. Questions of who has decision-making power and who has implementation power then become important for the timely execution of the required adaptation. The quality of adaptation, speed of identifying opportunities, and speed of implementation may vary depending on local circumstances. In the case of an event organizing committee it can be argued that certain countries present particular management challenges to the chain operator stemming from the differences in the organizational culture in the host city. The IOC faces the challenge of systemwide adaptation as it tries to lead NOCs and OCOGs towards particular activity and organizational behaviour.

Bradach (1998) claims that self-correcting, self-renewing organizations can meet the challenges of operating a chain. By incorporating attributes from all business sides (NOCs as company units and OCOGs as franchise units) the plural-form organization of the Olympic chain may be able to escape the natural tendency of internal arrangements to ossify over time and external relationships to suffer from entropy by creating a built-in constructive tension between the parts. Such a plural form then may be integral to the long-term sustainability of the Olympic chain organizations. Similarly, ambidextrous organizations (different structures are required for different circumstances) are better than hybrid forms. The plural form offers an intriguing alternative to the widely held view that the external variety in the environment needs to be matched with internal variety of structures and systems. In most theories of organization internal variety is said to be achieved through specialization. Bradach's research shows that another way to obtain that variety is by having different kinds of structures in tension in the same organization each generating different kinds of ideas (Bradach, 1998: p. 179). He claims that practitioners and academics alike need to move beyond simple models that search for the best way to organize or that seek to identify the unique fit between certain conditions and certain organizational designs.

We must entertain the notion that combinations of structures like the plural form offer attributes not available to any single arrangement. And we

45

need to embrace the counterintuitive idea that redundancy and variety can be intertwined in ways that set in motion a powerful set of dynamics that promote self-correction and self-renewal (Bradach, 1998: p. 185).

Company and franschise chains are not the only structures employed by the IOC. This organization also holds shares in a number of corporations which are its subsidiaries as discussed in Part Two of the book.

The IOC seeks to guide OCOG behaviour in order to improve their activity and aid positive impact formation. As IOC staff Dubi, Hug, and Griethuysen (2003) contend, it is necessary to have a strong vision for the entire games project. For the IOC, this vision is one of a project that lasts 15 years.

First we have to establish that framework of activities: this is what is referred to as the rules, the Charter, and the Host City Contract. Then we have the candidature phase, where the foundations are established. These are important, as every decision made during these phases will have an impact further down the road. From the IOC's standpoint, the questionnaires for candidate cities contain a number of criteria in themes, such as the concept of the games, etc, that are all linked to legacy. Where the situation will evolve further, or has evolved recently, is in the assistance and the educational services that the IOC provides to applicants and candidate cities. Not only will we need evaluation criteria, but we also need to provide information to the applicants and candidate cities that will help them build stronger foundations. This work is being carried out by a company created by the IOC, the Olympic Games Knowledge Services SA (OGKS). When looking at the project life cycle its foundation and strategic planning, the bid, the host city contract, and all the activities in these two phases are key because they will condition every activity down the line. For the actual management of the Olympic Games, the IOC has developed a project management tool called the Masterplan which helps us to analyse all the key events that are necessary to be delivered by an organizing Committee in a timely manner. It is a time and risk management tool. We have also developed a programme as of 1998, which is a concept of knowledge management. The objective here is to capitalize on experience and expertise from one edition of the games and transfer this to the next edition. Essentially, our objective is to speed up the learning curve of the organizing Committee. The Games have grown bigger: they are more spectacular, but more difficult to manage and to organize. Early in 2002, President Rogge established the OG Study Commission with the objective of looking at the product and try to find a way to ensure its success over time. The idea is to try to contain the growth and manage the growth and costs in a more efficient way.

During the games we have an observer programme in which experts look at the way the games operate and the issues or strong factors that should be replicated in the future. Following the games we have a formal debriefing with the OCOG that will produce an official report. In this exercise, we ask OCOG to take a step back and have a critical look at their activities and tell us frankly what they felt was good and should be replicated in the future and what should not. This is a very technical view of the organization of the Games. Recently we have also developed a methodology called Olympic Games Global Impact (OGGI) which aims to study the Games wider impact (social, environmental, and economic dimension). This is more a general evaluation than a technical one, and the idea of developing this method was to develop a consistent method that can be applied edition after edition. It was not developed to compare one edition with another, but really to analyse one edition in relation to the next one using a consistent approach (pp. 404–406).

Mega-event Research

Roche (2000) suggests that mega-events can be characterized in terms of whether they are modern/non-modern, national/non-national, and local/non-local. In addition, their study can be justified in terms of their presence and significance in modernity in personal (biographical), historical (national and cultural history), and sociological (substantive and abstract) terms. He proposes three levels of analysis by the essential temporal characteristics of any event seen as a process over time. These are the event related time periods of the present (and immediate past and future) (the 'event core' zone), the medium-term pre-event and post-event processes producing the event (the intermediate zone), and the long-term (pre-event) causes/motivations and (post-event) effects of the event (the zone of the 'event horizon'). Roche calls for the consideration of mega-events as multi-dimensional phenomena that require a multi-perspectival approach. He groups research that has taken place under the dramatological and contextual perspectives. The former can be divided into (a) ethnography that seeks to capture and map experiences and attitudes, (b) textualism where explicit and implicit interpretations of communications are the research foci, and (c) cultural functionalism with a strong anthropological orientation.

The contextual approaches reviewed by Roche include those exploring '(a) economic functionalism of the events in the host economies, (b) political instrumentalism (rational use of events to stimulate growth as well as non-rational use of events where decisions are made on a whim or for personal gain), and (c) critical functionalism as expressed by those informed by neo- Marxist approaches and critical theory' (pp. 11–19).

For MacAloon (1999), the modest beginnings of Olympic anthropology can be identified in the 1960s and 1970s intellectual context of semiotic and structural anthropologies of cultural performance theories. These were born from renewed interest in the old topoi of myth, symbol, and ritual, and of consequentially culturalist approaches to national and nationalist phenomena. Introducing the work of a group of Norwegian anthropologists edited by Klausen MacAloon (1999) claims that there is a maturing Olympic anthropology reflecting and taking advantage of a new theoretical state of affairs in the 'post-modern' human sciences. Reflecting on the work of Klausen (1999: pp. 12–13) he comments on the ways these studies are concerned with the familiar issues of the production of national identity on international occasions, traditional versus modern forms of each, and the recruitment and fate of individual actors in these mass-mediated public dramas. He contends that their commitment to attend as equally as possible to all the various social segments engaged with the making and the interpretation of the Olympic events in Lillehammer has as consequence, the negotiation of meaning and power from a post-structuralist mantra into a research finding, to be evaluated like any other scientific result according to its greater or lesser success against other disciplinary approaches in representing, interpreting, and explaining the events in question.

The concepts of contextual explanation and situational rationality introduced by Roche (1994) need to be illustrated through empirical studies. He proposes them as potentially useful concepts for the future development of explanation-oriented mega-event research and Parts Two and Three of this book employ them to structure the narrative of the *Olympic Event Organization*.

The two main contemporary approaches to understanding event production referred to by Roche (1994: pp. 11–12) as the planning and the political approaches are also evident in the literature. The planning approach of necessity focuses much more on developing the application potential of explanatory knowledge for presumptively rational actors and agencies, rather than on the genesis and construction of such knowledge per se. The political approach appears to address more directly the problem of describing and explaining real-world hallmark and mega-events than the planning approach.

The need for ethical behaviour by managers and planners is discussed by Chappelet and Theodoraki (2006) in the context of the discussion of issues related to the use of sport for development in modern societies. The links to improvements in health, education, and sound corporate governance are made in light of evidence that participation in sport does also have unwanted consequences. Faced with positive and negative outcomes they identify the key questions that need to be debated before blanket policies are employed for the use of sport to combat social evils and trigger economic development. It is relevant to note a recent initiative to better link sport management and ethical sustainable development. Industry bodies are encouraged to take up ethically considered action that will strengthen the field and enhance the use of sport for education and economic development purposes whilst safeguarding future generations from the identified threats existing in the sports environment.

Self-regulating and incitement mechanisms for athletes, sponsors, and the media must be established in order to fight the lethal dangers in sport, permitting sport to remain safe for those who practice it, for society in general and to serve harmonious human development everywhere, as the preamble to the Olympic Charter states. To this effect, the regulatory intervention of public authorities is indispensable, in close partnership with the governing bodies of sport:

It is becoming urgent to defend a certain notion of sport. This notion can be resumed by the slogan 'SAFE sport' (i.e. sport that is Sustainable, Addiction-free, Fair, and Ethical).

Sustainable to avoid sport leading to the construction of inappropriate facilities or organizing gigantic events, and on the contrary for sport to facilitate balanced development.

Addiction-free to avoid sport leading to the abnormal use of all kinds of substances that are harmful to the individual, and instead for sport to contribute towards better health.

Fair to avoid sport degenerating into physical or moral violence, and to ensure that sport remains an incomparable educational tool.

Ethical to avoid sport becoming corrupted or criminal, and for it to remain a factor contributing towards a sound, effective economy.

By promoting, managing, and financing an SAFE sport managers and planners can contribute to a harmonious human development everywhere and meet the needs of the present sportsmen/women, athletes, and fans without further harming sport or compromising the ability of future generations to enjoy sport at its best. Calls for corporate social responsibility were also made at the declaration (p. 22–23).

Social responsibility can be achieved through customer and employee trust, customer satisfaction, employee commitment, and investor loyalty can lead to better organizational performance. McAlister, Ferrel, and Ferrel (2005: p. 20) review the evidence that resources invested in social responsibility programmes reap benefits for organizations and stakeholders.

Social responsibility can be ranging from contractual responsibilities to dialectic stakeholder development and there are economic, legal, ethical, and philanthropic considerations to be made. It is grounded in effective and mutually beneficial relationships with customers, employees, investors, competitors, government, the community, and others who have a stake in the company. Increasingly, companies are recognizing that these constituents both affect and are affected by their actions (p. 11).

Business must be aware of and abide by the laws and regulations that dictate acceptable business conduct. They can also influence government by participating in the public policy process. Strategic philanthropy is a related concept where business seeks to align resources and expertise with needs and concerns of stakeholders not just any social causes and a social audit is an important part of demonstrating commitment and ensuring the continuous improvement of the social responsibility effort (p. 29).

Ferrel, Fraedrich, and Ferrel (2005) proceed to provide a comparison of the philosophies used in business decisions. These range from teleology that stipulates that acts are morally right or acceptable if they produce some desired result, such as realization of self-interest or utility.

Egoism defines right or acceptable actions as those that maximize a particular person's self-interest as defined by the individual. Utilitarianism defines right or acceptable actions as those that maximize total utility, or the greatest good for the greatest number of people. Deontology focuses on the preservation of individual rights and on the intentions associated with a particular behaviour rather than on its consequences. A relativist philosophy evaluates ethicalness subjectively on the basis of individual and group experiences. Virtue ethics assumes that what is moral in a given situation is not only what conventional morality requires, but also what the mature person with a 'good' moral character would deem appropriate. Finally, justice evaluates ethicalness on the basis of fairness: distributive, procedural, and international (p. 96). Three types of justice provide a framework for evaluating the fairness of different situations. Distributive justice is based on the evaluation of the outcomes or results of the business relationship (e.g. benefits derived and equity in rewards). Procedural justice is based on the processes and activities that produce the outcome or results. Evaluations of performance that are not consistently developed and applied can lead to problems with procedural justice (decision-making process, level of access, openness, and participation). Interactional justice is based on evaluating the communication processes used in the business relationship. Because Interactional justice is linked to fairness in communication, it often involves the individual's relationship with the business organization through the accuracy of the information the organization provides (goes both ways – employees, too) (e.g. accuracy of information, truthfulness, respect, and courtesy in the process) (pp. 105–106).

In retrospect the literature provides three frameworks for the research. In light of the principles of social corporate responsibility (Ferrel et al., 2005; McAlister et al., 2005) and SAFE sport (Sport and Development International Conference, 2003) the notions of phronesis in mega project planning (Flyvbjerg, 2004), contextual explanation and situational rationality (Roche, 1994) guided the structures of Parts Two and Three that follow.

Part Two: The Olympic Movement

Having reviewed the literature on organizational structures and mega-event management contexts, this part seeks to (a) identify the constituents of the Olympic Movement and the relationships that bind them together and (b) discuss the specificity of the context in which the Olympic Movement operates and the processes by which it is managed.

3

Olympic organizations

The Olympic Movement is defined (International Olympic Committee, 2005d) as the movement led by the IOC and represented by the Olympic Games and those organizations, athletes, and other persons who accept the authority of the Olympic Charter. Its official goal is to contribute to building a peaceful and better world by educating youth through sport practised without discrimination of any kind and in the Olympic spirit of friendship, solidarity and fair play.

Domiciled in Lausanne, Switzerland, this international non-governmental non-profit organization in the form of an association seeks to lead the Olympic Movement in accordance with the Olympic Charter (the codification of the fundamental principles, rules, and bye-laws adopted by the IOC). It governs the organization and operation of the Olympic Movement and stipulates the conditions for the celebration of the Olympic Games (Host City Contract IOC 2004). According to the Olympic Charter,

the Olympic Games are the exclusive property of the IOC which owns all rights and data relating thereto, in particular, and without limitation, all rights relating to their organization, exploitation, broadcasting, recording, representation, reproduction, access, and dissemination in any form and by any means or mechanism whatsoever, whether now existing or developed in the future. The IOC shall determine the conditions of access to and the conditions of any use of data relating to the Olympic Games and to the competitions and sports performances of the Olympic Games. The Olympic symbol, flag, motto, anthem, identifications (including but not limited to 'Olympic Games' and 'Games of the Olympiad'), designations, emblems, flame, and torches, as defined in Rules 8–14 below, shall be collectively or individually referred to as 'Olympic properties'. All rights to any and all Olympic properties, as well as all rights to the use thereof, belong exclusively to the IOC, including but not limited to the use for any profit-making, commercial, or advertising purposes. The IOC may licence all or part of its rights on terms and conditions set forth by the IOC Executive Board (International Olympic Committee, 2004c: p. 17).

The Olympic Movement encompasses a number of organizations, athletes and other persons, including, in addition to the IOC, the IFs, the NOCs, and the OCOGs. In addition to the above there are also the following organizations and programmes: The Olympic Museum (OM), a foundation governed by the provisions of the Swiss Civil Code which has been entrusted by the IOC with the task of depicting the history and development of the Olympic Movement and to associate the movement with art and culture for specialists and the public at large worldwide. The Olympic Foundation (OF), a foundation also governed by the provisions of the Swiss Civil Code that has been entrusted by the IOC to give support to the activities of the Olympic Movement notably in the areas of culture, education, and sports. The Olympic Solidarity (OS), a programme developed jointly by the IOC, and the NOCs whose purpose is to assist the officially recognized NOCs, to fulfil their mission or send a national team to the summer and winter games and promote Olympism in the respective country. The IOC Television and Marketing Services (IOC T & MS) SA which was established by the IOC in 2005 following the acquisition of its exclusive marketing agency, Meridian Management SA, and the centralization of Olympic broadcasting and marketing responsibilities. The Olympic Partners (TOP) programme, the IOC's worldwide sponsorship programme which is managed by the IOC T & MS SA. The Olympic Broadcasting Services SA (OBS), a company that supplies all services relating to the establishment and management of the Host Broadcasting function of the Olympic Games, and in which the OF holds a 99% shareholding. The Olympic Games Knowledge Services SA (OGKS), a company which supports the IOC in the transfer of knowledge and expertise from one OCOG to another, and in which the OF holds a 100% shareholding. La Maison du Sport International SA (MSI) Lausanne, a new office building infrastructure, owned equally by the City of Lausanne, the Canton of Vaud, and the IOC which brings together under one roof several players from international sports administration, notably 20 or so headquarters of IFs and also 10 active companies in the field of sport.

The activities of the OM, the OF, the OS, the IOC T & MS, the TOP programme, the OBS, the OGKS, and the MSI have been combined with those of the IOC on the basis of the fact that the latter has a majority shareholding or control of the boards of each organization and of each programme (International Olympic Committee, 2006). Any person or organization belonging in any capacity whatsoever to the Olympic Movement is bound by the provisions of the Olympic Charter and is expected to abide by the decisions of the IOC (International Olympic Committee, 2004c: p. 10). For the Olympic Movement a brand is a message, either visual or verbal or both, that (a) communicates the identity and image of a product or service and (b) conveys a set of and associations with a product or service and can take the form of a word, a mark, a symbol, a design, a term, or a combination of these (International Olympic Committee, 2005b).

The IOC holds the monopoly over the Olympic brand, of the sales of the rings, the term Olympic, Olympic Games, etc. and the local OCOGs ensure that the Olympic logos linked to a particular games are also protected by copyright laws. In fact one of the conditions signed for in the host city contract is that the country introduces laws to protect the Olympic brand. Being the registered owners of the Olympic Games, no other organization can organize Olympic Games of any size and scope unless they have permission by the IOC. Very important, the IOC owns the signal of the Olympic media coverage and sells it to various broadcasters for a fee. Any sponsor wanting to associate with the Olympic Games brand also enter into the monopoly of the IOC having to buy such association from the IOC (as is the case for the global TOP sponsors) or its local representative, the OCOG (as is the case for national sponsors). NOCs can similarly not represent the country unless they are recognized by the IOC and if they were to be established international copyright legislation would apply and they would be in breach for using the term Olympic in their name.

References to the power of the IOC can be found in the fundamental principles of Olympism presented in the Olympic Charter:

1 Olympism is a philosophy of life, exalting and combining in a balanced whole the qualities of body, will, and mind. Blending sport with culture and education, Olympism seeks to create a way of life based on the joy of effort, the educational value of good example and respect for universal fundamental ethical principles.
2 The goal of Olympism is to place sport at the service of the harmonious development of man, with a view to promoting a peaceful society concerned with the preservation of human dignity.

3 The Olympic Movement is the concerted, organized, universal, and permanent action, carried out under the supreme authority of the IOC, of all individuals and entities who are inspired by the values of Olympism. It covers the five continents. It reaches its peak with the bringing together of the world's athletes at the great sports festival, the Olympic Games. Its symbol is five interlaced rings.

4 The practice of sport is a human right. Every individual must have the possibility of practising sport, without discrimination of any kind and in the Olympic spirit, which requires mutual understanding with a spirit of friendship, solidarity, and fair play. The organization, administration, and management of sport must be controlled by independent sports organizations.

5 Any form of discrimination with regard to a country or a person on grounds of race, religion, politics, gender, or otherwise is incompatible with belonging to the Olympic Movement.

6 Belonging to the Olympic Movement requires compliance with the Olympic Charter and recognition by the IOC.

(International Olympic Committee, 2004c: p. 9).

The Olympic Charter contains the rules and bye-laws adopted by the IOC and serves three main purposes: (i) to present the fundamental principles and essential values of Olympism; (ii) to serve as statutes for the IOC, and (iii) to define the main reciprocal rights and obligations of the three main constituents of the Olympic Movement, namely the IOC, the IFs, and the NOCs, as well as OCOGs, all of which are required to comply with the Olympic Charter (International Olympic Committee, 2004c: p. 7).

As regards the organization of the Olympic Games it is entrusted by the IOC to the NOC of the country of the host city as well as to the host city itself and the NOC becomes responsible for the establishment, for that purpose, of an OCOG which, from the time it is constituted, reports directly to the IOC Executive Board. The OCOG needs to have the status of a legal person in its country and its executive body must include: the IOC member(s) in the country, the President and Secretary General of the NOC, at least one member representing, and designated by, the host city. The executive body of the OCOG may also include representatives of the public authorities and other leading figures and from the time of its constitution to the end of its liquidation after the end of the games, the OCOG shall conduct all its activities in accordance with the Olympic Charter, with the agreement entered into between the IOC, the NOC, and the host city and with any other regulations or instructions of the IOC Executive (International Olympic Committee, 2004c).

In accepting to host the Olympic Games the NOC, the OCOG, and the host city are jointly and severally liable for all commitments entered into individually or collectively concerning the organization and staging of event whilst the IOC has no financial responsibility whatsoever in respect of its organization and staging (International Olympic Committee, 2004c: p. 74–75).

The International Olympic Committee

The Olympic Charter defines the IOC as an international non-governmental not-for-profit organization, of unlimited duration, in the form of an association with the status of a legal person, recognized by the Swiss Federal Council in accordance with an agreement entered into on 1 November 2000. Its seat is in the Olympic capital of Lausanne and its object is to fulfil the mission, role, and responsibilities as assigned to it by the Olympic Charter. The decisions of the IOC are final and any dispute relating to their application or interpretation may be resolved solely by the IOC Executive Board and, in certain cases, by arbitration before the Court of Arbitration for Sport (CAS). In order to fulfil its mission and carry out its role, the IOC may establish, acquire, or otherwise control other legal entities such as foundations or corporations (International Olympic Committee, 2004c: p. 26).

As an organization it can be separated into the elected, voluntary, non-paid part, and the professional paid administration part (Figure 3.1).

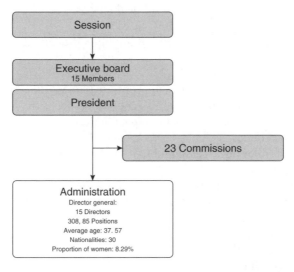

Figure 3.1 IOC structure (*Source*: International Olympic Committee, 2006)

The former includes all 111 IOC members that make up the IOC membership. The members are natural persons, and representatives of the IOC in their respective countries, not their country's delegate to the IOC. They meet at least annually at the IOC session and many of them serve and make up the IOC commissions that are established to study certain subjects and make recommendations to the executive board and the IOC President.

The Session elects a President for a term of eight years, renewable once for four years, and executive board members for terms of four years. The executive board, founded in 1921, consists of the IOC President, four Vice Presidents, and ten other members. All the members of the executive board are elected by the Session, by secret ballot, by a majority of votes cast, for a four-year term. The Board's role is in managing the affairs of the IOC as follows:

- attends to the observance of the Olympic Charter;
- assumes the ultimate responsibility for the administration of the IOC;
- approves the IOC's internal organization, its organization chart, and all internal regulations relating to its organization;
- is responsible for the management of the IOC's finances and prepares an annual report;
- presents a report to the Session on any proposed change of rule or bye-law;
- submits to the IOC Session the names of the persons whom it recommends for election to the IOC;
- conducts the procedure for acceptance and selection of candidatures for the organization of the Olympic Games;
- creates and allocates IOC honorary distinctions;
- establishes the agenda for the IOC Sessions;
- upon proposal from the President, it appoints the Director General and Secretary General;
- keeps the records of the IOC;
- enacts, in the form it deems most appropriate (codes, rulings, norms, guidelines, guides, and instructions), all regulations necessary to ensure the proper implementation of the Olympic Charter and the organization of the Olympic Games;
- performs all other duties assigned to it by the Session.

The executive board meets when convened by the President on the latter's initiative or at the request of the majority of its members. (International Olympic Committee, 2007a).

There are currently 20 commissions as follows: Athletes, Culture and Olympic Education, Coordination Commissions for the Olympic Games, Ethics, Finance, International Relations, Juridical, Marketing, Medical, Nominations, Olympic Philately Numismatic and Memorabilia, Olympic Programme, Solidarity, Press, Radio and Television, Sport and Environment, Sport and Law, Sport for All, TV Rights and New Media, Women and Sport. These commissions may include IOC members, representatives of the International Olympic Sports Federations and the NOCs, athletes, technical experts, advisers and sports specialists.

The IOC paid administration has evolved quite significantly during the past four years, with a number of changes over the quadrennium taking the organization towards an increasingly professional and service-orientated focus. Changes began with a series of audits initiated by President Rogge shortly after he took up office following his election in summer 2001. A number of operational and financial audits were conducted covering areas that included human resources, technology, games management, information management, and marketing

At the extraordinary session in Mexico in 2002, IOC members were informed of the changes recommended by the audits, specifically a new functional organizational chart for the IOC administration, a dedicated Olympic Games Department was born out of the former Department of Sports, Olympic Games Co-ordination and Relations with IFs. This department was tasked with ensuring the co-ordination of Olympic Games preparations, including the operational integration of all IOC functions and activities related to the Games; acting as the interlocutor within the IOC for the organizing committees; and developing and managing the Olympic Games candidature process. The creation of the Olympic Games department led to the development of a Department of Sports which has been mandated with ensuring efficient relations with IFs, Recognized Federations, and Recognized Organizations, supporting the Olympic Games Department in co-ordinating all aspects of sports operations and providing the Sport for All, Athletes', and Olympic Programme Commissions with administrative and operational support. An IOC Communications Department was also established in 2002, grouping together all aspects of communications, including media relations and editorial services. The audits also initiated the creation of an Information Management Department which now manages the information legacy of the Olympic Movement, including Olympic archives and video and photographic images. The OM and the Department of International Cooperation and Development also saw the appointment of new directors and the IOC Technology Department saw a change of director, too. Moreover, the IOC administration saw a change at the top, with the appointment of a full-time director general who replaced a part-time director general. The role of director general was reoriented and all operational business functions of the IOC administration and its satellites were placed under its direction. Then the IOC took over the running of functions critical to the organization of Olympic Games and the Movement by incorporating the work of some of its previous subsidiary companies, namely, OGKS, the company in charge of the knowledge transfer services; Olympic Broadcasting Services SA to undertake from 2010 onwards the host broadcasting function which had previously been the responsibility of the organizing committee; IOC T & MS SA, which bring all marketing activities under one umbrella (International Olympic Committee, 2006: p. 30–31).

The IOCT & MS SA was established by the IOC in 2005 following the acquisition of its exclusive marketing agency, Meridian Management SA, and the centralization of Olympic broadcasting and marketing responsibilities. Led by a Managing Director, the IOC T & MS is a wholly owned company of the IOC with offices outside Lausanne and in Atlanta, US. The IOC Television & Marketing Services SA is responsible for a broad portfolio including the development and implementation of the Olympic broadcast rights and marketing strategy. This includes the negotiation of Olympic broadcast rights and TOP sponsor contracts, and the management and servicing of the TOP programme and Olympic brand management.

Other Olympic Movement organizations that perform a subsidiary role to the IOC are the OF and the OM, which are governed by the provisions of the Swiss Civil Code. The former's objective is to support the activities of the Olympic Movement notably in the areas of culture, education, and sports by investing on behalf of the IOC. The operating funds are provided by the IOC and the OF had 50% voting and a 25% economic interest in Meridian Management SA which managed the International Olympic Marketing TOP programme and has now been replaced by the IOC Televisions and Marketing Services SA (Olympic Foundation, 2001: p. 5–6). The Olympic Museum Foundation (OMF) has been entrusted by the IOC with the task of depicting the history and development of the Olympic Movement over the years and through its various activities, its role is to associate the Olympic Movement more closely with art and culture, for specialists as well as for the general worldwide public (Olympic Museum, 2001: p. 5).

In 1995, the IOC established the Olympic Television Archive Bureau (OTAB) with headquarters in London, UK to manage and market the IOC's extensive Olympic Games Archive, provide rapid fulfilment of Olympic footage clips, as well as administer all related licencing procedures.

OTAB was established in 1995 by the IOC and is managed by Trans World International (TWI), the world's largest independent sports television producer. OTAB co-ordinates the management of the historical moving image archive of the Olympic Movement and special Olympic broadcast programming, such as 'The Olympic Series', commemorative DVDs/video cassettes of the Games, and in-flight programming (International Olympic Committee, 2006). Broadcast agreements vary from territory to territory, although the general policy is that a broadcast rights holder has a 6–12 months period of exclusivity (for broadcast rights only) after a specific Olympic Games, at the conclusion of which, all rights revert back to the IOC. At this point, the broadcaster no longer has any rights to sub-licence their material, but may use limited amounts of their own Olympic coverage (no more than 20 minutes) within their own broadcast programming, on their own network (The Olympic Television Archive Bureau, 2006). In 1996, the Olympic Photographic Archive Bureau (OPAB) was established by the IOC and is being managed by AllSport, the official photography agent to the IOC (a division of Getty Images, the world's largest sports photographic library). Its aim is to develop special Olympic photographic projects (including marketing service support at each Olympic Games) (International Olympic Committee, 2006).

Financial Flows

The IOC's Marketing Fact file (International Olympic Committee, 2005a) provides a rich account of the financial transactions between the various agencies in the Olympic Movement and this section summarize its key features. Many financial agreements are drawn up far ahead of the staging of the Games, to help host cities as it allows them to plan their budgets more efficiently. When the 2008 Olympic Games were awarded to Beijing in 2001 at the 112th IOC Session in Moscow, the IOC had already signed a television deal worth more than US $1 billion for whichever city was going to host those Summer Games. The Salt Lake City Organizing Committee (SLOC) received about US $1.39 billion from Olympic marketing programmes, of which 40% or US $570 million came from the broadcast and marketing programmes managed by the IOC. The Olympic properties of the United States, the joint marketing programme of SLOC and the USOC generated the remainder. Similarly for the Games of the XXVIII Olympiad, the IOC's marketing and broadcasting deals have given support to the OCOG. Prior to 2004, the IOC contributed 60% of the broadcasting revenue for the Games to the OCOG. With the increased value of the rights, this dropped to 49%, leaving the remainder going to the Olympic Movement to serve worldwide development and the progress of sport. The Athens Organizing Committee received about US $960 million from the IOC's sale of broadcast rights and worldwide sponsorship. This was approximately 50% of the OCOG's operating budget. NOCs participating in the Salt Lake City and Athens Games received approximately US $318.5 million, compared to US $198.7 million for the 1997–2000 period. This was made up of broadcast revenue via OS of US $209.5 million and the TOP programme of US $109 million. Such funding helps the NOCs with the cost of sending teams to the Olympic Games, and for the training and development of athletes. IFs revenue generated from Salt Lake City 2002 provided the seven winter IFs with US $92.4 million, compared with US $17 million from 10 years earlier in Albertville. Revenue generated from Athens 2004 provided the 28 summer IFs with US $253.9 million. For most IFs, whether winter or summer, the Games are their largest single source of revenue. In addition, the IOC makes contributions from its revenue from the Games to several recognized international sports organizations, including the International Paralympic Committee (IPC), the World Anti-Doping Agency (WADA), and CAS (p. 35).

Understandably, Olympic marketing programme has become the driving force behind the promotion, the financial security, and stability of the Olympic Movement and the IOC claims that the challenge of financing the Olympic Games has been a recurring theme throughout Olympic history. Since its founding in 1894, the Olympic Movement has depended on partnership with the business community to stage the Olympic Games and to support the Olympic athletes and marketing partners are considered part of the Olympic Family.

61

Table 3.1 Marketing revenue

Source	1997–2000 (US $)	2001–2004 (US $)
Broadcast	1,845,000,000	2,230,000,000
Top programme	579,000,000	663,000,000
Domestic sponsorship	655,000,000	796,000,000
Ticketing	625,000,000	411,000,000
Licencing	66,000,000	87,000,000
Total	3,770,000,000	4,187,000,000

Source: International Olympic Committee (2005a).

The Olympic Movement generates revenue through broadcasting, The Olympic Partners (TOP) and domestic sponsoring, ticketing, and licencing (see Table 3.1). The IOC manages broadcast partnerships and the TOP worldwide sponsorship programme while the OCOGs manage domestic sponsorship, ticketing, and licencing programmes within the host country, under the direction of the IOC.

The IOC distributes approximately 92% of Olympic marketing revenue to organizations throughout the Olympic Movement, to support the staging of the Olympic Games and to promote the worldwide development of sport whilst retaining approximately 8% of Olympic marketing revenue for the operational and administrative costs of governing the Olympic Movement. TOP programme contributions and Olympic broadcast revenue is provided by the IOC to the OCOGs to support the staging of the Olympic Games and Olympic Winter Games. The summer and winter OCOGs of each Olympic quadrennium generally share approximately 50% of TOP programme revenue and value-in-kind contributions and 49% of the Olympic broadcast revenue for each Games to the OCOG. The TOP programme is the worldwide sponsorship programme managed by the IOC that operates on a four-year term that aligns with the Olympic quadrennium. The IOC created the TOP programme in 1985 to develop a more diversified revenue base for the Olympic Games and to establish long-term corporate partnerships that would ensure the future viability of the Olympic Movement. The TOP programme generates support for the OCOGs of summer and winter Games, all active NOCs in the world, and the IOC. The TOP programme provides each Worldwide Olympic Partner with exclusive global marketing rights and opportunities within a designated product or service category. This includes partnership with the IOC, all active NOCs and their Olympic teams, and the two OCOGs and the Games of each quadrennium. For 2005–2008 the revenue from TOP was US $866 million and in return they may exercise these rights worldwide and may activate marketing initiatives with the various members of the Olympic Movement that participate in the TOP programme (see Table 3.2).

Table 3.2 The Olympic Partners

Name of TOP	Country	Category
The Coca-Cola Company	USA	Non-alcoholic beverages
Atos Origin, the worldwide information technology partner	Spain	Information technology
General Electric diversified group of 11 businesses	USA	Energy, healthcare transport, infrastructure, consumer and industrial, advanced materials and equipment services
Kodak	USA	Film/photographics and imaging
Lenovo Group (previously Legend Group Limited)	China	Computing technology equipment
Manulife Financial	USA	Life insurance/annuities
McDonald's	USA	Retail food services
Panasonic brand, Matsushita Electric Industrial Co., Ltd.	Japan	Audio/TV/Video equipment
Samsung	Korea	Wireless communications equipment
Visa International	USA	Consumer payment systems

Source: International Olympic Committee (2005a).

Understandably, TOP provides vital financial support and contributions of goods and services to the Olympic Games and the Olympic Movement. The IOC subsequently, distributes TOP revenue and contributions as follows: 50% to OCOGs, 40 to NOCs, and 10% to the IOC.

The Olympic Games domestic sponsorship programme (with three tiers of sponsors, suppliers, and providers) is managed by the OCOG within the host country under the direction of the IOC. The programmes support the operations of the OCOG, the planning and staging of the Games, the host country NOC, and the host country Olympic team. The Olympic Games domestic sponsorship programme grants marketing rights within the host country or territory only. The host country NOC and the host country Olympic team participate in the OCOG sponsorship programme because the Marketing Plan Agreement requires the OCOG and the host country NOC to centralize and co-ordinate all marketing initiatives within the host country. Sydney 2000 had 93 partners and raised US $426 million whilst Athens 2004 with smaller home market had 38 domestic sponsors and raised US $302 million. Nagano 1998 had 26 and raised US $163 million whilst Salt Lake City had 53 and raised US $494 million.

Olympic broadcast partnership has been the single greatest source of revenue for the Olympic Movement for more than three decades. Increases in the Olympic broadcast revenue generated in recent decades have contributed greatly to the success of the Olympic Games and ensured the future viability of the Olympic Movement. The global broadcast revenue figure for the 2004 Olympic Games of US $1,331,550,000 represents a fivefold increase from the 1984 Los Angeles broadcast revenue of US $286,914,000 two decades earlier. The global broadcast revenue figure for the 2002 Salt Lake City Olympic Winter Games of US $736,135,000 represents a sevenfold increase from the 1984 Sarajevo broadcast revenue of US $102,682,000 less than two decades earlier. Olympic broadcast revenue is distributed throughout the Olympic Family, providing financial support to the OCOGs (49%) and the IOC/OS and IFs (51%).

The Olympic Games ticketing programme is managed by the OCOG, with the approval of the IOC Executive Board to enable people to experience Olympic Games ceremonies and competitions and to generate financial revenue to support the staging of the Olympic Games. The OCOGs and the IOC work to ensure the availability of tickets priced to accommodate the wide-ranging economic circumstances of the public, to establish ticket prices in accordance with the domestic market prices for major sporting events, and to ensure the transparency of the ticketing programme. The OCOGs retain 95% of the revenue generated from Olympic ticketing programmes to support the staging of the Games. The remaining 5% is delivered as a royalty to the IOC to support the operations of the Olympic Movement. In Athens 2004, 3.8 out of the available 5.3 million tickets were sold and generated a revenue of US $228 million.

Olympic Movement organizations can develop programmes to create Olympic Games-related products, merchandise, and souvenirs for consumers through licencing agreements that grant the use of Olympic marks, imagery, or themes to third-party companies that market and manufacture the products. Licenced products generally commemorate the Olympic Games or a particular Olympic team. Olympic Games licencing includes the numismatic and philatelic programmes that create Olympic Games commemorative coins and stamps. The licencee pays a royalty to the Olympic Movement organization for the right to use Olympic marks, imagery, or themes. The standard percentage royalty paid by the licencee in the numismatic and philatelic programmes is between 10% and 15% of the product sales revenue. In Athens 2004, 23 licencees generated a revenue of US $61.5 million.

The International Paralympic Committee

Representing the vast majority of athletes with a disability, the IPC has taken sport to a new level, providing opportunities from a developmental to an elite sport level. Founded in 1989 it claims to have a democratic structure, its membership includes more than 160 National Paralympic Committees (NPC) and 5 International Organizations of Sport for the Disabled. In 2001,

Phil Craven from Great Britain was elected president of the IPC. This organization not only organizes, supervises, and co-ordinates the Paralympic Summer and Winter Games, but also other competitions including world and regional championships in 13 sports. For these sports, the IPC also acts as the IF. The Paralympic Movement began when Dr Ludwig Guttmann introduced sport as a form of recreation and rehabilitation therapy at the Spinal Cord Injuries Centre at Stoke Mandeville Hospital in Great Britain in 1944. Dr Guttmann's work and zeal lead to the increasing prominence of sport for people with spinal cord injuries and to the organization of the first International Stoke Mandeville Games in 1952. In the beginning, only wheelchair athletes competed, but as the Paralympic Movement grew, other athletes (with visual impairments, cerebral palsy, amputations or intellectual disabilities) were included. Elite competitions developed over the next 12 years to become the Paralympic Games. In 1960, the first Paralympic Summer Games took place in Rome, where the Olympic Games had just been held. Since then the Paralympic Movement has seen tremendous growth and now thousands of athletes participate in the more than 300 international competitions taking place every year all over the world (International Paralympic Committee, 2003).

The seat of the IPC is in Bonn, Germany, and it is registered with the 'register of associations' at the county court Bonn under the number VR 7414 with the stated vision to: enable Paralympic athletes to achieve sporting excellence and inspire and excite the world. To fulfil its vision, the IPC has created the following mission statement:

1 To ensure the growth and strength of the Paralympic Movement through the development of NPCs in all nations, and support the activities of all members.
2 With respect to the Paralympic Games, supervise and ensure the organization of successful Paralympic Games.
3 With respect to the IPC Sports, act as governing body of these sports, including the awarding and sanctioning of World and Regional multi-disability Games and Championships.
4 Promote sports for athletes with disabilities without discrimination for political, religious, economic, disability, racial, gender, or sexual orientation reasons.
5 Support and encourage educational, cultural, research, and scientific activities that contribute to the development and promotion of the Paralympic Movement.
6 Ensure that, in sport practiced within the Paralympic Movement, the spirit of fair play prevails, violence is banned, the health risk of the athletes is managed, and fundamental ethical principles are upheld.
7 Contribute to the creation of a drug-free sport environment for all Paralympic athletes in conjunction with the WADA (International Paralympic Committee, 2003).

The structure of the IPC includes a paid management team directed by the Chief Executive Officer and a number of voluntary positions like the General Assembly and other meetings of the membership; a governing board; the Councils, standing Committees, and the following commissions: Anti-Doping Committee, Athletes with a Severe Disability Committee, Classification Committee, Development Committee, Education Committee, Ethics Committee, Audit & Finance Committee, Legal Committee, Paralympic Games Committee, Sport Science Committee, Therapeutic Use Exemption Committee, and Women in Sport Committee.

The governing board has the full power of authority to represent the IPC and in exercising this authority, the responsibilities of the governing board include:

- to interpret the Vision set by the Membership at the General Assembly;
- to approve the IPC Policies;
- to ensure that the directions set by the Membership at the General Assembly are implemented;
- to set the broad goals of the Strategic Plan;
- to monitor the performance of the delivery of the goals;
- to mandate, as appropriate, the chief executive officer to represent the IPC in accordance with the rules and regulations laid down;
- to appoint a certified auditor.

The members of the IPC include (a) the National Paralympic Committees (NPC) (a national organization recognized by the IPC as the sole representative of athletes with a disability in that country or territory to the IPC); (b) the International Organization of Sport for the Disabled (IOSD) (an independent organization recognized by the IPC as the sole worldwide representative of a specific disability group to the IPC); (c) the International Paralympic Sports Federation (IPSF) (an independent sport federation recognized by the IPC as the sole worldwide representative of a sport for athletes with a disability that has been granted the status as a Paralympic Sport by the IPC); and (d) Regional/Continental Paralympic Organization (an independent Regional/Continental Organization recognized as the sole regional continental representative of the IPC members within a specific region/continent as recognized by the IPC) (International Paralympic Committee, 2004) (see Figure 3.2).

According to its constitution the IPC pursues its objectives directly and exclusively as a non-profit-making association as defined in the relevant section of the German fiscal code. Its activities need to be altruistic, not be aimed primarily at commercial purposes and the IPC claims not to work with a view to profit. Members may not have a share in the IPC's assets or in the surpluses attained and shall not receive any payments out of the association's financial resources. The IPC's funds must only be used for

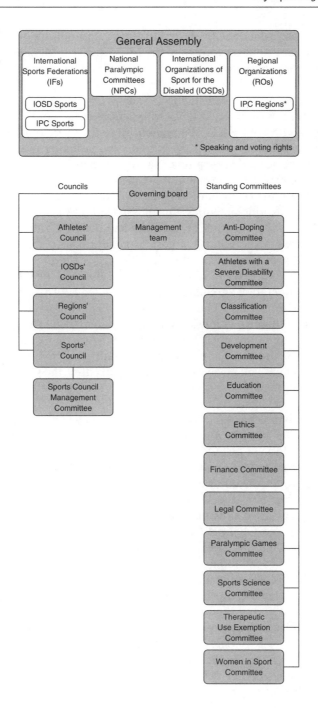

Figure 3.2 IPC general structure (*Source*: International Paralympic Committee, 2007)

purposes in accordance with the constitution and nobody may be bene-fited by payments that are foreign to the IPC's Vision & Mission and objects or by disproportionate remuneration (International Paralympic Committee, 2004).

The IPC had a successful financial year in 2005 and closed the books reporting a surplus of EURO 84,593, with a total revenue of Euro 3.4 million and an expenditure of EURO 3.33 million. More than 50% of IPC's revenues were generated through the Paralympic Games marketing and broadcasting rights sales. The second largest financial source came from grants from the IOC and the German Government (City of Bonn, North-Rhine Westphalia, Federal Government). In addition, the IPC raised Euro 150,000 income from other sponsoring activities. On the expenditure side personnel costs amounted to 40% of the total expenditure and the grants allocated directly to the sports were the second largest expenditure with 15% of the total (International Paralympic Committee, 2006).

In the period 2001–2006, the links between the IOC and the IPC have grown stronger. A cooperation agreement had been signed between the two organ-izations at the Paralympic Games in Sydney in 2000 to confirm their rela-tions. In June 2001, the relationship was further strengthened as an agreement was signed between the IOC and the IPC aiming to secure and protect the organization of the Paralympic Games. It confirmed that, from 2008, the Paralympic Games will always take place shortly after the Olympic Games, using the same facilities, and that, from the 2012 bid process onwards, the city that wins the rights to host those Olympic Games will be required to stage the Paralympics as well. While this agreement will not come into effect until the Games in 2008 and 2010, the OCOGs for Salt Lake City and Athens decided to use one Organizing Committee for both Games, with the Salt Lake Organizing Committee being the first Organizing Committee to totally integrate the organization of both the Olympic and Paralympic Winter Games. In August 2003, the agreement was then amended to strengthen the ties even further. It ensures that the IPC will receive, from the Organising Committees of the Olympic Games, US $9 million for the Games of the XXIX Olympiad in 2008, US $4 million for the XXI Olympic Winter Games in 2010 and US $10 million for the Games of the XXX Olympiad in 2012, in return for the broadcasting and marketing rights related to the 2008, 2010, and 2012 Paralympic Games (International Olympic Committee, 2006). In June 2006, the IOC and the IPC signed an extension to their current agree-ment, which will continue to see the IOC support the IPC and the Paralympic Games through to 2016. The existing accord, which runs through to 2012, is to be extended to the Games of 2014 and 2016, respectively. Furthermore, the IPC is represented on several IOC Commissions and Committees and vice versa. For example, it has a representative on the IOC Athletes' Committee, the Co-ordination Commissions of the Olympic Games, the IOC Medical Commission, the Women and Sport Commission, the Press Commission, and the Radio and Television Commission.

The International Federations

As mentioned earlier, one area where the IOC has a monopoly is on selection of sports and events to be included in the Olympic Programme. According to the Olympic Charter, in order to develop and promote the Olympic Movement, the IOC may recognize as IFs international non-governmental organizations administering one or several sports at world level and encompassing organizations administering such sports at national level. The statutes, practice, and activities of the IFs within the Olympic Movement must be in conformity with the Olympic Charter, including the adoption and implementation of the World Anti-Doping Code. Subject to the above, each IF maintains its independence and autonomy in the administration of its sport.

The mission and roles of the IF within the Olympic Movement are:

1 to establish and enforce, in accordance with the Olympic spirit, the rules concerning the practice of their respective sports and to ensure their application;
2 to ensure the development of their sports throughout the world;
3 to contribute to the achievement of the goals set out in the Olympic Charter, in particular by way of the spread of Olympism and Olympic education;
4 to express their opinions on the candidatures for organizing the Olympic Games, in particular as far as the technical aspects of venues for their respective sports are concerned;
5 to establish their criteria of eligibility for the competitions of the Olympic Games in conformity with the Olympic Charter, and to submit these to the IOC for approval;
6 to assume the responsibility for the technical control and direction of their sports at the Olympic Games and at the Games held under the patronage of the IOC;
7 to provide technical assistance in the practical implementation of the OS programmes.

In addition, the IFs have the right to formulate proposals addressed to the IOC concerning the Olympic Charter and the Olympic Movement, collaborate in the preparation of Olympic Congresses and participate, on request from the IOC, in the activities of the IOC commissions (International Olympic Committee, 2004b: pp. 58–59).

The sports governed by the following IFs are considered as Olympic sports:

Summer Olympic Games

■ International Association of Athletics Federations (IAAF)
■ International Rowing Federation (FISA)

- International Badminton Federation (IBF)
- International Baseball Federation (IBAF)
- International Basketball Federation (FIBA)
- International Boxing Association (AIBA)
- International Canoe Federation (ICF)
- International Cycling Union (UCI)
- International Equestrian Federation (FEI)
- International Fencing Federation (FIE)
- International Association Football Federation (FIFA)
- International Gymnastics Federation (FIG)
- International Weightlifting Federation (IWF)
- International Handball Federation (IHF)
- International Hockey Federation (FIH)
- International Judo Federation (IJF)
- International Federation of Associated Wrestling Styles (FILA)
- International Swimming Federation (FINA)
- International Union of the Modern Pentathlon (UIPM)
- International Softball Federation (ISF)
- World Taekwondo Federation (WTF)
- International Tennis Federation (ITF)
- International Table Tennis Federation (ITTF)
- International Shooting Sport Federation (ISSF)
- International Archery Federation (FITA)
- International Triathlon Union (ITU)
- International Sailing Federation (ISAF)
- International Volleyball Federation (FIVB)

Winter Olympic Games

- International Biathlon Union (IBU)
- International Bobsleigh and Tobogganing Federation (FIBT)
- World Curling Federation (WCF)
- International Ice Hockey Federation (IIHF)
- International Luge Federation (FIL)
- International Skating Union (ISU)
- International Ski Federation (FIS).

(International Olympic Committee, 2004c: pp. 86–88).

The IOC provides financial support from Olympic marketing to the 28 IFs of Olympic summer sports and the seven IFs of Olympic winter sports. These financial contributions, drawn from Olympic broadcast revenue, are provided to the IFs to support the development of sport worldwide. The IOC distributes Olympic broadcast revenue to the summer IFs and the winter IFs after the completion of the Olympic Games and the Olympic Winter Games, respectively. The continually increasing value of Olympic broadcast partnerships has enabled the IOC to deliver substantially increased financial support to the IFs with each successive Games. After the 1992 Barcelona games the summer IF received US $37.6 million whilst after Sydney 2000 the same organizations received US $190 million. Revenue to winter IFs also increased from US $17 million at the 1992 Albertville games to US $85.8 million after he 2002 Salt lace City games (International Olympic Committee, 2005a).

The National Olympic Committees

Being franchisees of the IOC, NOCs' mission is to develop, promote, and protect the Olympic Movement in their respective countries, in accordance with the Olympic Charter (International Olympic Committee, 2004c). The British Olympic Association (BOA) which is the NOC for Great Britain, for example, is involved in encouraging interest in the Olympic Games and fostering the aims and ideals of the Olympic Movement throughout Britain. It exploits its assets and connections with the Olympic Movement to generate commercial income, which is expended to send the best possible team to the Olympic Games. Therefore, it is responsible not only for the organization, and co-ordination, of Britain's participation in the Olympic Games but also for the technical development of the team, its welfare and scientific and medical backup. It does this specifically in order to further the team's accomplishments and thereby the BOA's attractiveness as a promotional conduit for commercial organizations (British Olympic Association, 2005).

Overall, NOCs aim to promote the fundamental principles and values of Olympism in their countries, in the fields of sport and education, by promoting Olympic educational programmes in all levels of schools, sports and physical education institutions and universities, as well as by encouraging the creation of institutions dedicated to Olympic education, such as National Olympic Academies, and other programmes, including cultural, related to the Olympic Movement. Furthermore, NOCs are required to ensure the observance of the Olympic Charter in their countries, to encourage the development of high-performance sport as well as sport for all, to help in the training of sports administrators by organizing courses and ensure that such courses contribute to the propagation of the fundamental principles of Olympism and finally to take action against any form of discrimination and violence in sport and to adopt and implement the World Anti-Doping Code.

The NOCs have the exclusive authority for the representation of their respective countries at the Olympic Games and at the regional, continental, or world multi-sports competitions patronized by the IOC. In addition, each NOC is obliged to participate in the Games of the Olympiad by sending athletes. The NOCs also have the exclusive authority to select and designate the city which may apply to organize Olympic Games in their respective countries. In order to fulfil their mission, the NOCs may cooperate with governmental bodies, with which they are expected to achieve harmonious relations but the charter requires that they should not associate themselves with any activity which would be in contradiction with it. The NOCs may also cooperate with non-governmental bodies but always seek to preserve their autonomy and resist all pressures of any kind, including but not limited to political, legal, religious or economic pressures which may prevent them from complying with the Olympic Charter.

NOCs have the right to designate, identify, or refer to themselves as NOCs, benefit from the assistance of OS; use certain Olympic properties as authorized by the IOC, take part in activities led or patronized by the IOC, including regional Games; belong to associations of NOCs recognized by the IOC; formulate proposals to the IOC concerning the Olympic Charter and the Olympic Movement, including the organization of the Olympic Games; give their opinions concerning the candidatures for the organization of the Olympic Games; participate, on request from the IOC, in the activities of the IOC commissions; collaborate in the preparation of Olympic Congresses and exercise other rights as granted to them by the Olympic Charter or by the IOC.

The IOC helps the NOCs fulfil their mission through its various departments and OS. Apart from the measures and sanctions provided in the case of infringement of the Olympic Charter, ultimately, the IOC Executive Board may take any appropriate decisions for the protection of the Olympic Movement in the country of an NOC, including suspension of or withdrawal of recognition from such NOC if the constitution, law, or other regulations in force in the country concerned, or any act by any governmental or other body causes the activity of the NOC or the making or expression of its will to be hampered. The IOC Executive Board shall offer such NOC an opportunity to be heard before any such decision is taken (International Olympic Committee, 2004c: p. 60–62).

The NOCs receive financial support for the training and development of Olympic teams, Olympic athletes, and Olympic hopefuls. The IOC distributes TOP programme revenue to each of the 203 NOCs throughout the world and contributes Olympic broadcast revenue to OS, the body responsible for managing and administering the share of the television rights of the Olympic Games that is allocated NOCs. OS assists the NOCs and the Continental Associations with their efforts for the development of sport through programmes carefully devised to match their specific needs and priorities. The continued success of the TOP programme and Olympic broadcast agreements has enabled the IOC to provide increased support for the NOCs and it provided approximately US $319.5 million (US $209.5 million of broadcast revenue and US $110 million of TOP programme revenue) to NOCs for the 2001–2004 quadrennium. Substantial additional indirect financial support is provided to the NOCs through the provision of a free athletes' village accommodation and travel grants to the Olympic Games (International Olympic Committee, 2005a). The IOC provides approximately 40% of the TOP programme's quadrennial revenue to all participating NOCs and for the 2005–2008 Olympic Quadrennium US $139 million was given to NOCs from this source.

The IOC contributes Olympic broadcast revenue to OS and from it the NOCs receive financial support for the training and development of Olympic teams, Olympic athletes, and Olympic hopefuls. Increased support in the region of US $209.5 million from this source was distributed by OS in recent years and has enabled more nations throughout the world to develop Olympic Programmes and Olympic teams (International Olympic Committee, 2005a, 2006).

The 203 IOC recognized NOCs around the world that aim to serve the Olympic Movement exhibit a range of sizes and structures, from having hardly any paid staff, as is the case in certain African countries to having very big NOCs like the Comitato Olimpico Nazionale Italiano (CONI) in Italy which not only runs Olympic affairs but also administers public sector facilities and is involved in the distribution of funding to NSFs.

Taking the example of the Australian Olympic Committee (AOC) its objects are: to develop, promote, and protect the Olympic Movement in Australia in accordance with the Olympic Charter and all regulations and directives issued by the IOC; to effect its exclusive power for the representation and participation by Australia at Olympic Games, Olympic Winter Games, and at Regional Games and do all matters incidental thereto, including the selection and discipline of all members of the teams to represent Australia at those Games. The Committee is obliged to participate in the Olympic Games and Olympic Winter Games by sending athletes; to promote the fundamental principles of Olympism within the framework of sports activity and otherwise contribute to the dissemination of Olympism in the teaching programmes of physical education and sport in schools and other education establishments including the encouragement of the creation of institutions devoted to Olympic education; to encourage the development of high-performance sport as well as sport for all; to discourage discrimination and violence in sport and to fight against the use of substances and procedures prohibited by the IOC or International Federations; to participate in the functions of the IOC, including but without limitation, to make proposals, and where appropriate, to make recommendations to the IOC concerning the Olympic Charter, the Olympic Movement and the organization and holding of the Olympic Games and the Olympic Winter Games, and to collaborate in the preparation of Olympic Congresses; to preserve its autonomy and resist all pressures of any kind, whether they be of a political, religious, or economic nature, that may prevent the Committee from complying with the Olympic Charter; and to do all such other acts and things incidental to the attainment of these objectives, including cooperation with private or government organizations providing that the Committee will never associate itself with any undertaking which would be in conflict with the principles of the Olympic Movement and the Olympic Charter (Australian Olympic Committee, 2004: p. 8).

Under the AOC constitution, the power, management and control of the AOC will be vested in and will reside in the Executive and all major, non-confidential decisions made by it must be circulated to all National Federations and State Olympic Councils. The Executive is committed to achieving and demonstrating high standards of corporate governance. Although best practice recommendations in the country have been articulated to apply to companies and other types of listed entities, the Executive has adopted them to protect members' interests whilst at the same time recognizing and balancing the supreme authority of the IOC under the Olympic Charter. The AOC reported a total revenue of AUS$21,195,595 for 2005, $14,195,695 of which was distribution from the Australian Olympic Foundation (AOF) and $5,959,184 from corporate sponsorship sales and licence fees. Expenditure totalled $12,397,100 for the year and went to areas such as assistance to national federations $2,277,750, Australian youth Olympic festival 2,288,955, medallists and their coaches $924804, finance and administration, miscellaneous 1,837,051. In 2004 the equivalent funds for the youth festival were spent on the Olympic teams (Australian Olympic Committee, 2006).

Solidarity and NOCs

OS has been the body responsible for managing and administering the share of the television rights of the Olympic Games that is allocated to NOCs and it exercises this responsibility in accordance with the specific programmes of technical and financial assistance approved by the IOC's Olympic Solidarity Commission. The section that follows gathers material from the IOC (2006), report that explains the ways in which OS assists the NOCs and their Continental Associations with their efforts for the development of sport through programmes that are devised to match their specific needs and priorities. For the 2001–2004 quadrennial period, the development and assistance budget was US $209,484,000, almost double the amount of US $121,900,000 from the previous quadrennium, and reflected a development, geared towards greater decentralization of the programmes and their management towards the continents and an increase in the number of world programmes available (from 12 to 21). More than 14,000 activities in the 202 NOCs were realized during the 2001–2004 period. The OS programmes are aimed at different protagonists in the world of sport and Olympism: athletes, coaches, sports leaders, NOCs, and Continental Associations. The focus of the 2001–2004 quadrennial plan was increased programme decentralization, with a budget of US $99,800,000 for the world programmes, managed from Lausanne, applied in an individual way to all NOCs and with a budget of US

$69,944,000 for continental programmes, managed by the five Continental Associations, whose application and management were specific to each continent. The rest of the OS budget was made up of the following: US $31,240,000 – Olympic Games (financial assistance to NOCs for participation) and US $8,500,000 – administration and communication.

OS offered NOCs 21 programmes covering a range of varied and complementary activities, divided into four areas: athletes, coaches, NOC management, and special fields. US $43,500,000, the biggest single amount allocated by OS, was for the five programmes in the athletes' category:

- Salt Lake City 2002 – NOC preparation;
- Olympic scholarships for athletes "Athens 2004";
- Athens 2004 – Team sport support grants;
- Regional and Continental Games – NOC Preparation;
- Youth Development Programme.

The success of the programme was evident from the Olympic Winter Games in Salt Lake City in 2002. Funding was made available through OS to 59 NOCs, 690 individual athletes and 4 ice hockey teams. From that, 402 athletes, from 56 NOCs, qualified and took part in 72 out of 78 events and 6 of the 7 sports on the programme. OS provided assistance to 17% of the total number of athletes who took part in these Games. In preparation for the Athens Olympic Games, OS offered 55 team support grants to specific teams that had the possibility to qualify, or had already qualified for the Games. Nine hundred and thirty-nine individual Olympic scholarships (652 men and 287 women) were allocated to athletes from more than 140 NOCs to allow athletes to qualify and prepare themselves for the Athens Olympic Games in 2004. Five hundred and eighty-three Olympic scholarship holders from 141 NOCs managed to qualify for the Athens Olympic Games. Included in these, OS made a special effort in relation to the athletes from the NOCs of Afghanistan and Iraq as they were rejoining the Olympic Movement at the Athens Olympic Games; 57 medals and 105 diplomas were won by the Olympic scholarship holders and 23 NOCs had over 50% of their delegation made up of Olympic scholarship holders.

The different options offered to the NOCs to train their national coaches are the programme of technical courses, the scholarships for coaches, and the development of national coaching structures, which allows the NOCs to benefit from the visit of an international-level expert designated by the IF in the country to train the local coaches. The NOC may also propose a coach to be sent abroad to a university or high-level training centre to attend a training programme in sports sciences or a specific programme in his/her sport. During the 2001–2004 quadrennial period, a total of 1,040 technical courses were organized worldwide with the support of the IFs. Furthermore, 417 coaches from 130 NOCs benefited from the scholarships programme and finally, 141 development programmes were successfully conducted by the NOCs.

Using a fund of US $20,500,000, the NOC management programme concentrated on NOC infrastructure, sports administration, high-level education for sports administrators, NOC management consultancy, and regional forums. The key to the efficient running of an NOC is an appropriate management structure, ensuring the development of sport at a national level. One option was a university training network where participants who work for NOCs and National Federations are offered one of two possibilities: an Executive Masters in Sports Organization Management (MEMOS) or scholarships for high-level training at a university of their choice. Each year, about 10 regional forums in collaboration with the respective Continental Associations were organized on various themes in collaboration with groups of NOCs to discuss and debate topical issues.

The following programmes, which fall under the special fields area, are aimed at assisting the NOCs in their task to promote and disseminate the values and ideals of the Olympic Movement: Sports Medicine; Sport and Environment; Women and Sport; International Olympic Academy; Sport for All; Culture and Education; and NOC Legacy. All the recognized NOCs have benefited from one or more of these programmes, for which a budget of US $12,800,000 was allocated.

The Olympic Foundations

Some NOCs have established OFs as the long-term investment arm of the NOC. The example of the AOF is listed below as an illustration of the moduls operandi of such organizations.

The AOF was formed in 1996 and aimed to develop and protect the Olympic Movement in Australia in accordance with the Olympic Charter including, in particular, funding the preparation and participation of the Australian Teams in the Olympic Games, Olympic Winter Games, and Regional Games and the costs and expenses of the AOC. The stated investment objectives of the AOF are to protect and grow the capital base whilst providing sufficient income and liquidity to provide a base distribution to the AOC toward its known commitments. The Directors of the corporate trustee of the AOF are the voting members of the AOC Executive. They continue to receive the advice of the AOF Investment Advisory Committee and the AOF's funds have been invested in accordance with the Committee's recommendations. The Directors of the AOF and the members of Investment Advisory Committee are assisted in their work by Mercer Investment Consulting, the largest and most experienced investment consulting firm in the world. Mercer monitors each of the managers and the overall portfolio on a continuous basis and provides quarterly reports on performance and developments to the Investment Advisory Committee, as well as drawing attention to any significant event affecting a manager or the AOF's investments. The AOF Limited is a company limited by guarantee and

is the Trustee of the AOF. The Articles of Association of the Company prescribe that the members of the Company shall be the voting members of the
Executive of the AOC Inc. from time to time. The Articles of Association
further prescribe that a voting member of the Executive of the AOC Inc. on
being deemed to be admitted to membership of the Company shall likewise
be deemed to be appointed a Director and that the President of the AOC
Inc. preside as Chairman of the Company (Australian Olympic Foundation
Limited, 2006: p. 11).

The AOF is a very long-term investor intended to assist in financing the
AOC's activities over the indefinite future and concentrates its investments
in growth assets – property and equities, including international equities.
Over time these assets can be expected to provide stronger returns and
growth than investments in bonds and cash.

At the end of 2005 the Foundation had 49% of the Fund's assets in
Australian shares, 24% in overseas shares, 17% in property, 4% in overseas
tactical asset allocation funds, 4% in overseas multi-strategy funds, and 2%
in cash. To reduce foreign currency risk, 45% of the currency exposure in the
Barclays International Equity Fund investment is hedged back to the
Australian dollar. At the same time the AOF's investments in managed funds
were valued at $123.5 million (2004: $107.7 million) with net assets totalling
$116.4 million (2004: $112.1 million). The unrealized gain in valuation is
attributable to the AOF's investments in the Australian and International
equities funds. The surplus for the year arising from distributions from the
managed funds, sale of investments, dividends band interest of $14.9 million
(2004, $5.3 million) was distributed to the AOC with $6.1 million being paid
in cash in 2005. Subsequent to year-end the AOC settled $8.8 million on the
AOF. Despite continuing concerns over the Middle East, terrorism, high oil
prices, and economic conditions in some regions, world markets generally
achieved satisfactory returns in 2005. In this environment the AOF produced an overall return of 19.8%. This was 0.8% ahead of its benchmark
return (what it would have achieved with index performance in each asset
class) and compares with a pretax return of 18% achieved by the median of
the Mercer Specialist Investment Fund Surveys. Since inception the AOF
has returned 1.8% per annum ahead of its benchmark (Australian Olympic
Foundation Limited, 2006).

The Continental NOC Associations

NOCs come together approximately every two years under the umbrella of
the Association of National Olympic Committees (ANOC) to lobby the IOC
for the use of funding and exchange information and experiences but there
are also the five continental associations of NOCs: (i) the Association of
National Olympic Committees of Africa (ANOCA), (ii) Pan American Sports
Organisation (PASO), (iii) Olympic Council of Asia (OCA), (iv) European

Olympic Committees (EOC), and (v) Oceania National Olympic Committees (ONOC). The following extract from the work of EOC is illustrative of the structure of these bodies and the work processes they undertake.

The creation of the Continental Association of European NOCs goes back to the Assembly of Versailles in 1968, under the leadership of its first President, Count Jean de Beaumont. The 1980 General Assembly, which had reached 33 members by that time, elected Franco Carraro as President of the European NOCs while the secretariat was entrusted to Adrien Vanden Eede from Belgium. The following year, five working groups were formed. Under different names and with a few changes, these groups kept supporting the Association's activities as years went by. During the 1980's, the Association's traditional meetings – the General Assembly and the Seminar for Secretaries General and Chefs de Mission – addressed the main topics: the preparation of the Olympic Games, the OS, marketing, etc. The OCOGs became permanent guests in these meetings. In 1989, the Presidency was entrusted to Dr Jacques Rogge also from Belgium and the Secretariat was opened in Rome, at the office of Secretary General Mario Pescante (from Italy). The activities of the European NOCs expanded under their leadership and starting in 1991, due to the political changes in Europe, 15 more NOCs joined the Association and they amount today to a total of 48. In 1995 its legal seat was established in Lausanne close to the IOC, while the operational headquarters settled in Rome, close to the Italian Olympic Committee.

After Dr Jacques Rogge's election as IOC President the EOC General Assembly elected Mario Pescante as President of the EOC while the General Secretariat was entrusted to Patrick Hickey, President of the Olympic Council of Ireland. The EOC is a non-profit making or distributing organization with public responsibilities which has the following main aims: (1) the spreading throughout Europe of the Olympic ideals as defined by the Olympic Charter, in close collaboration with the IOC, ANOC, and the NOC Associations of the other continents; (2) education of youth by sport in a spirit of better comprehension, friendship, and respect for the environment, contributing thereby to the construction of a better and more peaceful world; (3) promotion of cooperation between the European NOCs by research, study of common interests, exchange of information, and the defence of common attitudes; and (4) development of the OS programmes of the IOC in Europe.

The EOC is subject to the Swiss law, Article 60 and in line with the Swiss Civil Code it is fully responsible for the company obligations by means of its patrimony, with the exclusion of the direct responsibility of its members, organs, or employees (pp. 2–3).

The official organs of the EOC are: the General Assembly, the Executive Committee, the Commissions, the Working Groups, and the Auditors (p. 4).

The EOC currently has six commissions: (i) Technical Cooperation and Sport Development, (ii) Preparation of the Olympic Games, (iii) European Youth Olympic Festival, (iv) Medical and Scientific, (v) European Union, and (vi) Athletes (The European Olympic Committees, 2006).

Further to a proposal made by the NOC of Malta, in 1985 the EOC launched the Games of the Small States of Europe (GSSE), the first edition of which was organized in San Marino. Since then, this multi-sport event, for the athletes from the eight countries of our continent with less than one million inhabitants, has taken place regularly every two years, with ever growing success. In 1990 the EOC launched the 'European Youth Olympic Days' (EYOD), now called 'European Youth Olympic Festival' (EYOF), that is the only multi-sport event on this European continent. This event, which has a summer and a winter edition, is held every other year.

Similarly, PASO that represents NOCs in the American continent organizes the Pan American games that are a continental version of the Olympic Games including the Olympic Program sports and others that are not part of the Olympics. Conducted every four years, always one year before the Olympic Games, the first Pan American Games were held in 1951, in Buenos Aires, capital of Argentina. However, its origin dates back to 1932, in the Los Angeles Olympic Games. Inspired by the holding of the first Central American Games six years earlier, the Latin American representatives of the IOC proposed the creation of a competition that would include all the countries in the Americas, for the purpose of strengthening sport activities in the region (The Pan American Sports Organization, 2007).

4

Organizing in the Olympic context

Co-ordination in the Olympic Movement

According to Mintzberg (1979) the structure of an organization can be defined simply as the sum total of the ways in which it divides its labour into distinct tasks and then achieves co-ordination among them. The Olympic Charter claims that under the supreme authority of the IOC the Olympic Movement encompasses organizations, athletes, and other persons who agree to be guided by the Olympic Charter and an official view on the constituent parts of the Olympic Movement is available on the IOC website. This depicts all members in a series of satellites orbiting around a centrally positioned IOC (comprising of the President, the members, the executive board 15 members, the 23 commissions, and the administration) (International Olympic Committee, 2007b) (Figure 4.1).

By looking at the structures the aim is paraphrasing (Mintzberg, 1979: p. xi) to answer the question: how does the Olympic Movement structure itself? To address it synthesis of literature and organizational data needs to be weld together in a single integrated answer. Structure seems to be the root of many of the questions we raise about organizations (Mintzberg, 1979: p. xii)

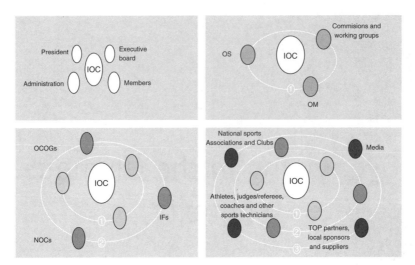

Figure 4.1 Olympic organizations: the official view (*Source*: International Olympic Committee, 2007b)

and investigating the structures of the organizations behind the Olympic Movement one can better understand the event's organization.

> To understand how organizations structure themselves, we should first know how they function. We need to know their component parts, what functions each performs, and how these functions interrelate. Specifically, we need to know how work, authority, information, and decision processes flow through organization (Mintzberg, 1979: p. 17).

Using the terms described earlier to define the parts of an organization the Figure 4.2 shows the various entities making up the Olympic Movement as respective parts of the overall organization.

The parts of the movement listed in Figure 4.2 perform individual roles in the division of labour in the Olympic Movement. Co-ordination – to include control and communication – between individuals and organizations who are part of the labour process, is important for the movement to run and the games to be delivered.

An organigram shows division of labour and how authority flows among divisions but does not capture informal relationships and does not necessarily show the work flows either. An alternative way of viewing the parts of the Olympic Movement is to consider the work constellations found in it Figure 4.3.

Mintzberg claims that there are five co-ordinating mechanisms that seem to explain the fundamental ways in which organizations co-ordinate their work: (i) mutual adjustment, (ii) direct supervision, (iii) standardization of work processes, (iv) standardization of work outputs, and (v) standardization of work skills. These should be considered the most basic elements of

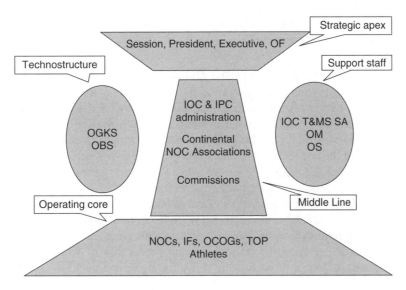

Figure 4.2 Parts of the Olympic Movement

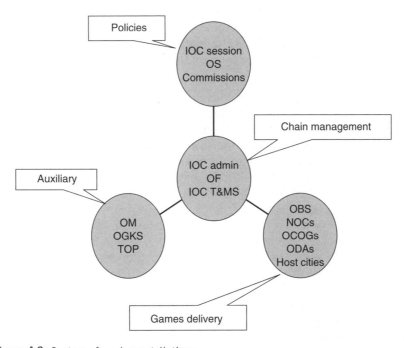

Figure 4.3 System of work constellations

structure, the glue that holds organizations together (Mintzberg, 1979; Mintzberg & Queen, 1992).

> Mutual adjustment achieves the co-ordination of work by the simple process of informal communication. Direct supervision achieves co-ordination by having one individual take responsibility for the work of others. Work can, however, also be co-ordinated without mutual adjustment or direct supervision. It can be standardized. Work processes are standardized when the contents of the work are specified or programmed. Outputs are standardized when the results of the work for example the dimensions of the product or the performance are specified. Skills (and knowledge) are standardized when the kind of training required to perform the work is specified. As organizational work becomes more complicated, the favoured means of co-ordination seem to shift from mutual adjustment, to direct supervision, to standardization preferably of work processes, otherwise of outputs, or else of skills, finally reverting back to mutual adjustment.

> In general, beyond some minimum size, most organizations seem to rely on standardization where they can; where they cannot, they use direct supervision or mutual adjustment, these two being partly interchangeable. When direct supervision fails, perhaps because the task of co-ordination is too big for one brain, the organization will resort to mutual adjustment. Alternatively, when mutual adjustment breaks down, perhaps because there is a need for one brain to guide others that cannot agree among themselves, the organization will turn to direct supervision (pp. 5–7).

It is evident that the Olympic Movement's structure is divisionalized and different organizations perform different roles according to the Olympic Charter. In Mintzberg's configurational terms the divisionalized form is not so much an integrated organization as a set of quasi-autonomous entities or divisions coupled together by a central administrative structure, the headquarters. This structural form is most widely used in the private sector but examples are also seen in multiple site universities and hospital systems made up of specialist units. It is not a complete structure from the strategic apex to the operating core, but rather a structure superimposed on others. Each division may have its own structure but divisionalization itself has a bureaucratizing effect on the composite structures that need to coexist and cooperate (Mintzberg, 1979; Mintzberg & Queen, 1992: p. 380–381). Divisionalized forms of structure evolve out of simpler structures as the age and size of an organization drive it towards diversification. In some cases divisions sell by-products produced in the process of delivering their main service or product to another division (e.g. continental games are produced by NOCs partly in preparation for NOC participation in the main product of the Olympic Movement, the Olympic Games). The Olympic Movements' involvement in international development more broadly, as well as conflict resolution through sport and promotion of the Olympic Truce can also be seen as Olympic by-products. By-products may become more important than end products for organizations and some divisionalized structures move even further to a production chain breakdown when products of divisions have no relationship with one another, as is the case in conglomerates.

In view of the above and the broader preceding discussion the organizational model of the Olympic Movement can best be described as a monopolistic chain corporation that is divisionalized through franchises and subsidiaries. The prime co-ordination mechanism in divisionalized structures is standardization of outputs expected by the various divisions and the key design parameter is the performance control system to effect headquarters' control of the divisions (Mintzberg, 1979). Similarly, the work of the Olympic Movement overall appears to be co-ordinated by the nature of the outputs expected of them. Nevertheless, individual parts or divisions of the movement can exhibit co-ordination in their structures through other means. For example, the work inside IOC commissions appears to be co-ordinated by the standardization of skill of the members who make them up whilst in OCOGs work is largely co-ordinated by outputs specified in the host city contract and the manuals of the event's organization.

Parameters of Design

The essence of organizational design is the manipulation of a series of parameters that determine the division of labour and the achievement of co-ordination. These include:

The parameters of design evidenced in the case of the Olympic Movement as follows:

Job specialization, may be performed horizontally and vertically of unskilled and professional jobs.

Specialization features in the IOC in the form of the 23 commissions and working groups. Similarly the IOC administration is specialized along 15 directors. NOCs exhibit related levels of specialization with a big membership body, an executive committee, various commissions and working groups, and an administration department of non-elected staff. OCOGs use horizontal and vertical specialization to perform the task of organizing the games. To a great extent horizontally specialized positions are affected by the bidding process which includes bid committees working under themes that the IOC decides upon (e.g. accommodation, sports concept, finance, security, and culture).

Upon formation of the OCOG the transfer of Olympic knowledge process affects the specialization of jobs as there is an expectation that the OCOG will follow the general structural pattern of past OCOGs as presented to them via the Transfer of Olympic Knowledge (TOK) process (which includes use of templates, proformas, and transfer of staff involved with past Games). During the life cycle of OCOG levels of specialization fluctuate to reflect organizational tasks and priorities. Approaching the event dates prior specialization patterns alter and the functional-based specialization changes to a venue based one as the event needs to take place at the venue. During the Olympic Games vertical specialization is very high with clearly demarcated jobs at all levels.

A number of subsidiary organizations of the IOC exist to perform particular roles in the management of the Olympic Movement. The OM, OF, the host city Olympic Broadcasting company e.g., the Beijing Olympic Broadcasting Co., Ltd (BOB), IOC T&MS SA, OGKS, La Maison du Sport MSI SA, OTAB, and OPAB are such organizations and they specialize in particular functions.

Allied Businesses such as Helios, David Grant, Sponsors, Satchi and Satchi are outsourced certain tasks, for example hospitality management (David Grant) sponsorship negotiations (Helios) ticketing sales (VISA) either on behalf of the IOC or the OCOGs.

Behaviour formalization occurs through the imposition of operating instructions, job descriptions, rules, and regulations.

Behaviour formalization at the IOC is evidenced in the admission criteria used to select IOC members and the Olympic protocol which is built on the premises of the Olympic Charter in terms of who performs what jobs and under whose authority. Following the IOC reforms (International Olympic Committee, 1999) extensive formalization measures were introduced to govern the behaviour of IOC members, candidate cities, and the host city selection process. The IOC administration operates in relatively informal and small groups of specialist staff who work with the support of the IOC President and Executive Committee. NOCs are dependant upon IOC recognition for existence and therefore have to abide by certain behaviour rules including the letter of the Olympic Charter. The availability of the IOC intranet supports and guides NOC activity in ways that also formalize acceptable behaviour on their part. This includes the composition of applications for Olympic Solidarity funding, and the training of NOC staff on administrative functions. The existence of statutes and requirements of the continental NOC Associations for example EOC, ANOCA, attendance at Chef de Mission, General Secretaries', and themed (e.g. Women, Environment) seminars also affect the formalization of rules, regulations, and acceptable behaviour.

OCOGs have a very formal framework of operation in the form of the host city contract that governs what they exist for, their responsibilities, as organizations and their boundary conditions. The tried and tested games master plan framework affects job specifications, planning processes, and progress assessment. Similarly, the explicit guidance of the TOK programme formalizes operating instructions that are complimented by the tacit knowledge of the staff with previous games experience.

Formalization in the roles of the subsidiary organizations in the Olympic Movement is relatively high as such organizations are foundations or corporations and their work is clearly described and regulated. Similarly allied businesses who carry out work for the movement play formal roles in the movement's work that is governed by business contracts.

Training through use of formal instructional programmes and indoctrination refers to programmes and techniques by which norms of the members of an organization are standardized. Training and indoctrination in the IOC is carried out during the meetings of the IOC assembly, working groups, and commissions. The majority of the IOC members have extensive involvement in the Olympic Movement in their country and one could argue, have already received extensive training and indoctrination in the movement in that capacity. Membership requirements and rules and regulations that govern IOC member activities train these parts of the Olympic Movement to behave in acceptable ways. In the relatively small – in size – IOC administration training and indoctrination are performed through staff development and informal interaction.

As regards the NOCs, Olympic Solidarity offers outside training to these bodies in the form of consultancy and scholarships to staff for Master's level studies. Norms are maintained by selection, recruitment, and promotion standards. Seminars for NOC Presidents' and General Secretaries are organized at continental and world level by Continental NOC Associations and the ANOC, respectively. OCOGs undergo training and indoctrination to particular norms partly through the transfer of games information systems and Olympic knowledge, partly by the IOC processes of authorizing main OCOG activity and partly by in house training processes and senior management expressions of culture, and acceptable employee behaviour.

The subsidiaries have been formed to accommodate particular needs of the IOC and are therefore pre-programmed to behave in certain ways but as time passes and these organizations develop their own identity, training and indoctrination of norms is carried out via responses to the reporting processes to the main shareholders, namely the OF. Participation and incorporation of representatives from the subsidiaries to a variety of meetings of the parts of the Olympic Movement ensures that the subsidiaries remain up-to-date and fine-tuned to the priorities of the Olympic Movement. Staff from allied organizations undergo training and indoctrination during their involvement in the Olympic Games and in the process of carrying out their contractual responsibilities whilst the IOC, OCOG, or NOC voluntary and paid staff who liaise with them also pass on explicit and tacit knowledge.

Unit grouping refers to the choice of the bases by which positions are grouped together into units, and those units into higher order units (typically shown on the organization chart) as well as unit size which refers to the number of positions contained in a single unit.

The IOC has a number of units; the executive board of 16 members, the 26 commissions, and the membership of 111 IOC members, the IOC administration similarly has 15 directors heading respective departments and a staff base of just over 300 staff. The two hundred and three NOCs have unit groupings similar to that of the IOC with an executive board, commissions, and working groups similar in orientation to those of the IOC, and a paid administration.

Some are relatively big organizations with dozens of staff whilst others are run by volunteers and possibly a few staff on loan from Ministries. OCOGs are grouped into departments that relate to the pre-bid activity of bid committee departments which in turn is modelled on the bid requirements of the IOC. As bid committees give way to OCOGs functional grouping along themes of for example, accommodation, security, sports, transportation, education, and accreditation is formed. Approaching the start of the event, functional grouping gives way to venue-based grouping for the venue teams to operate.

The subsidiaries in the Olympic Movement are units in their own right and are grouped in a variety of locations like Lausanne (OM, OF OT&MS SA, MIS) in host cities (BOB, Vancouver Olympic Broadcasting (VOB)) or London (OTAB, OPAB). The size of these units is relatively small and in the case of the Host City Olympic broadcasting organization, their existence is temporary. As regards the core allied independent business, again their number is relatively small, for example in relation to the TOP sponsors, the marketing brokers, global advertising, and event hospitality specialists. All are market leaders with strong standings in their respective sectors.

Strategic planning at the IOC takes place at the executive board level with conferment by the members during the annual session. The commissions are also involved with planning in their respective subject areas and report to the executive board and the members during sessions. Liaison between parts of the IOC takes place during the session and the various commission meetings. The decision-making power is quite diffused at the IOC level in that the members ultimately decide on nominations for new members, member re-elections, and the host city to be awarded the games. As regards the IOC administration it reports to and works under the guidance of the president and the executive board. Few liaison devices are needed at the IOC administration that works from the Lausanne headquarters but extensive liaison is carried out by IOC staff and the voluntary and paid staff at NOCs, IFs, and OCOGs. NOCs bring in the all important teams to the Olympic Games and the IOC and its administration seek to control their outputs by guiding NOC activity in the various countries. This can be achieved with the help of the IOC members in the respective countries and is also facilitated by the existence of strategic planning and reporting activities of the NOCs. With regards to the OCOGs, the IOC administration engages in protracted liaison processes to maintain standardization of the Olympic event in its planning and ultimate delivery. These control systems are engrained in the letter of the host city contract and facilitated by the work of the games co-ordination commission that inspects games progress, as well as by long standing and experienced staff that work in consecutive OCOGs. Decentralization is relatively low during the early years of the OCOGs formation as guidance and steering from the IOC is under way. As OCOGs gain experience and gravitas in their size and maturity, and as the complexity of the task increases so decentralization of power towards them is observed. Decision-making power within OCOGs is decentralized to maximum operational levels during the games to prevent delays in dealing with problems and challenges that arise in venues. The IOC and its administration is also heavily involved at the stage but in the venues OCOG staff deliver the games with the IFs.

The Olympic Movement subsidiaries work to facilitate the aims of the IOC but their planning and control is somewhat separate to maintain their relative autonomy of operations. These separate entities report to the IOC president and the executive board and are controlled by means of the shares that the IOC holds in them. Centralization is therefore relatively low. Allied organizations are controlled by the contracts with the IOC and liaison takes place in the form of joint and shared working with either the IOC administration itself, the NOCs, the IFs, or the OCOGs. It must not be underestimated that most allied organizations, the subsidiaries, and the IOC have established and tested working relations (with regards to the challenges of the event's delivery); something that cannot be said for the OCOGs. Decentralization of power can, therefore, understandably be relatively high towards the allied organizations.

Situational Factors

A number of contingency or situational factors influence the choice of the design parameters. These include the age and size of the organization which affect particularly the extent to which its behaviour is formalized and its administrative structure elaborated. As they age and grow organizations appear to go through distinct structural transitions, for example, from simple organic to elaborated bureaucratic structures or from functional grouping to market-based grouping.

The Olympic Movement and the IOC were officially established on 23 June 1894 at the Paris International Congress that was organized by Coubertin at the Sorbonne. From this small beginning, the IOC has grown in size to incorporate increasing numbers of members (111), IFs (28 summer and 7 winter),

NOCs (202), recognized sports and events. The increasing growth of the size of the movement presents a challenge to the IOC as such giganticism makes the games increasingly more expensive and difficult to manage. Therefore, measures were taken to respond to the challenges from NOC to send more athletes to the games and from IFs to be a part of the Olympic programme.

Similarly, the IOC took measures to curtail the phenomenon of games inflation where each host city sought to outperform the previous one for the title of the 'best games ever'. The IOC's administration has also grown in size as it aged. Having started as support staff to the volunteer IOC members, the IOC now resembles a formal bureaucratic structure albeit with strong professional control. Similarly the NOCs have grown in member as new countries were formed to a total of 202. Their size grew to include commissions that resemble those of the IOC and the paid administrative staff have grown in size as finances permitted and the growing scope of the NOC operations demanded. Although OCOGs are temporary organizations and have a predetermined end date as defined by the host city contract, their comparative size across host cities throughout the years has grown enormously. Linked to the giganticism of the Olympic Games and the increasing volume of the infrastructure works undertaken by the host city, were the growing demands on OCOGs to co-ordinate games preparations in partnership with an ever increasing number of IFs, NOCs, Government Departments, and private sector service providers. The average lifespan of OCOGs has increased greatly since the beginning of the history of the modern games and now OCOGs are established seven years prior to the year of the Games and liquidate approximately one year after the end of the event.

Subsidiaries to the Olympic Movement are relatively much younger than the IOC. The OM being established in 1993, the rest later than that; Meridian management SA in 1996 and OTAB and OPAB also in 1996. As regards the various allied companies their age and size varies. Some sponsors have been associated with the movement for many Olympiads whilst others just joined. Service providers like David Grant have been associated with the movement since 1996.

Another situational element is the technical system of the organization which influences especially the operating core and those staff units most clearly associated with it. When the technical system of the organization regulates the work of the operating core, as is done in mass production, it has the effect of bureaucratizing the organization by virtue of the standards it imposes on lower level workers. Alternately, when the technical system succeeds in automating the operating work, as is done in process production, it reduces the need for external rules and regulations enabling the structure to be organic. When the technical system is complex, as is often the case in process production, the organization has to create a significant professional support staff to deal with it and then decentralize selectively to that staff many of the decisions concerned with the technical system.

The technical system in the Olympic Movement exhibits certain variety. As regards the IOC's governance of the movement there is the intranet environment shared by the parts of the movement and the system of forward planning and reporting to the executive board and to the session. As regards the selection of the host city, the IOC's technical system allows evaluation of the candidates along certain criteria and subsequently a selection of the city by secret ballet of the IOC members.

Finally, in their role in the organization of the Olympic Games, the technical systems of the IOC are brought to OCOGs through the transfer of knowledge from past hosts, the application of master planning techniques, management software, databases, systems design documentations, etc. that are expected to be used in the OCOG as per its contractual responsibilities. The technical system is arguably more established in the production of the Olympic Games and although it does not automate the work of the operating core that delivers the games, it certainly does dictate the activity of the operating core and as Mintzberg reminds there is then a need to create professional support staff to oversee the work of the technical system. Such positions have in the past been filled by ex OCOG staff and supported by the work of OGKS and the later formed independent company Event Knowledge Services.

The technical systems of the NOCs are seen in the work of the production of the National Olympic Team and communication and cooperation with the IOC and the national federations. Not all NOC have elaborate administrative structures and some will have minimum technical systems available to them. As regards elite athlete development, NOCs liaise with national federations and coaches in the running of these technical systems. Scientific support (physiological, psychological) as well as life management support (finances, education, and post career planning) are delivered through such technical systems that seek to support the athletes' progression through the various development stages to reach qualification and possibly a medal at the Games.

Subsidiaries share access to the communication system of the IOC and have their own specialist ones for example collection management for the OM investment management for the OF; and broadcasting technology for the Olympic Broadcasting companies. Finally, allied businesses share selective access to the IOC communication system and become active players, facilitators, and/or controllers at various stages in the life cycle of the Games. For example, VISA as a TOP sponsor will help deliver the event ticketing process.

The environment of an organization can vary in its degree of complexity, in how static or dynamic it is, in the diversity of its markets, and in the hostility it contains for the organization. For Mintzberg (1979), the more complex the environment, the more difficulty central management has in comprehending it and the greater the need for decentralization. As regards the rate of change, the more dynamic the environment, the greater the difficulty in standardizing work, outputs, or skills and so the less bureaucratic the structure.

To define the environment of the IOC one needs to naturally consider the broader Olympic Movement. The IOC and its administration exist in a relatively complex (in relation to the number of interdependencies), stable (as regards the rate of change in the environment), diversified (considering the variety of operations – event, sport's governance, truce, development), and friendly (given the overall positive brand image) environment. NOCs exist in a variety of national and socio-political contexts and environmental assessment necessitates the evaluation of such particular features that are beyond the scope of this book. Nevertheless, as regards relationships with others in the Olympic Movement, NOCs operate in a complex, stable, non-diversified, and friendly environment. OCOGs are also affected by others in the movement in a variety of ways. The host city contract dictates particular processes in their management and the eventual service recipients (the NOCs, IFs, athletes, media, etc.) all have set standards of what the games' experiences should be like and therefore have certain expectations of OCOGs' behaviours. As they age and reach maturity OCOG environments change from being simple, dynamic, non-diversified, and friendly at the start to being complex, more stable, diversified, and occasionally hostile in the build up to the Games.

The management operations of the subsidiaries of the Olympic Movement are less open to public view and from the limited publicly available information it transpires that their socio-political environment is shared with that of the IOC and its administration having a geographical base in Lausanne (with the exception of OTAB, OPAB, and the broadcasting organization that is set up as another temporary organization in each host city). With regards to the allied industries these are often US based with global commercial activity.

The power factors of an organization include external control, personal power needs, and fashion. The more an organization is controlled externally, the more centralized and bureaucratic it tends to become, argues Mintzberg (1979). This can be explained by the fact that the two most effective means to control an organization from the outside are to hold its most powerful decision maker, the chief executive officer (CEO), responsible for his/her actions and to impose clearly defined standards on him/her (performance standards or rules and regulations). Moreover, because the externally controlled organization must be especially careful about its actions, often having to justify these to outsiders, it tends to formalize much of its behaviour and insist that its CEO authorizes key decisions. A second factor, individual power needs (especially by the CEO) tend to generate excessively centralized structures.

Seeking to capture power in and around the Olympic Movement is a very interesting exercise that reveals additional features of the relationships among the organizations that make up the Olympic Movement. Starting with the IOC and its administration, power is relatively decentralized to the executive board and the members, who have the power to modify the Olympic Charter, elect new members and choose the host city of future games. The position power of the President is also of particular note, and post-2001, Jacques Rogge replaced Juan Antonio Samaranch who for had considerable symbolic power as president of the IOC from 1980. As a general rule, NOCs have considerable power in elite sport development issues in their respective countries, being the administrators of such activity and responsible for its funding from Olympic Solidarity as well as government sources in some cases – often with the collaboration of government departments like the Ministry of Youth and Sports, etc. They are, however, externally controlled by the IOC to the extent that the IOC allows their existence. The presence of IOC member(s) in a country is an additional level of control of the IOC over the NOC with IOC members often holding senior positions in the NOCs. Given recent attempts by the IOC to address the issue of autonomy of the NOC from government intervention it is pertinent to mention the power of the respective nation state which the NOC represents and is based. Such a context also exists for OCOGs which are organizations that are affected both by the Olympic Movement and the nation state. Politically, socially, culturally, economically, technologically, and even anthropologically, OCOGs share organizational traits with others in the Olympic Movement as well as the public sector machinery of the host country. The host city contract explicitly defines the relative power of OCOG to any autonomous action and although contracts are enacted through programmes and processes it is the non-contractually bound power of the host country's governance group that goes relatively unrecognized up to the later stages of the games preparations when evidence (Malfas, 2003) suggest that it takes greater control of OCOGs. IFs also take power away from OCOGs as the games approach as IFs claim their rights in the event competitions in the field of play in all sporting venues.

Power in the subsidiaries of the IOC is depicted in the number and percentage of shares of the companies that are held by the OF (whose operating funds are provided by the IOC). Change in the organizational setups of subsidiaries (e.g. the formation of the IOC T&M SA Services SA out of Meridian Management SA) indicates the power of the IOC to restructure its subsidiaries whilst career moves of Olympic Movement staff to senior management posts in allied industries indicate the position power of individuals. The allied industries hold enormous power by way of their financial support of the Olympic Movement. Sponsors and broadcasters are attracted to the games because of the image of the Olympic brand and the spectacle provided. If the image was tarnished at any future stage, funding from sponsors would be affected and likewise, broadcasters could decrease spending.

Although the discussion has focussed on organizations as units of analysis it is also important to note the role of the individual and remember that in the long history of the Olympic Movement there have been many expressions of power from athletes, IOC members, politicians, and sports administrators.

The Olympic Chain

The monopoly of the IOC allows it to establish a transnational chain of organizations whose existence it ultimately controls. The IOC decides which IFs can have their events admitted to the Olympic programme and only the IOC may give the right to an NOC to operate in a country as a company chain. The IOC also allows an OCOG to come in existence as a temporary franchisee (to set up companies in host cities, to deliver the organization and management of the Olympic Games in the respective cities, bound by the host city contract rules and with the particular knowledge transfer in place). Evidently, the IOC shares characteristics of chain operators for whom franchising constitutes a vital facet of operations. Franchisees, typically purchase the right to operate a unit under the chain's brand name; the franchisee agrees to follow certain operating guidelines (to preserve the value of the brand), pays the chain operator a royalty fee based on revenue, and receives the income produced by the unit (Bradach, 1998: p. 3). Similarly, in the case of the Olympic Movement, an OCOG agrees to follow certain operating procedures, receives some money from the television rights and in return allows the chain operator, the IOC, to have the games organized in the host country at no extra cost to the IOC (or its company chains in the case of the NOCs) who subsequently sell the television signal to broadcasters and the advertising rights to various sponsors. The IOC's relationship with the NOCs also resembles that of a chain in that the IOC gives patronage and some funding to an NOC to operate in its host country (the IOC has a membership of IOC members in a country not of a country). In return the IOC expects from the NOC to send a team representing the country to the Olympic Games and Olympism and elite Olympic sport are promoted in the respective country. As regards the chain of OCOGs at everyone time there are a few temporary OCOGs operating. Some being at the start of their life cycle whilst others winding down their operations and approaching liquidation.

According to Bradach (1998) the building blocks of chain organizations (franchise as well as company arrangements) are as follows: (1) The contractual responsibility (in the case of the NOCs this comes in the shape of the Olympic Charter and the IOC recognition). (2) Chain operators economic benefit (this stems from the sale of television and other rights). (3) Local operators rewards and orientation (host city incentives through urban regeneration associated with the games). (4) Source of chain operator influence, (through the ownership of the Olympic Games and their trademarks). (5) Architecture of information that represents where how and what kind of information is captured by the organization; with consequences on management and decision making in chain organizations. (6) Federal or hierarchical, span of control. Broadly speaking, for company units the structure is hierarchical, for franchisees it is federal.

The IOC as a chain operator is using the above blocs having NOCs as company units and OCOGs as franchisees. In a chain, employees often have cross-cutting career paths. Similalry, career moves of individuals through parts of the Olympic Movement can also be observed. IOC members serving at continental level may advance to take up more senior posts in the IOC as in the case of IOC president Rogge who was previously president of the EOC. Staff from the IOC subsidiaries also move around the broader divisionalized chain. As the following example illustrates ex IOC staff now run private consultancy companies and help candidate cities with their bids. Helios Partners is a sponsorship consultancy with dedicated offices in Atlanta, Washington DC, and Beijing, and affiliate offices in London and Tokyo who specialize in: Sponsorship evaluation, partnership structuring and contract negotiation, strategic sponsorship plan development and management, media and sponsorship alignment, brand assessment and integration, and bid city consultation and management. Helios Chairman Frank Craighill was part of the team that developed the modern approach to global olympic sponsorship and developed the TOP programme. Helios Partners Chief Executive Officer, Chris Welton is the former President of Meridian Management and prior to that, he was the Vice President of market development for the Atlanta Committee for the Olympic Games. Helios President, Terrence Burns served as Senior Vice President and assisted in the creation of Meridian Management SA, following his role in managing Delta Air Lines' Olympic Sponsorship in 1996. IOC member for Canada, Richard Pound Chairman of WADA and Former Chairman of the IOC Marketing Commission is claimed (Helios Partners Inc., 2006) to suggest that during his tenure with the IOC's marketing agency, Meridian Management SA, Terrence was instrumental in introducing business-focused, brand-based strategies which enhanced the IOC's sales, marketing, and communications efforts. Similarly, Michael Payne, Former IOC Marketing Director (1983–2004) and now Special Advisor to Bernie Ecclestone, Formula 1 is claimed (Helios Partners Inc., 2006) to suggest that the founders of Helios – Frank Craighill and Terrence Burns – have been key players in the development of the Olympic Marketing agenda over the years. Clinton Dines, President of BHP Billiton China, one of the world's largest diversified resources company trading resources ranging from metals, energy, diamonds to iron and petroleum is quoted (Helios Partners Inc., 2006) explaining how the Helios Partners team was integral and instrumental in the development of the company's strategy and gave invaluable advice during negotiations to become the Official Diversified Minerals and Medals Sponsor of the Beijing 2008 Olympic Games. Helios partners now advise candidate cities and helped on the content development of the Sochi bid for the 2014 winter games Sochi 2014 Bid Committee (2006).

Bradach (1998: p. 61) provides a useful discussion on the underlying dynamics affecting the behaviour and performance of chain organizations. He claims that adding new units to the chain plays a crucial role in its success and management. The direct financial implications of new units being more revenue and profits from additional company units and more fees and royalties from new franchise units. Unit growth also produces important indirect effects in the form of leveraging the trademark to the benefit of existing and new units, increasing market presence and identity, and generating more funds for advertising. Adding new NOC units is relatively straightforward for the IOC given that most UN recognized countries have an NOC but in relation to OCOGs establishing and maintaining the corporate identity and uniformity of/to the IOC as chain operator, poses great challenges.

Management information systems have the possibility to make the operational detail of a local franchisee almost transparent. Superiors are able to view performance, and data may be accompanied with a comparison to a budget, to the previous year's performance or to averages in the company chain. Variances from expected performance could be identified at a glance. Senior managers can then identify projects and numbers that are out of bounds and ask subordinates for explanations and action plans (Bradach, 1998: p. 90). The NOC intranet allows some management of information and in OCOGs, master planning and key milestone planning, ensures that late projects are identified and remedial action then follows.

By presenting public results the chain operator has the opportunity to force rhetoric to rise or fall in level or intensity by deliberately applying pressure in various stages. When ex IOC president Samaranch warned Greece about venue construction delays in preparation of the Athens 2004 games he was putting pressure on the OCOG as well as the public authorities in the host city to speed up operations.

Similarly, benchmarking the work of an OCOG has in the past been associated with leading to games inflation of ever increasing expenditure as one OCOG raises the performance bar and the next one seeks to be the next 'best games ever'. Modelling often takes place in chains and if the company arrangement is successful then units have an incentive to emulate the designs that produced such performance (Bradach, 1998: p. 108). The games knowledge transfer is one way in which this has been achieved as the successful model moves from one host city to the next. Uniformity of procedures and standards is central in chain operations and performance related field audits of OCOGs in the Olympic chain are carried out in the form of games co-ordination commission visits. Local responsiveness is also instrumental for the success of the chain. Issues of pricing, variations of the products (e.g. exhibition sports, local mascots, etc.) access to key suppliers, a knowledgeable labour force, and local marketing are very important. Responding locally also creates challenges to NOCs and OCOGs in that the local chain units need to be trusted with execution. When the IOC offers the games organization to a host city and notwithstanding the safety net of the host city contract, there is a risk that the city may not be able to deliver the games as per the IOC requirements because of socio-political pressures, civil unrest, war, preparation delays, etc.

Along with being seen as a critical factor in the chain's increasingly competitive environment, systemwide adaptation is one of the most complex management challenges that chain organizations face. The particularities of diverse local markets, the difficulty of implementing a new activity in diverse units, the potential conflicts of interest between franchisers and chain operators, and the absence of authority in the franchise arrangements are a few of the problems that make systemwide adaptation a major challenge. The process of adaptation may involve: generating of ideas, testing and evaluating them, decision making and implementation (Bradach, 1998: p. 133). The leadership role of the IOC as chain operator is reinforced by fundamental economics. As NOC and OCOG units operate to serve it, it is motivated to introduce adaptations that grow the business and enhance profitability. Nevertheless, there is a fundamental difference between company units and chains units as chains can 'tell' company people but 'sell' to franchisees (Bradach, 1998: p. 157); in the case of OCOGs the IOC as chain operator is motivated to search for adaptation that improves performance so that revenue increases which in turn leads to more royalties and enhanced brand name recognition. Therefore, the IOC has an overarching interest in investing in corporate resources related to systemwide adaptation, including corporate marketing staff as well as research and development departments. This investment in resources to support companies and franchisees is also evidenced in the activity of the IOC subsidiaries, namely,

- the OM (foundation),
- the OF (foundation),
- the IOC T&MS SA – OF had a 50% voting and a 25% economic interest in its predecessor Meridian Management SA – (corporation),
- the OBS OF holds 99% of shares (corporation),
- OGKS SA holds 100% of shares (corporation), and
- MSI OF holds 33% of shares (corporation).

It is pertinent to note that by not allowing the NOCs to be controlled by national politics in the country in which they operate the IOC, as chain operator, safeguards this valuable chain operator control.

It is possible that not all franchisees are enthusiastic about systemwide adaptation. Questions of who has decision-making power and who has implementation power then become important for the timely execution of the required adaptation. The quality of adaptation, speed of identifying opportunities, and speed of implementation may vary depending on local circumstances. In the case of OCOGs it can be argued that certain countries present particular management challenges to the chain operator stemming from the differences in the organizational culture in the host city. As recent examples from managing the IOC reform illustrate, ridding the IOC of corrupt members also needs to include reform in the sports bodies that nominate these members to the IOC. Similar to differences between companies in the chain and franchises in the chain so differences in host countries present varied challenges for the management of the overall chain.

It is claimed that self-correcting, self-renewing organizations can meet the challenges of operating a chain. By incorporating attributes from all business sides (NOCs as company units and OCOGs as franchise units) the plural-form organization of the Olympic chain is aided in escaping the natural tendency of internal arrangements to ossify over time and external relationships to suffer from entropy by creating a built-in constructive tension between the parts (Bradach, 1998). Such a plural form then may be integral to the long-term sustainability of the Olympic chain organizations. Similarly, ambidextrous organizations (different structures are required for different circumstances) are better according to Bradach (1998) than hybrid forms. 'The plural form offers an intriguing alternative to the widely held view that the external variety in the environment needs to be matched with internal variety of structures and systems. For some, internal variety is said to be achieved through specialization' (p. 179). Another way to obtain that variety is by having different kinds of structures in tension in the same organization each generating different kinds of ideas. Bradach (1998) claims that practitioners and academics alike need to move beyond simple models that search for the best way to organize or that seek to identify the unique fit between certain conditions and certain organizational designs. 'We must entertain the notion that combinations of structures like the plural form offer attributes not available to any single arrangement. And we need to embrace the counterintuitive idea that redundancy and variety can be intertwined in ways that set in motion a powerful set of dynamics that promote self-correction and self-renewal' (p. 185).

Autonomy, Commercialization, and Sustainability

The organizations that make up the Olympic Movement have faced a number of important changes to the context in which they operate. Firstly, legal frameworks have challenged the long-standing autonomy of organization in the Olympic Movement. Secondly, the autonomous power of such organizations is being undermined by private entities (with their professionals and their associated management practices and norms) that seek to further control sport as a commodity. Thirdly, commodification of Olympic sport and games organization is threatening the sustainability of the movement that is becoming gigantic. The presence of private enterprise in the Olympic

Movement ultimately raises the question of how their interests will be served without the Olympic Movement being compromised or loosing its guarded autonomy.

Autonomy

As a Swiss Verein (German for association – similar to the Anglo-American voluntary association), neither the IOC nor any of its member organizations have any liability for each other's acts or omissions. Each of the member organizations is a separate and independent legal entity operating under the various countries. The protection of the autonomy of the movement is linked to the IOC's monopoly and power that allows it to exercise pressure on its various member sports organizations to remain autonomous. It is a selective form of autonomy, however, that the IOC want, most profoundly, autonomy of its member organizations from government involvement and legislation. At the same time the IOC expects its member organizations to follow its guidance or face significant pressure and even expulsion from the Olympic Movement.

The case material below draws from the debriefing of the Beijing OCOG organizers by the Athens Organising Committee for the Olympic Games (ATHOC) staff and gives examples of pressures on this OCOG to use particular contractors and suppliers. Obviously the sponsors of the Olympic Games have exclusive access to some categories (value in kind) for provision (technology, catering, vehicles, etc.) but as Athens games organizers claimed, their OCOG faced the task of reconciling conflict of European Union (EU) legislation on public contracts with binding instructions from the IOC.

In the course of the organization of the Games, ATHOC's mission faced great difficulties in cases where the IOC, based on its experience and expertise, strongly recommended specific contractors to undertake certain tasks of the Olympic preparation.

Although the context of legal issues for an OCOG will vary from host country to host country, the approach to legal issues is very similar. In almost every case, the OCOG must work with the host country to modify existing laws or create new laws to protect the OCOG in the areas of risk, brand protection, venue use, etc. The EU has added a level of complexity to the legal conditions under which an OCOG must operate. The Charter grants to the IOC full authority and responsibility for all issues related to the Olympic Games. This also applies to the OCOGs. Furthermore, as far as the OCOGs are concerned, the Charter imposes on them the obligation to conduct all their activities in accordance with the Olympic Charter, the host city contract, and the instructions of the IOC Executive Board. However, in view of the fact that the contracting parties undertaking the organization of the Games are states and administration units of the public sector (cities, i.e., municipalities), the OCOGs are in most cases incorporated and operate as entities of public law. In the majority of states worldwide, there is a specific legal framework governing all activities of such entities, which, for obvious reasons, is much stricter than the rules applying to the entities of private law (Papathanasopoulou, 2004: p. 31).

The issue has been experienced in its most complex parameters, in the process of the organization of the 2004 Athens Games, particularly in relation to the procurement contracts concluded by ATHOC. Apart from the national legislation applicable on the operations of ATHOC and due to the fact that Greece is a member state of the EU, ATHOC, as a state-owned organization, has been obliged to abide by the European legislation as well. This involved also the observance of the EU procurement rules as stated in the EU Directives 93/36/EEC on public supply contracts, 92/50/EEC on public service contracts, and 93/37/EEC on public works contracts. The aforementioned EU Directives (already amended by Directive 2004/18/EC, which has not been implemented by the EU member states yet), the provisions of which are in force in all EU member states, regulate the procedures of assignment of public procurement contracts, imposing quite strict rules of objectivity, transparency, and competition on equal terms, in order to safeguard competition within the EU market. It is worth noting that the Athens Olympics was the first games in history with an obligation that legal regulations be consistent with European Law and where a blending of important and strict areas of the community law with those of the Olympic Movement was tested for the first time. Greece, therefore, has been the first EU country which undertook the organization of Olympic Games after the application of the strict legal framework on the assignment of public procurement contracts in the EU. ATHOC could not choose a certain number of potential contractors and directly proceed to negotiations with them, as a company of private economy would do, but it needed to follow the specific procedures of the EU procurement rules referring to supply and service contracts (as far as public works contracts are concerned, ATHOC has not been involved in constructions and therefore it has not faced the application of Directive 93/37/EEC). Under the said rules, direct negotiations are allowed only exceptionally, in cases specifically mentioned in the relevant legislation, and always on condition that the selection of the contractor is adequately justified. In the course of the organization of the Games, ATHOC's mission faced great difficulties in cases where the IOC, based on its experience and expertise, strongly recommended specific contractors to undertake certain tasks of the Olympic preparation. On the one hand contractually bound to abide by the instructions/recommendations of the IOC and on the other legally obliged to follow the EU procedures for the selection of its counter parties, ATHOC was confronted with the following question: Which rules supersede, the EU legislation or the rules deriving from the Olympic Charter and the Host City Contract? How should a country confront a possible conflict between the 'binding instructions' of the IOC and the provisions of the Directives on public contracts? As a Greek entity of public law established and operating in a EU member state, ATHOC could in no case act in breach of the EU procurement rules, which even prevail over the Greek national legislation. The said approach was confirmed by the European Commission as well, which refused to grant any derogation from the application of EU law, even in the case of the Olympic Games. Therefore, ATHOC had no choice but to observe the EU legislation, complying with the instructions of the IOC to the extent that they did not entail any infringement of the EU law (pp. 25–26).

The level of autonomy of sport organization in general has been the focus of the Independent European Sports Review which Sports Ministers of France, Germany, Italy, Spain, and UK, decided to launch in the context of the UK Presidency of the EU, to consider and provide tangible recommendations for the implementation of the Nice Declaration of 2000 on the European model of sport. The report claims (Arnaut, 2006) that sport has a specific nature that sets it apart from any other field of business activity and the Nice Declaration attempts to describe what some of these unique features are.

According to the Nice Declaration, the independent nature of sports bodies should be supported and protected and their autonomy to organize the sports for which they are responsible should be recognized. The Declaration further confirms that it is the federation that should continue to be the key form of sporting organization providing a guarantee of cohesion and participatory democracy. Self-regulation of the sports sector is an aspect of the principle of freedom of association, recognized and protected as a fundamental element of personal liberty in all EU member states' constitutions and in the European Convention on Human Rights. The self-organization and self-regulation of the sports world is an important expression and legacy of European civil society from the end of the 19th to the beginning of the 21st century. Regulatory functions in sports are performed by private authorities – sports governing bodies – rather than by governments. For historical and cultural reasons, all EU member states have, to various degrees and to a large extent, left the regulation of sport to the sports bodies. As noted, the Nice Declaration confirms that the sports federation should continue to be the guarantor of cohesion and should have a central role in ensuring solidarity between all different levels of sporting practice. In the context of European sport, this means that, to discharge their functions effectively, both the European and the national federations should be independent and their autonomy to regulate should be recognized and respected. This implies, however, that these bodies also enjoy the necessary margin of discretion to perform their duties.

At the same time, however, it is necessary that the various stakeholders in sport must be properly represented at both European and national association level because this is a precondition for ensuring that these authorities are best equipped to speak on behalf of all interests in the game.

There is perhaps no other economic sector where private bodies have the same scope of regulatory latitude as in the sports sector. Nevertheless, this scope for autonomous regulatory activity is by no means unlimited. In particular, the potential application of EU law has resulted in a situation where it has become increasingly difficult for the sports authorities to judge when they are acting legally or not. It is also fair to say that both the European Commission and national courts in the EU have, on occasion, struggled to find appropriate solutions to cases involving sports matters. The EU institutions have treated sports governing bodies in a similar manner to 'public authorities' meaning that their private rules do not escape the application of EU Treaty principles (in particular, regarding free movement of workers). At the same time, however, the EU has been less willing to recognize that sports governing bodies must enjoy a margin of appreciation, such that they are able to exercise their regulatory functions in a meaningful sense (pp. 29–31).

The report concluded that there needs to be a clearer delineation as to those matters where sports bodies may act autonomously and with a legitimate and wide margin of discretion, without fear of their decisions being undermined by the application of European Community law.

This is not because sport should seek a blanket 'exemption' from the rigours of EU law: it is rather because certain matters (in particular, pure sports regulatory matters) are best left to the bodies with the expertise to deal with these issues (p. 31).

In light of the above examples it appears that the autonomy of sport organizations can not be allowed at the expense of the application of EU law. The host city contract of the IOC may bind a host city to certain behavior but EU countries are not immune to pressures that limit the autonomy of the IOC (as a sporting organization) in its operations in EU countries.

Commercialization

Foster (2005) considers the likely changes to the regulation of sport if the process of globalization continues and contends that as the political economy of sport is now ruled by global capital this will hasten the Americanization of sport and lead to the development of a single model of globalized sport.

The present system, of governance, as represented to a large extent by the traditional sports federation, will be dismantled in favour of elite sports managing themselves, especially in the key area of profit maximization. Even the minimum level of regulation represented by the EU approach will be resented by capital and it will strive to recreate unregulated, autonomous structures. Law and regulation needs to rise to this challenge by subjecting globalized sport, and its commercial forms of governance to the full legal consequences of its commercial logic (pp. 85–86).

The IOC can not be immune to such changes and its monopoly power and associated autonomy are affected. As Allison (2005) suggests it is important to consider (a) whether some International Non-Governmental Organizations (INGOs) really pre-empted the power and influence of states and of a range of intergovernmental organizations and (b) what are the extents of power of sporting INGO (SINGO) and business INGO (BINGO).

In any case, the forces of globalization do not offer a single coherent challenge, but a fragmented contest between different visions of sport. The BINGO offer sport as the commercial opportunity of the future, an entertainment industry of almost unlimited potential. But the SINGO talk of it as a mission a social, cultural, even quasi religious entity which must be governed as such. In many ways they are dependant on each other's logic, but the difference is mirrored by a completely different set of assumptions about the regulation of sport in Europe and the United States. And a final question that emerges about global regulation simply concerns whether it will be effective, given the money to be made, in dealing with the problems of doping and gambling and the force of the lowest common denominators argument (absorbing the normative approach to corruption of the most corrupt) (p. 163).

For Forster and Pope (2004) the IOC has the biggest impact as an event organization.

As a global sport organization, the IOC deserves its own treatment on several counts. First it is an event global sport organization as opposed to a sporting one. A second major reason is the concept of the Olympic family, a set of affiliations that gives it extraordinary power and makes it a legitimizing force in the eyes of many both inside and outside the sports' movements. A third and enormously important difference is also apparent. The IOC does not exist at the behest of the Olympic Committees of various nations but exactly the reverse. And so it is with the individuals that belong to the IOC as members. The IOC has helped create some of the most important specialist global sports organization like the World Anti-doping Agency, the International Court for Arbitration of sport, and the International Federation of Sports Medicine (pp. 96–99).

As sport commercialization intensifies and broadens, this will create new structural forms where private enterprise will increasingly demand a share in the governance mechanisms or create its own. One way in which this may occur (Forster and Pope, 2004) is through the vehicle of joint venture between private enterprise and the global sports organizations whereby the North American model is likely to become a feature of global sports structures.

> Rather than the political assembly structures seen in Europe the private corporation may become the dominant organization form and ownership of sports may then become private rather than public (p. 100).

Given the above it is possible to conclude that the autonomy of the Olympic Movement will be affected by the levels of commercialization of business activities, commodification of the Olympic experiences and privatization of organizational structures. As the giganticism of the Olympic Games also suggests growth control is not always possible and concerns over the sustainability of the movement have been raised in relation to the events' impact as well as the movement's future.

Sustainability

The official position on sustainability offered by the IOC finds expression in Agenda 21 (International Olympic Committee, 1999). This aims to encourage members of the movement to play an active part in the sustainable development of the planet and sets out the basic concepts and general actions needed to ensure that this objective is met. It has been inspired by the UNCED Agenda 21, adapted to the characteristics of the Olympic and sports Movement and suggests general outlines which should guide the activity of the Olympic Movement in the fields in which it can bring an effective contribution. It is meant to provide a theoretical and practical guide for all members of the Olympic Movement and suggests to governing bodies areas in which sustainable development could be integrated into their policies. It also points out ways in which individuals can act so as to ensure that their sporting activities and their lives in general play a part in this sustainable development in a climate of respect for different social, economic, geographical, climatic, cultural, and religious contexts which are characteristic of the diversity of the members of the Olympic Movement. In order to satisfy the general objectives of Agenda 21, the Olympic Movement developed a programme of action built around the following three objectives: (a) Improving socio-economic conditions, (b) Conservation and management of resources for sustainable development, and (c) Strengthening the role of major groups. The following discussion takes them in turn and illustrates examples of actual practice.

The first objective of improving socio-economic conditions relates to the satisfaction of those cultural and material needs that are essential for all individuals to live with dignity and play a positive role in the society to which they belong. With this principle in mind, Agenda 21 claims to pays attention to the fate of minorities and the most disadvantaged members of society. Oxfam GB's & International Confederation of Free Trade Unions' (2004) report on the sportswear industry claims that global sportswear companies are careful to distance themselves from accusations that their business operations – the way in which they place orders and negotiate price cuts – are having negative consequences in the workplace. They point to statements of corporate responsibility and codes of conduct covering labour practices as evidence of their good intent. But according to the report

> the industry's business model creates clear market signals to suppliers, placing a premium on the creation of low wage, temporary workforces, and denied basic workers' rights (p. 6).

> Yet the sporting world – apart from a few exceptions – has done very little to call for change on the part of the sportswear companies, despite years of campaigning (p. 47).

> The organizing committee for the Olympic and Paralympic Games in Sydney 2000 adopted a code of Labour Practice for the productions of licenced Olympic Goods and although the organizing committee gave the Textile Clothing and Footwear Union of Australia the right of access to information about workplaces and the right to send representatives to speak to workers by this time most of the garments for the Sydney Olympics had already been made. Similarly in 1996, Fédération Internationale de Football Association (FIFA) agreed to a 'Code of Labour Practice' for FIFA licenced products, as requested by the trade unions. Labour-standards criteria – based on the International Labour Organization (ILO) Declaration on Fundamental Principles and Rights at Work – have now been included in the licencing agreements. The Clean Clothes Campaign has, however, repeatedly targeted FIFA for not implementing this code, presenting it with evidence of non-compliance (pp. 48–49).

Oxfam GB & the International Confederation of Free Trade Unions (2004) claims that the Olympic Movement is a particularly stark example of this indifference. In spite of its rhetorical commitments to fair play, international solidarity, and valuing the worth of human beings, it has not taken any practical action at the global level to challenge the sportswear brands on the exploitative and abuse working conditions in their supply chains. As the leading governing body in world sport, the report suggests that the IOC has a moral and legal obligation to make these calls. Their obligation includes making sure that companies that use the Olympics logo respect fundamental workers' rights.

To date, however, the IOC has done little apart from 'encourage' the efforts of the World Federation for Sporting Goods Industry (WFSGI) in this area. This lack of commitment seems irresponsible, particularly given that the officials' uniforms, parade uniforms of the various national Olympics teams, athletes' kits, and souvenir sportswear, all bearing the Olympics emblem, may well be produced under the kinds of exploitative working conditions described in this report. Currently, those sportswear companies that act as official suppliers of uniforms or kit to the IOC (e.g. Mizuno, the supplier of official clothing to IOC officials) or to the organizing committee of the host nation (e.g. Adidas, as the official sponsor of Sport Clothing for Uniforms at the Athens 2004), or the national Olympics teams through their national Olympics committees are under no obligation to ensure that these products are not made by exploited workers.

At factory I, manufacturing sportswear which bears the Olympics emblem, workers (interviewed in October 2003) reported the following conditions: When there are export deadlines to meet, workers are forced to work shifts as long as 17 hours over six consecutive days. Workers are exhausted. Many pregnant women suffer miscarriages because of the long working hours. A quarter of the 2000-strong workforce are employed on temporary contracts. They are paid half the standard monthly wage of permanent workers and are forced to do unpaid overtime when they do not complete their piece-rate targets in the normal working hours. Union activists are harassed and verbally abused. Workers, especially temporary workers, are subject to sexual harassment. Workers are verbally abused: 'They call us "dogs" and tell us to go and die.' Workers are not receiving any social security pay. None of the workers knows about labour codes of conduct, nor are they aware of any inspections having taken place.

The report concludes that the Olympic Movement can directly influence the sportswear companies by including contractual obligations on labour standards in its licencing and marketing agreements relating to products bearing the Olympics emblem. At the very top of the hierarchy, the IOC is the owner of the rights to all Olympic marks, including the five-ring emblem, and is responsible for the overall direction and management of all Olympics marketing and licencing programmes. While it is the NOCs and the OCOGs that actually issue the licences and marketing contracts, the IOC has the power to determine the overall policies and set the rules.

If the movement as a whole made a commitment to respect labour standards, similar to its commitments on protecting the environment, it could play an important role in achieving improvements to working conditions for the many workers who produce sportswear worldwide (pp. 50–51).

As regards the second objective of conservation and management of resources for sustainable development, this is developed by the IOC through environmental defence policies and efforts to achieve the 'greening' of the Olympic Games (International Olympic Committee, 1999).

Research on the various impacts of the Olympic Games as a mega-event has been discussed by Malfas, et al (2004) who review conflicting evidence in the literature on mega sporting events and the Olympic Games as case examples to illustrate the forms of impact on the host city and country.

> Drawing examples from recent mega-events discussion on impacts high-lights positive as well as negative ones and provides examples of how structures as well as acting human agents affect outcomes. Increased city awareness, economic development, job creation and urban regeneration have been witnessed along with high inflation, expensive housing, threats to civil liberties of certain groups, terrorist acts and even city defamation after revelations of bribery scandals. Despite the widespread criticisms surrounding the institution of the Olympic Games, which mainly challenge the connection between the ideas of Olympism and the contemporary nature of the event, the Games continuously grow in magnitude and significance. In effect, the contemporary Olympics sustain the status of a mega-event, and economic benefits are the prime motive for all the interests involved in the hosting of the Games, be it the local Government, which seeks urban development of the region through infrastructure made for the staging of the event, or the corporation that becomes a sponsor of the event to attract publicity. While bidders battle for the kudos of winning the hosting of a mega-event, the desired economic, fiscal, social, cultural and political outcomes are expected to justify their actions but further research in the area is necessary to judge the benefits of such undertakings in light of costs and potential negative impacts (p. 218).

The final Agenda 21 objective relates to strengthening the role of major groups through democratic practices such as access to sources of information, involvement of all interested groups in the process of arriving at decisions relating to sustainable development, strengthening of the roles of women, young people, and indigenous communities who represent a significant percentage of the global population and who also often suffer social exclusion. Despite such efforts there is evidence to suggest that the actions of parts of the Olympic Movement do not go far enough. In 1997, as part of its Women and Sport policy, the IOC established targets for women's membership of NOC Executive Committees. These were for women to hold at least 10% of executive decision-making positions in NOCs by December 2001 rising to at least 20% by December 2005. Research conducted on the effects of that policy (International Olympic Committee and Institute of Sport and Leisure Policy, Loughborough University, 2004) suggests that although minimum targets has had a clear and positive impact on the proportion of women in NOC Executive Committees (a) they cannot affect all levels of the pyramid that women climb to reach NOC, (b) some NOCs see the achievement of targets as an end in itself rather than a means towards a more effective Executive Committee, and (c) universal percentages do not take account of the social and cultural conditions in different countries and therefore there is scope for further emphasis of the desirability for NOCs to strive to achieve higher levels of equality in their governance structures from whatever base they start.

Financial flows in the movement also have the potential to affect levels of sustainability. Al-Tauqi (2003) conducted an evaluation of the process of the establishment of Olympic aid through Olympic Solidarity and its forerunner the International Commission for Olympic Aid and he concluded that Olympic aid may be seen as liberating as well as constraining.

> Liberating, because it provides new resources and widens the sporting services the country may offer. Olympic Solidarity provides programmes that give NOCs the opportunity to enhance the level of available sport services in terms of the quality and of the nature of the knowledge provided. In collaboration with IFs and Continental Associations, selected qualified sport experts are appointed to deliver the assistance programmes through courses, clinics, and training for coaches and sport managers. This wide range of programmes offers the NOCs an opportunity to choose technical assistance according to their own needs and enhance their performance in the Games. However when Olympic sport aid promotes values which are different from those of the recipients, it becomes conflictual and constraining given different ways of viewing the world, the body, social values, and moral systems. Traditional sport may then become a commodity for tourist consumption and Olympic aid by ignoring or undermining indigenous culture may be constraining as when it limits the definition of participation by focusing on the achieving of qualification standards and success in the Olympic Games. This notion of high performance tends to discourage rather than encourage mass participation in sport especially in those countries which have less of a sporting cultural tradition and have economic difficulties whether in Europe, Asia, Africa, and Latin America (p. 271).

Conclusion

Olympism and the Olympic Movement is evolving, affected by broader, geopolitical, socio-cultural, and economic world events. Along with its increased rhetoric of universal ideas, access for all, and fair play coexists its increased identification as a global elitist business which has the potential to affect greatly the cities and countries that host its megaevents, the summer and winter Olympic Games.

For Wamsley (2004) the Olympic Games provide a venue to celebrate competitiveness and the extracts below point to the incommensurability of such competition with the values of peach and quality.

to place the strong on the podium as the winner of a fair contest – the obfuscatory signature of global capitalism.

Of course, the physical achievements of the individual and the team are paramount and the defeat of others is a critical part of the spoils. There are tremendous symbolic, cultural and economic rewards available for a limited population that benefits directly from the games. Elite sport competition is intense, cut-throat, and sometimes comes at many costs – there is really nothing peaceful about it. But people love it, participants, coaches, parents and spectators alike, now more than ever (p. 240).

Tearing away the layers of hyperbole, the glorious rhetoric and grandiose ethical proclamations, revealing the Olympics as the sport spectacle they are just might make the games of the twenty-first century a bit more honest. Make no mistake, there is and always will be hope for peace and understanding in the world. Such things are worth striving for but not through something as abstract as the Olympic Games; indeed if we are really prepared or motivated to take on these challenges and find peace, then we would best start with an honest engagement with the people around us ...

When people are prepared to engage one another without coveting, without trying to get ahead materially, socially, culturally, nationally, intellectually, physically then we will have honestly addressed the idea of competition. Indeed, the best indication on the world's cultural landscape that we are prepared for peace and equality, that Olympism and these often quoted values have finally triumphed, is that the Olympic Games will be gone (p. 242).

This second part of this book has sought to identify the constituents of the Olympic Movement and the relationships that bind them together. The discussion of the situational elements in which the Olympic Movement operates, the processes by which it is managed and the organizational model of the Olympic Movement reveal a multifaceted organization precariously situated as a divisionalized structure. As Mintzberg (1979) and Mintzberg and Queen (1992) suggest there are advantages and disadvantages to the divisionalized form of structure. Divisionalization allows headquarters the choice of where to focus its resources, enables middle managers to train in various divisions and develop their career better, spreads risk when divisions rather than the whole organization fails, and finally increases strategic responsiveness. On all the above a divisionalized structure would perform better than a functional structure. However, the real alternative to the divisionalized structure is through eliminating the headquarters and allowing divisions to function as independent organizations. Being a Swiss Verein, risk does not spread to the other organizations partly or wholly owned or established as regional units of the IOC. With the IOC as the headquarters of the Olympic Movement their role is to oversee the divisions (company or franchise units and sub-sidiaries) and this may encourage headquarters' managers to usurp divisional powers, to centralize certain market decisions at headquarters and so defeat the purpose of divisionalization. As Mintzberg (1979) suggests

> headquarters managers may believe they can do better; they may be tempted to eliminate duplication; they may simply enjoy exercising the power that is already theirs; or they may be lured by new administrative techniques. An enthusiastic technostructure may oversell a sophisticated management information system. Lack of time to understand many business is precisely the reason why organizations are divisionalized in the first place, to give each business the undivided attention of one manager. So that high-speed transmission lines lure some headquarters managers into making decisions better left to the divisions (pp. 419–420).

The monopoly of the IOC notwithstanding, the performance control system of the IOC on its divisionalized Olympic Movement is the main aspect of its economic efficiency. Yet, this system also produces one of its most serious social consequences. For Mintzberg (1979) the divisionalized form requires the headquarters to control their divisions primarily by quantitative performance criteria and that often means financial ones. As a result, the control system of the divisionalized form drives it to act, at best, socially unresponsively, at worst, socially irresponsibly (p. 424).

As organizations grow and divisionalize they face the potential economic costs to bigness, notably the threat to the competitive market. It is difficult to deny that sheer size can affect competition, for example, through the ability to use massive advertising expenditure to restrict entry to markets. In the case of conglomerate diversification, there is the added danger of what is known as 'reciprocity'. 'I buy from you if you buy from me' deals between corporations Mintzberg (1979) (p. 426). Big size may also mean higher levels of bureaucracy and the concentration of enormous amount of power in very few hands.

> Furthermore and paradoxically the concentration of power leads to further divisionalization and the concentration of power in spheres outside the divisionalized form as Unions federate and governments add agencies to establish countervailing powers (p. 427).

Having considered structures, design parameters, and co-ordination mechanisms in the broader Olympic Movement attention turns in the next chapter to the particular organizations involved with the production of the main 'products' of the Olympic Movement, the events themselves (summer and winter Olympic Games) as well as related by-products, like the continental games.

Part Three: Event
Organization Phases

The organization of the Olympic events starts with the bidding phase and if successful the planning and hosting phases that follow. Whilst local political and growth regimes are often behind the visions expressed in the bid, the sporting establishment also needs to approve as a city can only apply if the country's NOC is in agreement. Although the Olympic Movement operates through a number of units as discussed in the previous part, some of the units are more centrally involved in the organization of the sporting events themselves. These include most significantly the organizing committee that is established in each host city, the IF that runs the competitions just as it would do when hosting a world championship, the host government ministries or departments as well as local authorities that deliver the necessary infrastructure, the broadcasters, and the sponsors that offer 'value in kind' services.

The following two chapters discuss the roles played by the various organizations, the parameters of design engaged, the situational elements found around them, the coordinating mechanisms, and the overall structural shapes during the bidding, planning, and hosting phases. In conclusion, the discussion considers challenges of the processes involved and pressure points that emerge in the various interorganizational relationships.

Dimensions of Olympic Events

The Olympic Games are said to be competitions between athletes in individual or team events and not between countries. They aim to bring together the athletes selected by their respective NOCs, whose entries have been accepted by the IOC and they compete under the technical direction of the IFs concerned (International Olympic Committee, 2004c).

The Olympic event is referred to in the Olympic Charter as the games of each Olympiad to be staged in and around a host city. They include the Paralympic Games, all preliminary, qualifying, trial heats, semi-final, and final competitions in all sports; opening, closing, awards, and other official ceremonies; athletic exhibitions and sport demonstrations as approved by the IOC. A cultural programme known as the Cultural Olympiad is also conducted before and during the games under the authority, and patronage of the OCOG. Other Olympic related mega-events include the continental games that are organized under the auspices of each Continental NOC association and the host country's NOC. In the case of the EOC this event is called the European Youth Olympic Festival; it is the only multi-sport event in the European Continent, and has a summer and a winter edition that is held every other year.

Understandably, the Olympic Charter that governs the organization and operation of the Olympic Movement also stipulates the conditions for the celebration of the Olympic Games. In it, it is claimed that the organization of the games is based on a partnership between the IOC and the OCOG. Being the guardian of the Olympic Games, the IOC's role is one of supervision and support. It oversees their staging and ensures that the event is run smoothly and that the principles and protocol of the Olympic Charter are followed (International Olympic Committee, 2004c). Another important document is the host city contract that sets out the legal, commercial, and financial rights and obligations of the IOC, the host city, and the NOC of the host country in relation to the Olympic Games. In case of any conflict between the provisions of the host city contract and the Olympic Charter the provision of the host city contract takes precedence and it is signed by the above parties immediately following the announcement by the IOC of the host city elected to host the Olympic and Paralympic Games. As such, the host city contract is specific to each edition of the Olympic Games, and may vary from games to games due to necessary changes and modifications (International Olympic Committee, 2005d: p. 51).

5

Bidding and selection phase organizational activity

Once a city has put together an Olympic bid that is subsequently endorsed by the NOC, the structural foundations of the committee predispose/ determine the structural setup of the future OCOG. The nature of the relationship with the host government plays a very important role in defining this structure. In countries where the private sector is well established significant activity related to the hosting of the event is undertaken by the private sector. On the contrary, in countries where the public sector is predominant in the city's governance then the OCOG is more likely to resemble and be perceived as a branch of the government. A bid committee often comprises of individuals representing local politicians and city governors, and or public administrators. The bidding procedure as laid out by the IOC means that often bid committees create positions in the committee to deal with the various aspects of the bid document: sports, security, accreditation, etc.

Understandably, the idea behind the bid is conceived by certain individuals or sector representatives long before any bid committee is formed.

Once the bid is accepted by the IOC and the IOC starts its evaluation procedure the committee also starts its lobbying and advertising in an attempt to convince the IOC voting members and to create a good brand name and image.

Bid committees start life small and as time passes they grow in size till the election period. Their structuring is reflecting the functional areas of the games organization to a great extent and a code of conduct decided upon by the IOC governs the activity of a candidate city which needs to adhere to the rules. The selection process includes two phases and. The IOC first rank order the expressions of interest and then eliminate some cities from the race. This is a development that was introduced to protect candidate cities from unnecessary expenditure as in the past all cities reached the final selection stage that meant that they invested a lot of resources in going all the way.

It is important to note that the strength of the Olympic bid is affected by the political and economic situation in a candidate city. The bid portfolio comprises of guarantees, information on the host city generally, demography, environment, economy, politics, information about the sports and the sports concepts. Plans of all the facilities, plans about the accommodation of the Olympic family and the Olympic village, and plans about activities linked to the cultural Olympiad and Olympic Education activities are also included in the bid documents.

Typically a bid portfolio is a number of volumes and is submitted in multiple copies to the IOC. Following the IOC reform and the creation of the two step process, host cities cannot be visited by the IOC members. Instead, members of a bid evaluation commission write a report following the visits to all candidate cities along the themes ofsports concepts, security, accommodation, etc. and credit score each candidate city.

This report is normally available before the IOC session when IOC members vote for the host city. The reports are available for reading and digest but the cities then embark on a last days lobbying to build up their chances of success. During the IOC session the candidate cities are present in hospitality suites in big hotels or conference centres and the IOC members and the press have the opportunity to ask questions and obtain more material from the candidates. The last days before the election see enormous diplomatic activity as often heads of states of the aspiring countries join the bid committee for the final lobbying. The 2012 host city race in Singapore in 2005 saw the British Prime Minister and the French President battling for the right to host the games till the very last stages of the race.

Other activity that takes place in the IOC session involves the general assembly to discuss issues related to the governance of the Olympic Movement, but such an IOC session truly culminates in the selection of the host city.

During the bidding certain rules apply for the conduct of individuals (bid committee as well as IOC members).

It is important to remember that the IOC asked bidders for the 2012 race to withdraw some promises of extra packages for NOCs should the games be granted to the city as such promises were seen by the IOC as inflating a last minute war by the candidate cities.

Before reaching the final candidature stages the host city has to convince its own country that the bid is worth supporting. Communication Campaigns are not only aimed at the international audiences but also at home audiences too where bid committees want to convince the people at large of the benefits that the games will bring.

The bid committees outsource opinion polls to ascertain the public support for the games as such data is also used in the bid document and by the IOC bid evaluation commission to assess candidatures. Percentages of support are often quoted by candidate cities. Typically the press in the candidate city and nation also takes part in the bid race as they have the potential to create certain messages and affect public opinion. The bid committee also organizes a series of events in the candidate nation to showcase the bid and promote public perceptions of support to the bid. As a selection of the bid team set out to the IOC session (that is hosted in various places around the world) the host city also prepares for the announcement as there are public gatherings in central location in the candidate cities and supporters of the bid gather to hear the final announcement.

The bid committee is often housed in a public building centrally in the candidate city and its resources come from the local government and sponsors.

Often Olympic bids become linked to ideas of regeneration in the host city and country at large. The winter games have become associated with presenting opportunities for tourism development, regeneration of the transport system (as in the High Speed train connection in the case of Torino) redeveloping certain areas and offering new employment opportunities. Similarly, the summer games have been linked to the regeneration of old parts of cities (as was the case in Barcelona, Sydney, and London). Behind the links to regeneration are planners and politicians who see the opportunity of earmarking federal or national money for local causes. They also see political opportunities for themselves as they aspire to gain the kudos associated with succeeding in attracting the games to the city and the composition of the committee reflects the interests of such key players. Local and national business interests are also present in a bid committee and can provide political and financial support from the bid (Sochi, 2006).

Bid committees typically exist for two to three years and see a life cycle punctuated by key events such as its creation, its successful bidding, and ultimately its voluntary liquidation. It is interesting to note that bid committees and an OCOG coexist in the early phase on OCOG's life. At the start of its lifecycle the bid committee has the strategic apex as the key part of the organization. Key senior staff are appointed not without some political interference and subsequently they appoint middle and junior level staff. Associated consultants also get involved at this stage as well as experts and academics who either know the Olympic Movement or have a professional reputation in a specialist area (e.g. public relations, architecture, etc). Staff are also sometimes on loan from ministry departments or local councils and public sector administration.

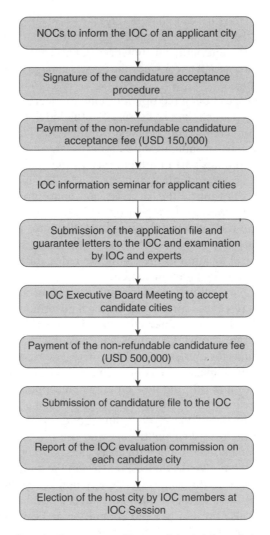

Figure 5.1 Host city selection process (*Source*: Adapted from International Olympic Committee, 2005c)

As regards guidance to candidate cities by the IOC, it is argued that the procedure leading to the election of the Host City for the Olympic Games is governed by and detailed in the Olympic Charter (Rule 34 and its bye-law) (International Olympic Committee, 2005c).

Throughout the entire bid process (pre-application, application, and candidature phases), great emphasis is placed on the role and responsibilities of the NOC which is expected to supervise and be jointly responsible for the actions and conduct of the applicant city in relation to its application. Figure 5.1 lists the aspects of the host city selection process.

Close cooperation is required between the NOC and city, and according to the IOC (2005c). It is also important to note that all cities wishing to organize the Olympic Games and their NOCs are required to comply with the Olympic Charter, the IOC Code of Ethics, the rules of conduct applicable to all cities wishing to organize the Olympic Games and all other rules, instructions, and conditions which may be established by the IOC.

Candidature Committee Structures

Candidate committees start organizational life as relatively small organizations. Their constitution is often heavily influenced by the growth and development agendas of the city and region and their membership reflects the power structure and to some extent the source of the idea behind the bid. Although representatives of the Olympic Movement may have been instrumental in materializing the bid, it is the city administration that takes the lead at the formative stage as the bid needs political support to move forward. Fundamentally, those that underwrite the projected costs of the games (infrastructure as well as hosting) are represented in these structures and have a major say in the committee's activities. Nevertheless, it can be argued that the host city selection race is not won by local politicians alone. In addition to the various planners, public relations experts are employed to facilitate the committee in developing a winning image and a promising brand name for potential sponsors.

Examples of the structures of the Vancouver 2010 Candidature Committee that has since been superseded by the Vancouver Organizing Committee for the Olympic Games (VANOG) and of the Sochi 2014 Bid Committee illustrate the various representations in the bid committees.

The Vancouver 2010 Candidature Committee membership is broad and diverse, representative of the wide support for Vancouver's candidature as Canada's bid. The Vancouver 2010 Board of Directors is currently composed of 96 Directors (53 voting and 43 non-voting, ex officio) from British Columbia and other regions of Canada. An Executive Committee made of 12 members monitors the day-to-day affairs of Vancouver 2010. The Board includes representation from each of the Member Partners (Canadian Olympic Committee (COC), Government of Canada, Province of British Columbia, City of Vancouver, RMOW), local First Nation governments, the Canadian Paralympic Committee (CPC), the Calgary Olympic Development Association, sports organizations, transportation organizations, community organizations, labour organizations, tourism organizations, members of the cultural and business communities and athletes who have competed in both summer and winter games. Nineteen of our Directors are Olympians and three are Paralympians. Our Board of Directors also includes all IOC Members in Canada (Vancouver

Organizing Committee for the 2010 Olympic and Paralympic Winter Games, 2006).

The Sochi 2014 Bid Committee is structured as an autonomous non-profit organization, according to Russian Federation (RF) Civil Code, Federal Law on Non-Profit Organizations. Sochi 2014 registered with the Russian Federal Tax Service on 29 November 2005, with the corresponding entry made into the Unified State Register of Legal Entities. The RF has created an Supervisory Committee to support the Sochi 2014 Bid Committee. Government Order No. 2047-r of 26 November 2005 declared that an advisory committee was formed to act in support of the nomination of Sochi as a candidate city to host XXII Olympic Winter Games and XI Paralympic Winter Games in 2014. The Head of the Committee is Deputy Chairman of the RF Government; the Committee members are the Mayor of Sochi, the President of the RF Olympic Committee, the Head of Rossport, the RF Minister of Finance, the RF Minister of Economic Development and Trade, the RF Minister of Health and Social Development, the RF Minister of Transport, the RF Minister of Foreign Affairs, the Head of Rosstroi, Olympic Champions, famous cultural figures, and other officials (Sochi 2014 Bid Committee, 2006).

Although these bodies are expected to be independent legal entities their composition reveals the strong local political control. As the case of the Beijing Olympic Games Bid Committee (BOBICO) illustrates the committee needs to be approved by the State Council of the People's Republic of China before it is recognized as an independent legal entity. The Executive Committee of BOBICO was Presided by the Mayor of Beijing and comprised of a number of other senior public sector figures.

Its Executive President who was also the Minister in Charge of the State Sport General Administration of China and President of the Chinese Olympic Committee. The Co-Secretary General was Deputy Secretary General of the People's Government of Beijing Municipality, Executive Vice President and President of All-China Sports Federation. The Executive Vice President was Vice Mayor of Beijing. The Director of Sports was President of the Chinese Athletic Association. The Co-Secretary General was Secretary General of the Chinese Olympic Committee. The Executive Committee was the executive body of BOBICO, and under it were the following departments: General Office, Research & Analysis, External Relations, Press & Publicity, Sports & Venues, Construction & Project Planning, Finance & Marketing, Technology, and Environment & Ecosystem.

Funding for BOBICO was primarily provided by sponsorship and donations from various enterprises and social associations, as well as through special Beijing Municipal Government funds and financial support from the Central Government. In the bid files the Beijing Municipal Government confirmed that BOBICO is empowered to sign contracts and other documents related to

Figure 5.2 Information on OCOG obligations (*Source*: International Olympic Committee, 2005c)

its bid for hosting the 2008 Olympic Games on behalf of Beijing (Beijing Olympic Games Bid Committee, 2000).

The information available to bid committees and subsequently OCOGs is available through a number of means as illustrated in Figure 5.2.

Technical Manuals produced by the IOC with the help of OGKS and companies like 'Event Knowledge Services' form an integral part of the host city contract and can be studied by applicant cities so that they better prepare their bid. These manuals contain information regarding a given subject/theme of the Olympic Games organization: detailed technical obligations, planning information, procedures and processes, and proven practices. Thus, they provide the technical requirements and information for the implementation of the key functions by the OCOGs and their partners.

The Olympic Games Knowledge Reports represent a description of practices and experiences from previous Games organizers, referring to a given local host city context and environment. The reports contain:

> Technical and organizational information from the OCOG's point of view referring to a given edition of the Olympic Games. This can include practice examples, scale and scope data, as well as information on resources, planning, strategy, and operations. They do not contain: Legal obligations and IOC recommendations (International Olympic Committee, 2005c).

These reports are part of the Olympic Games Knowledge Programme put in place by the IOC to facilitate the transfer of Olympic Games Knowledge and assist in the exchange of information from one Olympic Games to the next. The programme comprises several components (written information, workshops, etc.) and features the Olympic Games Knowledge Reports as one of its key elements.

During the Application phase, the IOC provides applicant NOCs/Cities with the following services:

- All documents/information produced by the IOC for Applicant Cities.
- Protection of the word mark '[City] 2014' outside the Applicant City's national territory.
- Access to the IOC's Olympic Games Knowledge Management programme.
- Participation in the IOC Applicant City information seminar.
- Participation in the Olympic Games Observer Programme.
- Assessment of the application by the IOC (International Olympic Committee, 2005c).

Co-ordination in Bid Committees

The work of a bid committee is initially coordinated by direct supervision. As new staff start work and the bid committee grows and delves more deeply into the preparation of the bid (prepare documents, affect public perception home and abroad have technically strong plans, designs concepts) work becomes coordinated by work processes such as those set by the IOC (i.e. evaluation commission visit performed successfully, delegation prepared for the IOC session when selection will take place). During the intense lobbying at the IOC session the bid committee coordinates its work more by mutual adjustment using the public relations skills of staff. Those attending the IOC session which will select the host city are carefully picked on the basis of their skills and to compliment the overall team. Staff present at the session are together for great lengths of time exchanging feedback and ideas and news about developments at the other candidate city camps. Post selection, the successful city passes on the work to an organizing committee (it is not uncommon for teams to change at that stage) within a typical time period of five months from one to the other. Unsuccessful cities close down their operations and audit their accounts but the impact of the preparations and aspirations lives on and lingers as some of the impetus for the associated regeneration can have a friendly reception by politicians, taxpayers, etc. In conclusion, it is important to note that an Olympic bid does not seem to be generated from the sports organizations in the country, or the federations. The local NOC obviously plays a strong role in the bids formulation but it is mostly the local politicians and business representatives that lead Olympic bids.

Parameters of Design

A bid committee exhibits predominantly horizontal specialization with a relatively flat structure. Decision making is relatively decentralized during the bid team's establishment and becomes more centralized at the strategic apex during the period nearing the completion of the host city race. Formalization levels are high at the start of a bid committee's life cycle as it seeks to show its alliance to established bid processes and the Olympic protocol. This lowers during the last phase of the host city race when the IOC is in session. As regards training, it is affected by the guidance set by the IOC, with organizational norms of staff being reinforced by the staff selection process. It is important to note that some significant players involved with and/or working in bid committees are not staff but associated individuals appointed or selected on the basis of their political or position power.

The size of the units obviously grows as the host city selection process reaches its final stages and planning during the bid built-up period is structured as a result of the existence of certain outputs required of functional areas. Liaison devices take the form of progress meeting when functional area representatives present progress and ideas for development whilst staff present from other functional areas have the opportunity to identify interdependencies. Informal communication also accounts for a significant part of the liaison devices. With regard to centralization of decision making the main bid preparation phase sees high levels of horizontal decentralization interspersed with periods of intense cooperation as parts are coming together to ensure cohesion and deliverability of the overall bid concept.

Finally, vertical decentralization is limited as key decisions are reached by heads of functional areas and sections, accordingly.

Situational Factors

As a newly born organization, established to coordinate work related to the city's application and subsequent candidacy, a bid committee starts life in a simple structure centred around figures leading the bid. As the information exchange with the IOC becomes established, the criteria for success become clearer and the bid committee evolves towards a functional structure along the various themes of the questionnaire of the IOC (see Figure 5.3 of the structure of the Sydney bid committee).

Elements of market grouping are also evident in a bid committee as it tries to focus its work at home (liaising with local and national government offices) and abroad (liaising with the IFs and the IOC). Although bid committees are understandably populated by senior figures such as politicians, public sector

Figure 5.3 Sydney 2000 Bid Committee structure (*Source*: Adapted from Sydney Organising Committee for the Olympic Games, 1999)

managers, and sports personalities after the formative early stages, the bid is led by urban entrepreneurs who are headed by a symbolic leader.

Although the bid committee does not have a technical system as such the term may be used to mean the instruments used by the operators to transform inputs into outputs (Mintzberg, 1979: p. 250). With this definition in mind the technical system of the bid committee can be seen to include the host city manuals produced by the IOC and is available by the OGKS SA extranet facility that gathers facts and figures about games organization. Using such technology is required in order to prepare an Olympic bid. This technical system is therefore creating some regulation and its complexity and intricacies indicate its sophistication. A bid committee enters the host city race without any prior knowledge of the structural setup, the key stakeholders, the culture, and ideology of the movement. Understanding the composite parts of the movement, its language and code of conduct present a challenge of a technical nature and often members of staff or elected representatives from the IOC help the bid committee identify the rules of the game. The early periods in the life cycle of a bid committee involve significant learning on the part of the organization on how to behave presenting a candidate city. The technical system evolves after submission of the bid document in that attention then turns to hosting the evaluation commission visit (a number of people, over several days, visiting various facilities, politicians, heads of state, etc.) and finally committee representatives engage in a public relations frenzy during the final stages of the IOC session that will select the host city.

The environment of the bid committee can be discussed in terms of its complexity, dynamism, and hostility. After the euphoria of having secured political and financial backing to the idea of the bid, the business – rather than politics – constituents of the bid committee face a complex environment with numerous loosely defined interdependencies. The environment is also dynamic as rapid growth in staff creates new alliances as well as internal structural evolution. Nevertheless, the environment is friendly overall as the public and the politicians are predominantly supportive of the venture, as is shown in the cases of most recent Olympic Games. Complexity and dynamism remain as features of a bid committee's environment but hostility from other host cities (in the form of negative media coverage) emerges as the bid committee gets closer to selection and especially if it emerges as a host city race frontrunner.

The power issues in a bid committee are very interesting as they reveal the tensions and differences in visions between the ambitious elected politicians, the professional planners, and the urban entrepreneurs that seek capital growth. Notwithstanding domestic power issues a bid committee engages in international relations and diplomacy as it approaches the IOC session during which the selection will take place. IOC members must be convinced about what the candidate city can deliver and the committee is therefore right in the middle of a process that involves very senior country representatives lobbying for their country's candidacy. On successful selection by the IOC session the bid committee enters a new phase of power relations as some staff migrate to the OCOG that will subsequently be established. Political changes sometimes mean that the bid committee staff are not offered jobs in the OCOGs and this creates an additional challenge to the OCOG as there is a lack of continuity and lower levels of understanding of the Olympic undertaking.

Structure

A bid committee typically starts as a simple organic structure. It has little technostructure, some support staff, a loose division of labour, few divisions, and a small hierarchy. As the committee grows its structure becomes more bureaucratic and work is coordinated by the IOC required outputs. Special-ization and decentralization increases and the key part of the organization is the operating core. The expected outputs are delivered by specialist staff or outside consultants but when the host city race is approaching its pinnacle at the IOC session the committee structure evolves again to a more organic one with centralized decision making, direct supervision, and with the strategic apex as the key part of the organization.

6

Planning and delivering phase organizational activity

Planning for the games starts as soon as the host city is elected by the IOC.

As mentioned earlier, the foundations of the structure are in existence in the form of the bid committee structures and slowly the ex bid committee evolves into the organizing committee. It is not uncommon for leadership and some staff to change at that stage as was the case with the Athens 2004 and London 2012 Bid Committees.

The signing of the host city contract signifies the passing of an era and the setting of the clock against the opening of the games. Other elements of the contract, for example the protection of the rights of the IOC also set in motion legal processes in the host country.

An OCOG starts life as a small organization that grows as various sections and departments take shape. These sections represent the areas of activity against which the IOC judged the candidacy and typically, at the start, include a finance, marketing, personnel, sports, and legal department. As figure 6.1 illustrates there are numerous stakeholders in the organization of the games and an OCOG needs to work with the majority of these.

An Olympic Games Coordination Commission is also formed shortly after the election of the host city to oversee and assist the OCOG in planning, and in the implementation of the Olympic Games. This commission includes representatives of the IOC, the IFs, the NOCs, and a representative of the athletes, as well as experts in various games-related fields. The co-ordination commission provides supervision and support in the seven years leading up to the games and aims to ensure respect of the Olympic Charter and the host city contract. It validates the level of services and facilities proposed by the OCOGs through plenary sessions and technical working groups. There are regular visits to the host cities interspersed with frequent reports on the progress of such items as the building of facilities and completion of various infrastructure works. The IOC Olympic Games Department also supports this co-ordination commission with the aim of ensuring that the games are staged in the most efficient, effective, and harmonious manner possible. The department's mission begins at the candidature stage in the run-up to the host city being selected by the IOC. It establishes a technical brief and then evaluates the ability of the candidate cities to meet it. After the vote, the department provides the organizers with the appropriate knowledge and expertise and ensures the smooth preparation of the games. The department also draws up a master plan for staging the Olympic Games which in principle, is generic, and based on past experience. However, allowances are made for it to be adapted to each individual host city, according to specific local conditions. This plan covers areas such as: venues; the media; marketing; communication; culture; Games services; technology; and commercial and legal issues and finally gives recommended time scales for the implementation of these areas.

According to the IOC, the successful partnership between the IOC and the organizers depends on three main principles.

First, there has to be a clear definition of the contributions of each party, something which is achieved by the host city contract. Second, there must be mutual confidence between the parties. This is established through the IOC games co-ordination commission inspection visits, regular contact between the two partners; precise tools to monitor progress; early identification of potential problems and risks; and help from previous organizing committees, together with the accumulated knowledge of experts. Third, the collaborators must share common values. Two or three months after each celebration of the games, there is an extensive debrief about the strengths and weaknesses of the event. Over four days, 20–25 key areas are examined. Such practice is invaluable for future host cities. This is accompanied by the report produced by the OCOG, its last official document, which is divided into four parts: candidature; organization; 16 days of competition and official results; and the Games impact evaluation (International Olympic Committee, 2004d: p. 54).

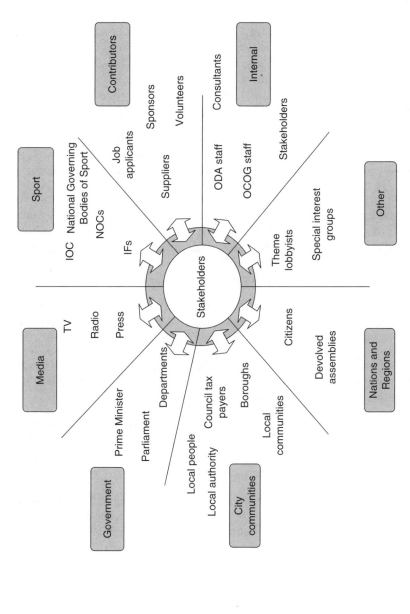

Figure 6.1 London 2012 Stakeholders in the organization of the Olympic Games (*Source*: With permission from Palmer, 2006)

The planning for the games also involves the IFs who have technical responsibilities at the Olympic Games. Each IF is responsible for the technical control and direction of its sport at the Olympic Games and all elements of the competitions, including the schedule, field of play, training sites, and all equipment must comply with its rules. For all these technical arrangements, the OCOG must consult the relevant IFs and the holding of all events in each sport is placed under the direct responsibility of the IF concerned. Nevertheless, it is the OCOG's responsibility to ensure that the various Olympic sports are treated and integrated equitably.

As to the schedule and daily timetable of events, the final decision lies with the IOC Executive Board. In more detail the IFs have the following rights and responsibilities regarding the technical arrangements at the Olympic Games:

> To establish the technical rules of their own sports, disciplines, and events, including, but not limited to, results standards, technical specifications of equipment, installations and facilities, rules of technical movements, exercises or games, rules of technical disqualification, and rules of judging and timing.

> To establish the final results and ranking of Olympic competitions. Such results shall be made available to the IFs by the OCOG, at its expense, immediately after each event in electronic form, in accordance with guidelines established by the IOC. The IF concerned then has the right to display such competition results for its own sport on its official website.

> Subject to the IOC's authority, to exercise technical jurisdiction over the competition and training venues of their respective sports during the competition and training sessions at the Olympic Games.

> To select judges, referees, and other technical officials from the host country and from abroad within the total number adopted by the IOC Executive Board upon proposal of the IF concerned.

> The Olympic Games referees and other technical officials coming from countries other than the host country shall be paid by the OCOG. The technical officials must be present at the site at least three days prior to the first event in their sport and at least one day after the last event.

> To appoint two technical delegates during the planning and setting up of the facilities for their sports in order to ensure that their rules are complied with and to review and validate all technical elements of the competitions including entries, venue standards, competition schedule, pre-Olympic events as well as the conditions regarding accommodation, food, and transport provided for the technical officials and judges (International Olympic Committee, 2004c: pp. 92–94).

From its establishment to its ultimate liquidation that OCOG's planning processes evolve to match the tasks at hand and the following section identifies the parts of that process as including the phases of: foundation and operational planning, test event planning, and operational readiness.

Approximately Games-98 months to Games-66 months. This initial foundation planning phase of each OCOG starts when the host city is selected and ends when operational planning starts. During this phase the board is formed, top management staff are recruited, the need for games-related legislation is identified, corporate governance structure is selected, and the image of the games is envisioned. Outputs during this phase are the IOC/OCOG Master Schedule, the first version of the Venue and Infrastructure Construction Schedule, the Venue and Infrastructure responsibility matrix, and the Global Strategic Plan.

Approximately Games-72 months to Games-12 months. During this operational planning phase the OCOG evolves through progressively more detailed phases of planning for games operations, according to an agreed structure, timeline, and methodology, designed to move the organization towards a state of readiness to deliver the Games. Initially, the focus is on Functional Planning, when each function develops its Strategic Plan. The evolution progresses, moving primarily to a venue based focus, but retaining a functional focus where required. Outputs during this phase are Functional Area Strategic Plans, Functional Area Concepts of Operations, Generic Competition Venue Concept of Operations, Draft Functional Area Operating Plans, Model Competition Venue Operating Plan, and Draft Venue Specific Operating Plans.

Approximately Games-20 months to Games-10 months. This is the test event planning phase during which the OCOG tests its games time preparations. This involves planning to conduct test events, mostly venue based but also function based. Feedback and lessons learned from these events are then incorporated into the Games planning documents. Outputs during this phase are Test Event Venue Specific Operating plans and Final Venue Specific and Functional Area Operating plans.

Approximately Games-12 to Games-1 month. This is the final stage of operational readiness planning during which simulation exercises and rehearsals take place.

The last phase is that of dissolution during which venues are reinstated to their owners, the Games Official Report is written, the OCOG is dissolved, and any assets are liquidated (International Olympic Committee, 2004b: pp. 22–23).

A strategic plan is the first step in the planning process. It is a short document that describes strategy; that is how a functional area intends to plan its work and some of the key parameters involved (e.g. strategy, timelines, budgets, operating principles). This document is superseded by the Concept of Operations. A concept of operations is the second step in the planning process. It involves the production of a more detailed document that clearly identifies the concepts or the outline of operations and identifies, in detail, what services are to be provided by each functional area, what the level of service is likely to be and who will provide these services. It is a logical progression from the strategic plan and provides the basis to move to the next level of detail – Venue Operating Plans. Another critical difference between a strategic plan and a concept of operation is that all Concepts of Operation will undergo a process of review and approval. This means that each concept of operations is completed as a draft and then circulated for comment amongst the stakeholders and interested parties. As part of this review and commenting process, at least one, and often a series of workshops are held to discuss and finalize any outstanding issues. After the workshops are complete and all comments are considered and incorporated, a concept of operations is recommended for approval by the operations management group. Once

Table 6.1 Athens 2004 Organizing Committee Functional areas

■ Health services	■ Generic Competition Venue
■ Catering	■ Energy supply
■ Overlay and site management	■ Merchandising
■ Telecommunications	■ Ceremonies
■ Sport division	■ Torch relay
■ Sport competition	■ Press operations
■ Information technology	■ Security
■ Sport entries	■ Ticketing
■ Risk management	■ OAKA Complex
■ Accommodation	■ Hellinikon Complex
■ Image and Identity (look)	■ Faliron Coastal Zone
■ Broadcasting	■ Doping control
■ Accreditation	■ Main press centre
■ IOC relations and protocol	■ Airports
■ Greeks abroad	■ Sponsor hospitality centre
■ NOC relations and services	■ Olympic Village
■ Pre-games training	■ Village overlays
■ Environment	■ International Broadcasting Centre
■ Olympic youth camp	■ Media Villages
■ Supply chain (procurement and logistics)	■ Olympic Family Hotels
■ Rate card	■ Olympic Logistics Centre
■ Human resources	■ Technical Officials Village
■ Test events	■ City (look)
■ Paralympic Games	■ Spectator services
■ Transport (generic venue)	■ Brand protection
■ Cleaning and waste management	■ Uniforms
■ Language services	

Source: Athens Organizing Committee for the Olympic Games, 2001.

approved, a concept of operations is the foundation for a functional area (see Table 6.1 with list of functional areas in ATHOC) to move to the detailed planning of Games time services and operations.

Concepts of operations follow the strategic plans and will be the next step before commencing venue operating plans. Concepts of operations development is complementary with other streams of planning such as time planning (functional plans), and budgets that are being prepared. Concepts of operations assist in educating and informing other programmes so that they understand the services provided and the key operational issues of each programme. This is an important step in the integration process. A concept of operations is a document that describes the key operational aspects of a functional area or geographic location (venue or complex). It takes the high-level information in the strategic plan and adds a layer of detail that not only explains the strategy of the functional area or geographic location but also the visions of the functional area or location, the scope of services and the levels of service, the stakeholders involved, the resources required, an overview of the delivery method, a list of any key policies to be developed, key milestones (as described in functional plans), draft operational budget, key operational risks, and identifies open or outstanding issues.

The process of writing, reviewing, and approving concepts of operations is as important as the information within the documents themselves. This process is the first step towards operational integration – where ultimately, all functional areas are cooperating and working together in a single multifunctional team. By reviewing each other's documents, the entire organization is being educated on the operations necessary to run an Olympic Games and, the services provided by each functional area are being defined and understood by the various stakeholders. With education and understanding across the organization, comes the confidence to move on to more detailed planning and operations within each specialist functional area. Workshops are the best way for an OCOG to: challenge and test concepts of operations, specifically to ensure key customer requirements are being met; define scope and levels of service for key operations and ensure they are appropriate; commence integration of functional areas and educate other functional areas; find possible improvement to the methods of delivery; identify critical issues and resolve as many as possible with all key stakeholders; and ensure that all parties' needs and concerns are aired and addressed, and they feel part of the team (Sloane, 2001).

Venue operating plans that follow are detailed descriptions of operations in a specific venue. These Operating plans are venue specific documents that bring together and integrate the operations of each functional area required to operate the venue. They take the services and operations from each functional area concept of operations and adjust them to suit the specific operational constraints of the venue and the venue team. The emphasis is on policies, procedures, timings, locations, detailed roles and responsibilities, procurement of furniture fixtures and equipment, and detailed staffing plans. To facilitate the formation of specific venue plans the generic venue concept of operations discussions are used to introduce key definitions concerning venue operations. To provide an introductory overview of the operations at a generic venue and form the foundation to move forward into detailed venue operating plans. Such discussions focus on the physical components of a generic venue, the typical venue management team structure, and description of responsibilities; a description of functional area activities at venue level and preliminary design of the command and control structure and to clarify any confusion with the terminology. Sloane (2001) provides the following guidelines on the differences between these documents (Table 6.2).

Table 6.2 Differences between a Strategic Plan, a Concept of Operations, and a Venue Operating Plan

Games – 4 years	Games – 3 years	Games –2 Years
Strategic Plans	**Concept of Operations**	**Operating Plans**
Vision	Scope	Policies
Goals	Level/s of service	Procedures
Stakeholders	General roles and responsibilities	Timings
Key principles	Delivery method concept	Locations
Key phases and critical milestones	Resources	Detailed roles and responsibilities
Definition stage	Budget	Procurement
	Detailed milestones	Staffing
	Risks	Very detailed

Source: Sloane, 2001.

As an OCOG moves from one phase to the next higher understanding is secured given that the detail of operations is made clear and staff confidence increases.

The IOC realized that this experience in the staging of the games should not be discarded and that is why the transfer of knowledge was initiated during the preparations of the Sydney Games in 2000 in cooperation with the SOCOG. This involved a process (which has been also mentioned earlier when reviewing the TOK activities of the IOC) through which the know-how of previous OCOGs is captured and codified in the form of written guides and operating materials including images and video that is sold to organizes of future Olympic Games as well as other event organizers.

Host City Contract and OCOG Legal Aspects

The host city contract signed by the successful candidate city has a number of parts that relate to the event's organization. More specifically, they relate to:

the entrustment of the organization of the games; the formation of the OCOG and it being party to this contract; the joint and several obligations of the city, the NOC, and the OCOG; the ensuring of respect of commitments undertaken by the government, the evolving nature of the contents of technical manuals, guidelines, and other directions; the fact that representation, statements, and other commitments are binding; that prior agreements are of no effect; the indemnification and waiver of claims against the IOC; finance-related agreements between the city and or the NOC and or the OCOG; Olympic identity and accreditation card; working in the host country on Olympic-related business; entry formalities for certain personnel, goods, and animals; rights and benefits provided by IOC to OCOG and NOC; and responsibility for the organization of the IOC session and other meetings.

Not later than six months after the formation of the OCOG, the OCOG shall submit a global strategic plan (which shall include a general organization plan) and the master schedule of the games to the IOC for its prior approval. All changes to both plans shall be subject to the prior written approval of the IOC. The OCOG shall provide to IOC at its cost, updates and details regarding the OCOG's general organization, generic planning process, and master schedule (International Olympic Committee, 2004a).

It is important to note that: This contract does not constitute either of the parties hereto the agent of any of the other parties nor create a partnership, joint venture, or similar relationship between any of the parties (International Olympic Committee, 2004a: p. 53). As regards the legal structures employed by OCOGs it is relevant to consider the example of the proposed entity in the case of Sochi 2014 (see Figure 6.2 for an illustration of the relationship between the proposed Sochi Olympic Organizing Committee (SOOC) and other relevant organizations). According to the bid document (Sochi 2014 Bid Committee, 2006), on winning the bid, SOOC will be formed to stage the 2014 Olympic Winter and Paralympic Winter Games and it will co-ordinate activities with local, regional, and national authorities and the Directorate for the Development of Sochi (DDS) to ensure the fulfilment of all obligations contained in this bid and in accordance with the host city contract.

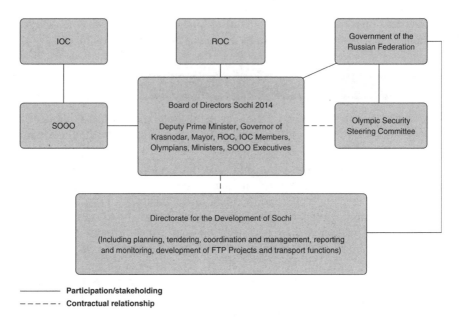

Figure 6.2 Illustration of relationship between SOOC and other relevant organizations (*Source*: Sochi 2014 Bid Committee, 2006)

The SOOC will interface with the IOC, the IPC, the NOCs, and the IFs to ensure compliance with their requirements and collaborate with them in delivering outstanding Games. All elements of this structure are in place and ready to begin work on the day that Sochi is awarded the right to host the 2014 Olympic Winter Games. Funding in the amount of $16.1 million is already provided in the Federal Target Programme for the Development of Sochi to finance the transition from the Bid Committee to the SOOC. This funding ensures an immediate transition into organizing for the Games on 5 July 2007, if the IOC elects Sochi as the Host City for 2014. The SOOC board membership will represent all the partners that have worked together on the Sochi 2014 bid: The President and General Secretary of the Russian Olympic Committee; the Russian IOC Members; the President and General Secretary of the Russian Paralympic Committee; Head of Rossport; Russian Olympic Athlete representatives; Representatives of the government of the Russian Federation; Governor of the Krasnodar Region; Mayor of Sochi; Representatives of DDS; and General members of the board, appointed for their particular expertise in various areas of sport and business, as well as additional representatives of the relevant ministries that will be key to delivering the infrastructure and services for the Games.

As regards the type of legal entity, the Sochi team claim that after analysing the Russian law and the host city contract they have reached the conclusion that it would be most advantageous to incorporate the SOOC as a foundation.

> The SOOC foundation will be a not-for-profit organization that may pursue charitable, cultural, educational, or other social purposes as set in its charter. There are no restrictions in Russian law that would prevent the Russian Olympic Committee, the City of Sochi, and the Krasnodar Region from establishing the SOOC. Russian law enables a foundation to draw assets from various sources, including property contributions from the founders, gifts, donations, government subsidies, and revenues from business activity. A board of trustees must supervise the foundation's activities, decision-making processes, and disposal of assets. Because trustees are not compensated, any person, including a federal, regional, or municipal public official may serve on the board. A foundation may carry out entrepreneurial activity that complies with the social purposes set in its charter. Thus the SOOC foundation may conduct business activities and direct revenue to benefit sport in Russia as required by the host city contract. Foundations are exempt from corporate profit tax on donations and governmental subsidies, provided that these revenues are used for the purposes established by the foundation's charter. Thus, all contributions from the IOC, considered to be donations, will be exempt from corporate profit tax. Although profit from entrepreneurial activities would be subject to corporate profit tax at 24%, corporate profit tax implications will be mitigated by adopting the Olympic Law that exempts from taxation income that is related to Olympic Games activities (Sochi 2014 Bid Committee, 2006).

Similar measures have been announced in relation to the UK tax treatment of the London Organizing Committee for the Olympic Games (LOCOG), the IOC, and competitors and support staff who will be temporarily present in the UK for the Olympics.

According to Deloitte and Touche LLP (2006), LOCOG will not be subject to corporation tax by specific statutory exemption. This will apply from the date of incorporation of the company, and provision will be made to allow the exemption to be extended to LOCOG's wholly owned subsidiaries as necessary. Powers will also be put in place for regulations to be made to ensure that the IOC and other non-UK entities owned or controlled by the IOC are not subject to UK corporation tax, income tax or capital gains tax on any revenues from the Games. Similarly, non-UK residents who are temporarily in the UK as competitors or support staff for the Games will not be subject to UK tax on income arising from their performances or duties at the Games. There will also be an exemption from UK withholding tax on interest, royalties, or other annual payments made to LOCOG, the IOC, or visiting performers and support staff.

Tax issues appear to be quite significant in the operation of OCOGs and related to this are all the financial projections on the budgets for the infrastructure works as well as the sporting competitions. OCOGs write their own history in the games organization albeit within a predetermined framework of activity (time and process wise). Their stories are unique as are the intricacies of their structural formations. The following section considers the examples of OCOGs as they evolve in the process of planning and delivering the Olympic Games.

It is important to also consider the finances of OCOGs, who finances them, how much do they spend, etc. The budget of ATHOC was US $1.7 billion and the government had committed to contributing US $1.6 billion for works that relate to the Games. Eighty-six percent of the income of ATHOC was expected to be received from the sales of broadcasting rights, national and international sponsors, the licencing programme, the sale of tickets, etc. with the remaining 14% of the budget to be covered from the Greek State (Athens Organising Committee for the Olympic Games, 2001: p. 54).

The expected profit of ATHOC was US $36.7 million (total revenues of $607 million minus total expenditure of $570.3 million). It was anticipated that ATHOC would invest US $142 million and that the public and private sector would invest another $1.411 billion making a total of capital investments of US $1.553 billion. The cost of Olympic operations was anticipated to be US $570.3 million and if added to total capital investments this gives an anticipated total expenditure on the Games of US $2.213 billion. Additional post Olympic Games data on the economic impact came in the form of the published accounts of ATHOC in May 2005. ATHOC's excess income of US $8.4 million was much less than the $36.7 million that was promised in the bid. In addition, although the total non-Games related capital expenditure has not been officially announced, figures quoted in the media range from US $5–10 billion, which is significantly higher than the original budget of US $2.123 billion.

Figures from Beijing are quite higher overall. The respective OCOG's budget estimates a US $16 million surplus (see Table 6.3) and even at bid stage the Beijing Bid Committee was estimating the non-OCOG expenditure at almost US $15 billion (see Table 6.4).

OCOG Structures

The structures found in OCOGs are broadly similar as they reflect the management guidance from the IOC and the host city contract requirements in relation to master planning. Examples from the Vancouver and Beijing Organizing Committees for the Olympic Games (VANOC, BOCOG) are included below to illustrate the similarities. A snapshot of organizational life in VANOC four years before the games shows that it is structured along wider functional areas than Beijing which two years before its summer games has broken these down more broadly to their component parts.

Table 6.3 Beijing 2008 Organizing Committee budget

Revenues	US $ m	%
Television rights	709.00	43.63
Top sponsorship	130.00	8.00
Local sponsorship	130.00	8.00
Licencing	50.00	3.08
Official suppliers	20.00	1.23
Olympic Coins Program	8.00	0.49
Philately	12.00	0.74
Lotteries	180.00	11.08
Ticket sales	140.00	8.62
Donations	20.00	1.23
Disposal of assets	80.00	4.92
Subsidies	100.00	6.15
National Government	50.00	3.08
Municipal Government	50.00	3.08
Others	46.00	2.83
Total	1625.00	

Expenditure	US $ m	%
Capital Investments	190.00	11.69
Sports facilities	102.00	6.28
Olympic village	40.00	2.46
MPC and IBC	45.00	2.77
MV	3.00	0.18
Operations	1419.00	88.31
Sports events	275.00	16.92
Olympic village	65.00	4.00
MPC and IBC	360.00	22.15
MV	10.00	0.62
Ceremonies and programmes	100.00	6.15
Medical services	30.00	1.85
Catering	51.00	3.14
Transport	70.00	4.31
Security	50.00	3.08
Paralympic Games	82.00	5.05
Advertising and promotion	60.00	3.69
Administration	125.00	7.69
Pre-Olympic events and co-ordination	40.00	2.46
Other	101.00	6.22
Surplus	16.00	0.98
Total	3234.00	

Source: Beijing Olympic Games Bid Committee, 2000.

Table 6.4 Beijing 2008 Infrastructure budget

Capital Investments	Construction cost (US $ m)								Total
	2001	2002	2003	2004	2005	2006	2007	2008	
Planned nonolympic specific expenditure									
Environmental protection	1000	1000	1500.00	1500.00	1500.00	1300.00	827.0	0.00	8627.00
Roads and railways	547	592	636.00	636.00	636.00	313.00	313.00	0.00	3673.00
Ariport	12	30	31.00	12.00	0.00	0.00	0.00	0.00	85.00
Olympic related expenditure									
Sports venues	0	0	212.57	425.13	495.99	283.42	12.01	0.00	1429.12
Olympic Village	0	0	0.00	0.00	110.62	158.87	134.74	38.25	442.48
Total	1559	1622	2379.57	2573.13	2742.61	2055.29	1286.75	38.25	14256.60

Source: Beijing Olympic Games Bid Committee, 2000.

VANOC is organized into the following areas, which continue to grow as the committee approaches the event's start date. By Games time, VANOC will have approximately 1,200 employees.

Sport, Paralympic, and Venue Management has responsibility for all sport services, competition management, medical services, doping control, and sport performance and legacy.

Venue Development is responsible for the construction of venues.

Service Operations and Ceremonies is responsible for the operations and services planning of all non-competition venues of the Games, including the Olympic and Paralympic villages and International Broadcasting Centre, as well as overlay, and fit out of the Games venues, the implementation of 'Look of the Games' and signage, and all aspects of culture and ceremonies.

Revenue, Marketing, and Communications is responsible for revenue generation through sponsorship sales and services, ticketing, and licenced merchandising. The torch relay programme and all external and internal communications, including communications services, community relations, media relations, image and creative services, and web development are also the responsibility of this division.

Technology and Systems has responsibility for all technology services and support, such as information technology, Internet, telecommunications, and audio-visual systems. This group is also responsible for press operations, accreditation, and is the Olympic and Paralympic broadcasting liaison.

Human Resources, Sustainability and International Client Services is responsible for the recruitment and training of the Games workforce, including volunteers and organizing committee employees while ensuring aboriginal participation and guaranteeing sustainability. This division is also responsible for all aspects of language services, official languages, and international and national client services.

Finance and Administration has responsibility for all financial aspects of the Games including budgets, procurement, risk management, project management, and administration.

General Counsel is responsible for all legal aspects of the Games, including the structure and governance of the organizing committee for both the Olympic and Paralympic Games (Vancouver Organizing Committee for the 2010 Olympic and Paralympic Winter Games, 2006).

BOCOG was established in 2001, five months after Beijing won the right to host the 2008 Games. In 2006 the Committee consisted of 22 departments looking after functions from venue planning to environmental management. BOCOG gradually expanded its departments and staff in line with the demands of the Olympic preparations. By the year 2008, it is estimated that there will be more than 30 departments and 4,000 staff under the BOCOG umbrella. BOCOG's general goal has been to host high-level Olympic Games and high-level Olympics with distinguishing features, to realize the strategic concepts of 'New Beijing, Great Olympics' and to leave a unique legacy for China and world sports. For the Chinese organizers the concept of high-level includes high-level sporting venues, facilities, and competition organizations, high-level opening ceremonies and cultural events, high-level media services and favourable press commentary, high-level security work, high-level volunteers and services, high-level transportation and logistics, high-level urban civility and friendliness, and high-level performances by Chinese athletes. Associated to the high-level performance are the three concepts that have been adopted for the Beijing Olympic Games, namely, the Green Olympics, the High-tech Olympics, and the People's Olympics (Beijing Organising Committee for the 2008 Olympic Games, 2006).

In BOCOG the Executive Board has ultimate leadership and decision-making authority. To achieve the 'high-level Olympic Games with distinction', the Supervision Commission of the Games of the XXIX Olympiad was set up at the same time as BOCOG was formally established. This commission's role has been to exercise independent and overall supervision of preparations for the Beijing Olympic Games as well as over the BOCOG staff, its expenditures and revenues, and procurement of goods and materials for the Games. In 2006, BOCOG had 25 functional departments, as follows, operating to prepare and develop critical plans and programmes required for the Games. What follows is a detailed account of the responsibilities of the various departments as described by BOCOG (Beijing Organizing Committee for the 2008 Olympic Games, 2006).

General Office: Responsible for co-ordination and liaison between BOCOG and various government departments and agencies as well as other co-host cities, the BOCOG internal administration activities and the management of city operations projects for the Beijing Olympic Games.

Project Management Department: Responsible for the compilation, project management, and adjustment of overall development plans for the Beijing Olympic Games and the Beijing Paralympics. It is also responsible for providing services for BOCOG's decision-making activity and for organizing and co-ordinating BOCOG's risk management programmes.

International Relations Department: Responsible for liaison and communications efforts with the IOC, NOCs, regional Olympic committees, and other Olympic Family members as well as providing other relevant services.

Sports Department: Responsible for the organization of all sports competitions of the Beijing Olympic Games and the Beijing Paralympics.

Media and Communications Department: Responsible for information preparation and news release activities, media relations, and general publicity as well as the contents of the BOCOG official website and the Olympic education efforts and programmes.

Construction & Environment Department: Responsible for the co-ordination and supervision of the Olympic venues and facilities construction and relevant environmental protection issues.

Marketing Department: Responsible for all fund-raising activities associated with the Beijing Olympic Games, the conduct of marketing activities, which include the sponsorship programme, licencing programme and the ticketing programme; and the implementation of the IOC's marketing plan within the jurisdiction of the Chinese Olympic Committee.

Technology Department: Responsible for providing the Beijing Olympic Games and the Beijing Paralympics with necessary technical services and support in effectively maintaining competition records, information, telecommunications, and other operations.

Legal Affairs Department: Responsible for the management of the contracts and other legal affairs of BOCOG and the protection of the Olympic Games' intellectual property rights.

Games Services Department: Responsible for accommodation, transportation, accreditation, catering, and spectator services as well as the operations of the Olympic Village and other venues for the Beijing Olympic Games and the Beijing Paralympics.

Audit and Supervision Department: An administrative institution of the BOCOG Supervision Commission, this department is responsible for supervising the use of BOCOG's funds and materials as well as the performance of its staff and their honesty and self-discipline.

Human Resources Department: Responsible for the organizational set up and human resource management of BOCOG, the recruitment, training, and management of staff and volunteers.

Finance Department: Responsible for the compilation and management of BOCOG's general budget, annual budget, and accounting, and the execution of Beijing Olympic Games' financial risks management, logistics management, and procurement.

Cultural Activities Department: Responsible for the organization and implementation of the Olympic youth camp and various ceremonies as well as other Olympic cultural activities, and the design and management of the look and image of the Beijing Olympic Games.

Security Department: Responsible for security affairs and maintenance of public order during the Beijing Olympic Games and the Beijing Paralympics.

Media Operations Department: Responsible for logistical planning and operations of the main press centre, the international broadcasting centre, and the venue media centres. Also charged with providing equipment and services to accredited news media personnel.

Venue Management Department (VMD): This is a functional department in BOCOG which is in charge of co-ordinating, promoting, and fulfilling venue-oriented management and also the game-time venue operations. During the preparation phase, the VMD is leading the managing work as well as planning and co-ordinating all the competition venues and non-competition venues as a whole in order to facilitate the venue-oriented tasks. During the Games time, the VMD will be part of the Main Operations Centre (MOC) in managing the team operations at every site. Meanwhile, the co-ordination among various departments during the transition period from Olympics to Paralympics on the venue operations is also the VMD's responsibility.

Olympic Logistics Centre: Aiming to provide materials and services for Olympic Games, Paralympic Games, and the relative activities. It is mainly responsible for the material planning, and for the procurement, storage, distribution, tracking, management, retrofit, and disposal of all the materials for hosting and staging the Olympic and Paralympic Games.

Paralympic Games Department: Responsible for making plans for the preparatory work of the 2008 Paralympic Games; facilitating the preparatory work and monitoring implementation of plans; liaising and communicating with the IPC, the IPSFs, the IOSDs, and the organizations for the disabled in China; providing guidance and suggestions on Paralympic-specific work; and assisting in training, promotion, and advertisement of the Beijing Paralympic Games.

Transport Department: Responsible for transport services and traffic management for Olympic Family the Beijing Olympic Games and Paralympic Games.

Olympic Torch Relay Centre: Responsible for the planning and implementation of the Beijing 2008 Olympic Torch Relay, including relay cities liaison, route arrangement, torchbearer operations, ceremonies, celebrations, public relations, media communications, image design, marketing, brand management, security, laws and regulations, logistics, and transportation.

Accreditation Department: Responsible for the accreditation of Olympic Family Members, Paralympic Family Members, and the workforce participating in Beijing 2008 Olympic Games and Paralympic Games.

Opening & Closing Ceremonies Department: Responsible for drawing and implementing the work programme as well as the organizational and operational policy for the opening and closing ceremonies of the Beijing Olympic Games, and forming working teams for the ceremonies to ensure the smooth integration of the processes that include the creation, production, rehearsal, and the final implementation of the schemes.

Olympic Village Department: Established in 2006, the Olympic Village Department is responsible for the preparation and operation of the Olympic Village of the Olympic Games and Paralympic Games. Its main task is to prepare the Olympic Village; to formulate and implement the service standards, operation policies, and master plan of the Olympic Village project; to co-ordinate the preparations and operations carried out by related departments; and to supervise the Olympic Villages in the co-host cities.

Ticketing Centre: Responsible for ticketing production, sales, delivery, and ticketing operation for the Beijing Olympic Games and the Beijing Paralympic Games (Beijing Organising Committee for the 2008 Olympic Games, 2006).

Continental Games Organization

These games are not part of the Olympic Games but are examined here as related Olympic related events by virtue of the fact that they are organized by the continental association of NOCs. A year prior to the Olympic Games these events represent qualifying opportunities for athletes and a chance for NOCs to assess their elite sporting performance strengths. The structures of the organizing committees of the continental games resemble those of Olympic Games OCOGs and the involvement of the local government is also prevalent in the committee constitution.

The legal model chosen for the management of the EYOF took the form of (the JACA 2007 Foundation) a foundation determined by the prevailing Spanish law which applies to the constitution of foundations.

The JACA 2007 Foundation was set up in 2004, and its objectives were as follows.

The promotion and improvement of the organizational capacity and the development of human resources with regard to Winter Sports activities and competitions in JACA and in the Province of Huesca as a whole. The promotion and development of all necessary or advisable activities for the organization of the EYOF 2007 in Jaca, including carrying out promotional activities, elaborating technical studies, obtaining sponsors, drawing up proposals, etc.

The JACA 2007 Foundation was made up of the following patrons and persons:

- The Spanish Olympic Committee, represented by its President; The Aragonese Government, represented by the Councillor for Education, Culture and Sports; and the Superior Council of Sports, represented by the Secretary General for Sports.
- The Huesca County Council, represented by its President.
- The Town Hall of Jaca, represented by the Mayor who is the acting President of the foundation (European Youth Olympic Festival 2007, 2007).

At the heart of the Foundation, there was an Organization Committee in charge of the practical organization of the EYOF. This Organization Committee centralized organizational activities and dealt with them through a technical office that was responsible for setting up the general organization plan and for overseeing its progress. In accordance with a process established in the plan, the organization chart evolved in terms of the number of personnel (see figure 6.3 for the organizational chart of the JACA 2007 Organizing Committee) .

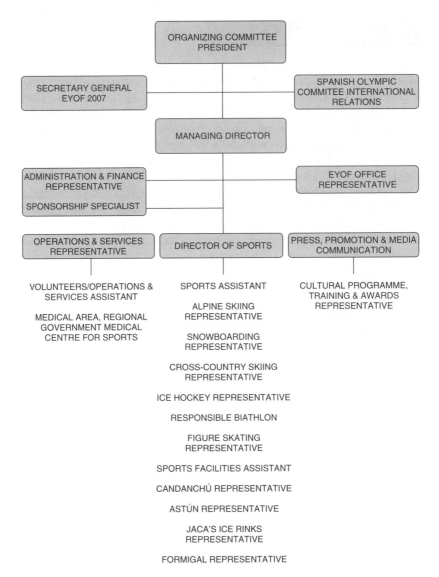

Figure 6.3 Jaca 2007 Organizing Committee structure (*Source*: European Youth Olympic Festival 2007, 2007)

Similarly, the Organizing Committee of the XV Pan American Games in Rio in 2007 (CO-RIO) was a non-government, non-profit entity directed by the Brazilian Olympic Committee (BOC), and with the participation of representatives of Rio de Janeiro's City Hall, of Rio de Janeiro's State Government, and of the Brazilian Federal Government. Structured according to the model of a Specific Purpose Society (SPE), having a limited term of duration, it was an

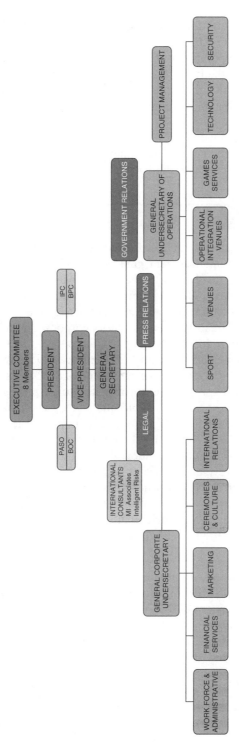

Figure 6.4 Rio 2007 Organizing Committee structure (*Source*: Organizing Committee of the XV Pan American Games Rio 2007, 2007)

independent organization for making agreements with government agencies and private entities (CO-RIO).

The structure and operation of the organizing committee strictly followed the terms provided by the PASO Statute, by the Olympic Charter, and by the host city contract for the XV Pan American Games, entered into by PASO, the BOC and Municipal Government of Rio de Janeiro with the support of the Federal Government of Brasil.

CO-RIO (see figure 6.4 for an illustration of its structure) was in overall charge of organizing the Games, including planning and implementation of all activities directly related to the Rio 2007 Pan American Games.

Change in OCOGs

Organizational change in OCOGs is affected by the time-scale of preparations for the event and the management guidance provided by the IOC. Others stakeholders who are involved with the Games also influence the rate and nature of change. Malfas (2003: p. 143) provide a thorough consideration of the organizational and structural evolution in the life cycle of the Sydney's OCOG. SOCOG was established in 1993 as a statutory corporation under the Sydney Organising Committee for the Olympic Games Act 1993 by the NSW Parliament, and became part of the host city contract, which involved the IOC, the AOC, and the City of Sydney. His examination of SOCOG's contextual and structural characteristics provides useful insights into the process of identifying critical events and decisions, which could qualify as transitional points in the organization's life cycle. Effectively, certain events or decisions in SOCOG's life cycle have been classified as 'critical' ones, in the sense that they provoked considerable changes in the organization as a whole. SOCOG's life cycle was marked by a series of events and decisions which had the potential to trigger organizational transitions. However, according to the perceptions of SOCOG's managers and the analysis of the relevant document data Malfas (2003) claims that only a limited number of such events and decisions had a transitional effect on the organization's operations. For SOCOG, these included the following:

- The observation of the Atlanta Games by SOCOG's staff, in August 1996.
- The appointment of NSW Minister for the Olympics, Michael Knight, to the position of President of SOCOG, in September 1996.
- The shift of SOCOG's operations to the Games' venues under the co-ordination of the Main Operations Centre (MOC), in May 2000.
- The end of the Games, in October 2000.

The two initial events, which occurred almost simultaneously, signified the transition of SOCOG's operations from a formative stage, which was termed by Malfas (2003: p. 220–221) as 'Start-up Period', to a stage of significant growth and development, namely the 'Build-up Period'. The establishment of the

Table 6.5 Sydney 2000 Organizing Committee organizational characteristics over its life cycle

Age	Start-up period	Build-up period	Games-time period	Close-down period
Size	Medium	Medium	Large	Small
Environment	Simple/dynamic	Complex/relatively stable	Complex/relatively stable	Simple/stable
Resource dependence	High	High	High	Moderate
Power	High external control	High external control	High external control	High external control
Strategic capacity	Low	Low	Low	Low
Specialisation	Little specialisation	Much specialisation	Much specialisation	Little specialisation
Unit grouping	Functional-based	Functional and place-based	Place-based	Functional-based
Liaison devices	Few liaison devices	Many liaison devices	Few liaison devices	Few liaison devices
Formalisation	Little formalisation	Much formalisation	Some formalisation	Little formalisation
Centralisation	Centralisation	Limited decentralisation	Decentralisation	Selective decentralisation
Training	Little training	Some training	Much training	Little training
Basic part	Strategic apex	Technostructure/operating core	Operating core	Technostructure/operating core
Basic co-ordination mechanism	Mutual adjustment	Standardisation of work processes	Mutual adjustment	Standardisation of outputs

Source: Malfas 2003.

MOC in May 2000 marked the shift of SOCOG to another organizational phase, that is the 'Games-time Period', which ended in October 2000, when the event was finished. The later event indicates SOCOG's shift to the last stage of its operations, the 'Close Down Period', which naturally ended in December 2000 when the organization officially dissolved. Malfas (2003) provides a summary of the structural and processual features of SOCOG in Table 6.5.

Malfas (2003) concludes that the fact that the IOC owns the Games, yet it delegates the responsibility for their organization to an OCOG, which is often dependent on governments and commercial organizations, inevitably creates a weak organizational model usually enabling more powerful and strategically located interests to prevail.

In effect, although the IOC's institutional framework concerning the organization of the Games seems solid, it is effectively adjustable to the conditions of the place and time in the name of the Games' success. For example, the Sydney Olympics occurred after the privately funded Olympic Games in Atlanta, which was in many respects an organizational failure. As a result, in the subsequent Olympics in Sydney the IOC encouraged the deep involvement of the public sector in order to guarantee the success of particular areas of the Games, such as security and transportation, both of which substantially failed in Atlanta. Besides, the increasing magnitude and organizational complexity of the Olympic Games is naturally beyond the scope of an OCOG, and therefore the IOC seeks the involvement of credible agencies, usually the host governments, which have the capacity to provide the necessary facilities and services for the event and guarantee its financial viability. Therefore, the role of OCOGs in the organization of the Games might be weakened in the future, and perhaps we might see the role of the host governments or the NOCs of the host countries to be strengthened Malfas (2003: p. 219).

Venuisation in OCOGs

The transitional phase of SOCOG's transfer of operations to the Games' venues under the co-ordination of the MOC is also known as the venuization process. This is further explored below drawing examples from the Turin organizers of the 2006 Winter Olympic Games.

The post-games reports of the Turin Organizing Committee for the Olympic Games (TOROG) provide valuable information on how the structure of this organization evolved.

Planning and development of structures and measures necessary for holding the Games were regulated by law (Interventions for the Torino 2006 Olympic Winter Games') and subsequent modifications that defined the skills and responsibilities of the parties involved in implementation. Within the legislative framework defined by law, TOROC was responsible for defining the series of works, on which implementation has began through the preparation of feasibility studies. To build the permanent structures, another law established the Italian (Italy) Agenzia per lo svolgimento dei XX Giochi Olimpici Invernali Torino 2006 (Torino 2006), a public institution with the twofold function of being the party responsible for carrying out the Interventions Plan and the contractor for their construction, in accordance with law (the so-called Merloni Law) (see Figure 6.5 for the organization tree of TOROG).

The organization of the Games required the committee to carry out activities which unfolded in time with increasing complexity: from the strategic planning phase, to operational scheduling, to the actual management of the competition within the venues (competition and non-competition venues in which the Winter Olympics were held). The evolution of activities was reflected in the Committee structure, which progressively transformed its internal organizational model to effectively manage the operability of the venues. During the Games, each venue worked as an autonomous decentralized structure, equipped with the proper resources and skills to manage the event and activities, within the scope of an organization that ensured professional support, guidance, and superior capability for interventions on a centralized level. The process of venuisation includes the passage necessary from an organizational model 'by function' to a specific model 'by venue' through the progressive assignment of human resources to the positions that they will fill during the games. A venue team is a basic organizational unit for each venue composed of people with supplementary skills able to meet the various needs associated with the event. The TOROG organizers (Torino 2006, 2006) describe the process as follows:

> The managerial activities of venues were planned and initiated through drafting the operational plans. These, together with the policies and procedures, are a tool to integrate activities for the individual functions at each venue and they identify the inter-functional nodes of the venue processes, rendering them more effectively manageable by the team; the development of useful simulation initiatives: analysis of activity planning for a typical day, round table meetings regarding purposely prepared critical scenarios and practical exercises; the beginning of risk assessment to identify, evaluate, and classify events or situations that may have a negative impact on the holding of the games. The analysis is followed by the establishment of mitigating activities to reduce the probability that a negative event will occur or to limit its impact. Starting from the venue preparation phase in view of the games the full responsibility for the management of activities is entrusted to the Venue Manager. The organizational model planned for non-competition venues during the games like the Olympic Village(s) and the media Village(s); the Olympic Stadium, dedicated to the Opening and Closing Ceremonies, and the International Airport, anticipated the attendance of two key figures guiding the venue team: the Venue Manager, in the capacity of the person responsible for co-ordinating the Venue team and the operational result of the event in its entirety; and the

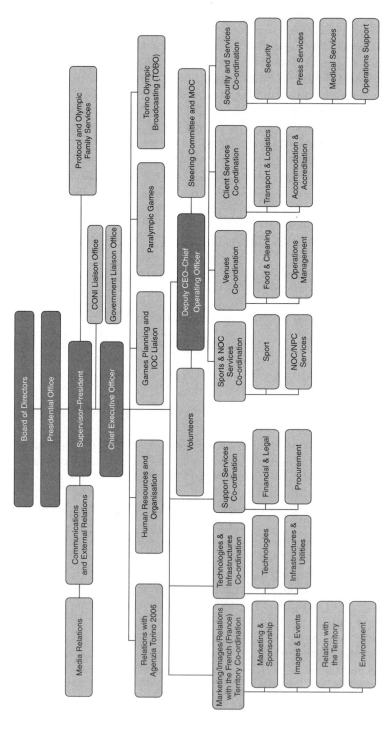

Figure 6.5 Torino 2006 Organizing Committee structure (*Source*: Torino 2006, 2006)

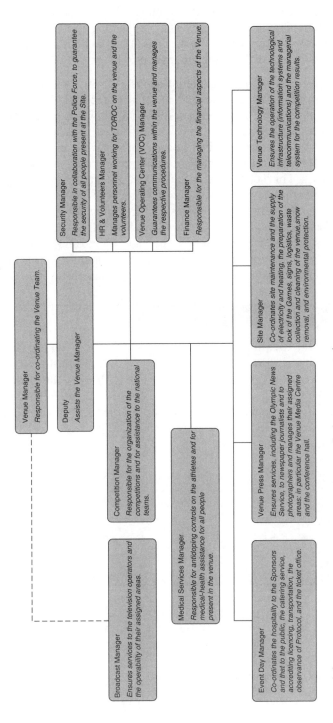

Figure 6.6 Torino 2006 Venue team structure (*Source:* Torino 2006, 2006)

The boxes in the figure contain the following text:

Venue Manager
Responsible for co-ordinating the Venue Team.

Deputy
Assists the Venue Manager

Security Manager
Responsible in collaboration with the Police Force, to guarantee the security of all people present at the Site.

HR & Volunteers Manager
Manages personnel working for TOROC on the venue and the volunteers.

Venue Operating Center (VOC) Manager
Guarantees communications within the venue and manages the respective procedures.

Finance Manager
Responsible for the managing the financial aspects of the Venue.

Venue Technology Manager
Ensures the operation of the technological infrastructure (information systems and telecommunications) and the managerial system for the competition results.

Site Manager
Co-ordinates site maintenance and the supply of electricity and heating, the preparation of the look of the Games, signs, logistics, waste collection and cleaning of the venue, snow removal, and environmental protection.

Competition Manager
Responsible for the organization of the competitions and for assistance to the national teams.

Broadcast Manager
Ensures services to the television operators and the operability of their assigned areas.

Medical Services Manager
Responsible for antidoping controls on the athletes and for medical-health assistance for all people present in the venue.

Venue Press Manager
Ensures services, including the Olympic News Service, to newspaper journalists and to photographers and manages their assigned areas: in particular the Venue Media Centre and the conference hall.

Event Day Manager
Co-ordinates the hospitality to the Sponsors and that to the public, the catering service, accrediting licencing, transportation, the observance of Protocol, and the ticket office.

Site Manager, responsible for maintaining all Site structures and their proper functioning and the supply of services to support the other functions (p. 41) (see Figure 6.6 for further detail on the lines of responsibility stemming from a TOROG venue manager).

On successful transition to the venue teams TOROG was involved with the test events that are used to check the levels of preparedness of plans and processes. In the case of TOROG the responsibility for the organization and conduct of the various tests events was entrusted to Local Organizing Committees (LOCs), non-profit institutions purposely set-up and in general composed of TOROC, the National Federation concerned, and of local institutions involved. For TOROC, the Sport Test Events were an important occasion to assess the level of preparation attained by its organization, the adequacy of its skills, and of the infrastructures built for the 2006 Winter Olympics. These test events project allowed the TOROC organizers to identify critical aspects and define impact levels. The majority of issues were recorded in relation to the operation of the (permanent and temporary) infrastructures and to the organizational model implemented to manage the events.

OCOGs and Government Departments

Examples of the relationships between OCOGs and a host country's national, regional and local government are considered in the case of the London and Beijing Games. The UK Government, through the Secretary of State for Culture, Media and Sport and the Mayor of London work in close and partnership to manage the preparation and staging of the Games in London. Other agents in the governance model are presented in Figure 6.7.

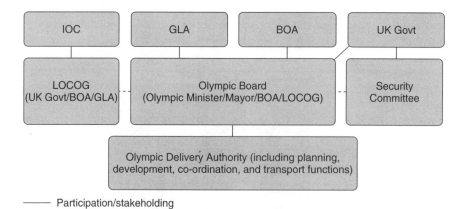

—— Participation/stakeholding
------ Contractual relationship/consultation

Figure 6.7 London 2012 Olympic delivery and co-ordination structure (*Source*: London 2012 Bid Committee, 2005)

It is interesting to note that the only contractual relationships identified in the diagram are those between the IOC and the OCOG, the Olympic Board and the Security Committee, while the rest, including those with the national and local government are identified as signifying stakeholding.

Under the direction of the Mayor of London, the London Development Agency (LDA) and Transport for London (TfL) are planning together for the 2012 Games. The five London boroughs around the planned Olympic Park also work under joint planning arrangements. This group is working closely with the Greater London Authority (GLA) and the LDA on planning for the Olympic Park. However, ultimate planning authority for the Games is with the specially formed Olympic Delivery Authority (ODA) and the Cabinet-level Minister responsible for delivering the Games. The ODA reports to the Olympic Board which comprises of the Olympic Minister, the Mayor of London and Chairmen of the BOA and the LOCOG. The London 2012 Bid Committee (2005) anticipated that:

> The ODA will ensure delivery of the physical infrastructure for the Games, including the construction of the new venues. To help do this, it will be granted special powers to purchase land, compulsorily if necessary, and to grant detailed planning permissions in the Olympic Park. The ODA will also ensure effective co-ordination of central and local government in the preparation and staging of the Games. The ODA will be granted special powers to enable it to operate as an Olympic Transport Authority, which will control and co-ordinate all the transport requirements of the Games.

In addition to the ODA, OCOGs have to work with local government departments and as Table 6.6 illustrates there are also local government departments outside the host city that get involved in games preparations to ensure venue availability and overlays, security, transport, and any necessary planning permissions.

The ODA of the London 2012 Games has the authority to deliver and co-ordinate every aspect of public sector support for the Games with the local authorities. It is a corporate body established by Section 3 of the London Olympic Games and Paralympic Games Act 2006, for administrative purposes it is classified as an executive non-departmental public body and for national accounts purposes, it is classified to the central government sector (see Figures 6.8 and 6.9 for ODA's budget approval processes). Further references to the organizational particularities and intricacies of the ODA are included below:

> Reference to the ODA includes any subsidiaries and joint ventures that are classified to the public sector for national accounts purposes. If such a subsidiary or joint venture is created, the arrangements between it and the ODA shall be set out in the normal corporate constitutional documents, such as the Memorandum and Articles of Association. Any additional understanding reached between the entity and ODA must also be set out in writing. Under Section 4(1) of the Act the ODA may take any

Table 6.6 London 2012 Cities and communities hosting the Olympic Games

Authority		Role
London	Corporation of London	Marathon
	London Borough of Barnet	Cycling (Road)
	London Borough of Brent	Football
	London Borough of Camden	Softball, Cycling (Road)
	London Borough of Greenwich	Gymnastics (Artistic/ Rhythmic/Trampoline), Equestrian, Basketbell, Badminton, Modern Pentathlon, Shooting
	London Borough of Hackney	Olympic Park
	London Borough of Haringey	Cycling (Road)
	London Borough of Merton	Tennis
	London Borough of Newham	Olympic Village, Olympic Park, Boxing, Judo, Wrestling, Taekwondo, Table Tennis, Weightlifting, Marathon, Race Walk, Water Polo
	London Borough of Tower Hamlets	Olympic Park, Marathon, Race Walk
	London Borough of Waltham Forest	Olympic Park
	Westminster City Council	Archery, Cycling (Road), Baseball, Beach Volleyball, Triathlon, Marathon
Outside London	Birmingham City Council	Football
	Cardiff City Council	Football
	Glasgow City Council	Football
	Manchester City Council, Trafford Metropolitan Borough Council	Football
	Newcastle City Council	Football
	Buckinghamshire County Council, South Bucks District Council	Rowing, Cance/Kayak (Flatwater)
	Hertfordshire County Council, Borough of Broxbourne	Canoe/Kayak (Slalom)
	Dorset County Council, West Dorset District Council, Weymouth and Portland Borough Council	Sailling
	Essex County Council, Brentwood Borough Council	Cycling (Mountain Bike)

Source: London 2012 Bid Committee, 2005.

Budget approval process

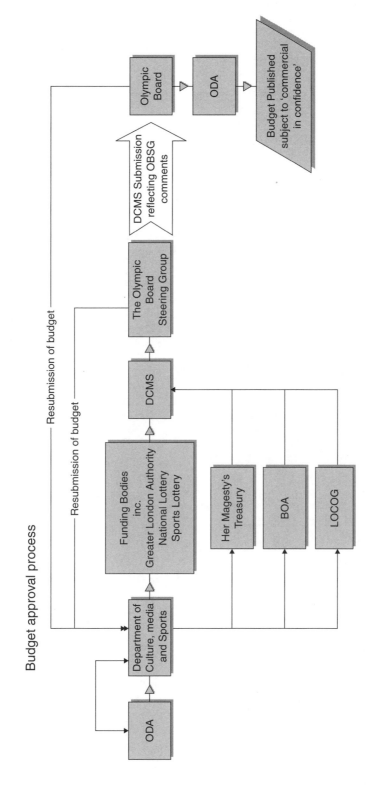

Figure 6.8 London 2012 ODA's budget approval processes (*Source*: Olympic Delivery Authority, 2006)

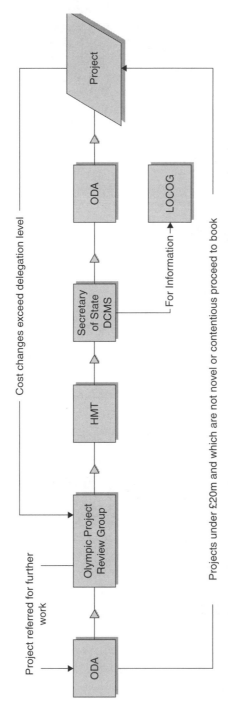

Figure 6.9 London 2012 ODA's budget approval processes for projects over £20 million (*Source:* Olympic Delivery Authority, 2006)

action that it thinks necessary or expedient for the purpose of preparing for the Games; making arrangements in preparation for or in connection with the use or management, before, during, or after the Games, of premises and other facilities acquired, constructed, or adapted in preparation for the Games; or ensuring that adequate arrangements are made for the provision, management, and control of facilities for transport in connection with the Games.

Section 4(3) of the Act requires the ODA to exercise its functions, where relevant, with regard to the desirability of maximizing the benefits that may be derived from the preparations for the Games, whilst contributing to sustainable development. The ODA's powers derive from these general functions, and from other sections of the Act granting specific powers to the ODA. In short, the tasks of the ODA are to deliver the Games venues and infrastructure in time for the Games in a way which embeds equality and diversity and contributes to the delivery of a sustainable legacy and to plan and co-ordinate the transport plans for the Games in line with the decisions taken by the Olympic Board in fulfilment of the host city's obligations within the host city contract (Olympic Delivery Authority, 2006: pp. 5–6).

As regards Beijing, the equivalent of the ODA is the Beijing 2008 Project Construction Headquarters Office. Under the leadership of the Beijing municipal government, it

takes unified command and comprehensive co-ordination of the construction of the Olympic competition venues and their affiliated facilities. The Beijing 2008 Project Construction Headquarters Office is an administrative body in charge of day-to-day operations of the Headquarters. The Headquarters is responsible for the following: (1) Overall planning of the construction schedule for the Olympic competition venues in Beijing, their affiliated facilities, and related urban infrastructure. It is also responsible for instructing the governments of concerned districts and counties and owners of the competition venues to work out comprehensive plans of construction schedule and detailed network plans, examining and finalizing the plans, and submitting reports to the Communist Party of China (CPC) municipal committee and the municipal government of Beijing on the execution of the plans. (2) Initiation of preliminary steps for the construction of the venues and related affiliated facilities in Beijing, co-ordination and overseeing of feasibility study, layout and design, land requisition and residents relocation, first-stage land development, groundbreaking, and other works. The Headquarters also co-ordinates the task of different departments of the municipal government in assembling the projects for examination and approval in order to ensure their commencement on schedule. (3) Deployment of the task for the construction of the venues and affiliated facilities in Beijing, resolution of any problems which may arise in the course of construction, with an aim at carrying out the construction in a unified and harmonious manner to meet all the requirements in the areas of safety, quality, construction time limit, function, and cost. (4) Co-ordination of the task for environmental improvement in places adjacent to the venues and affiliated facilities in Beijing. (5) Collection, clear-up, statistical compilation, and management of the information related to the construction of the venues and affiliated facilities, proper management of archives by relevant departments. (6) Overseeing the enforcement of contracts signed by the venue owners and government authorities, redressing any violations. (7) Supervising the implementation of compulsory criteria set up by the state in the areas of safety, quality, fire fighting, and environmental protection during the construction of the venues, overseeing and guaranteeing the implementation of the technical criteria and quality requirements set up by the IOC and IFs. (8) Managing a portion of the Olympic Special Fund for the municipal government, overseeing its use. (9) Superintending tender and bid activities of project entities and concerned departments of the Beijing municipal government to ensure transparency in every stage of construction. (10) Engaging in publicity of the Olympic venues in Beijing, strengthening links with the Beijing Organizing Committee for the Games of the XXIX Olympiad and with concerned departments of the state government. (11) Attending to other matters assigned by the municipal Party committee, the municipal government of Beijing, and BOCOG. The 2008 Project Construction Headquarters Office has established the following functional departments in to perform the aforementioned responsibilities: General Office, Project Planning and Key Project Construction Department, Competition Venue Construction Department, Training Venue Construction Department, Urban Facility Construction Department, Quality Control Department, Technology Department, Finance and Budget Department, Audit Department (audit room), and Communications Department (Beijing 2008 Project Construction Headquarters Office, 2006).

Related to the work of OCOGs and the organizations charged with delivery of the infrastructure works for the games is the task of broadcasting. The following section considers the organizations responsible for this task drawing examples from the Athens 2004 Games and Beijing 2008.

Olympic Broadcasting

In recent Olympic Games the broadcasting of the games has been the responsibility of a separate organization which according to the Athens organizers it aimed to be a multi-disciplinary organization that serves as eyes and ears of the world (Athens Organising Committee for the Olympic Games, 2001).

Our mission is to produce the best television coverage of the Olympic Games ever – coverage that will make Athens, Greece and ATHOC proud. We will also strive to provide services that the right holder broadcaster RHB appreciate and provide broadcasting coverage that billions of worldwide viewers will enjoy.

In terms of its key services, the Athens Olympic Broadcasting (AOB) produced the international television and radio (ITVR) signal from each venue. This signal was produced at the venues and sent to the International Broadcasting Centre (IBC) where it was distributed to each of the RHB. The AOB is also responsible for the IBC which serves the broadcasting function at games time (see Figure 6.10 for the structure of the IBC).

In the case of the 2004 Games the AOB designed, built, installed and operated the IBC where ATHOC was responsible for providing the various broadcasting services during the games. The AOB also retrofited the finished building into the IBC where it co-ordinated and provide facilities and services for the RHB on behalf of ATHOC (see Figure 6.11 with list of Athens 2004 RHB).

AOB was also responsible to produce features and maintain an Olympic archival service for the RHB, the IOC, and ATHOC.

AOB will develop features for use by the RHB concerning Athens, Greece and the Games. Further AOB will provide the official Games video archives to the IOC and ATHOC at the conclusion of the Games. AOB will assist ATHOC in the formation and design of the venues in order for ATHOC to provide the appropriate services for AOB and the RHB. This includes consultation on how the venues should be designed and operated in relation to camera positions/platforms, commentary positions, commentary Control Room, mixed zone, and the broadcast compound (Romero, 2001).

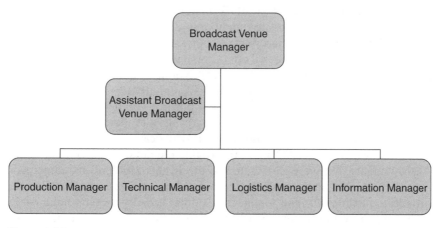

Figure 6.10 Athens 2004 IBC structure (*Source*: Athens Organising Committee for the Olympic Games, 2001)

- EBU (European Broadcasting Union)
- NBC (National Broadcasting Company)
- CBC (Canadian Broadcasting Corporation)
- Seven Network Ltd. (Australia)
- JC (Japan Consortium)
- OTI (Latin and South America)
- ASBU (Arab States Broadcasting Union)
- SABC (South Africa)
- CTP (Chinese Taipei Pool)
- URTNA (Africa)
- CBU (Caribbean Broadcasting Union)
- PTNI (Phillipines)
- KP (Korea Pool)
- TVNZ (New Zealand)
- ABU (Asia-Pacific Broadcasting Union)

Figure 6.11 Athens 2004 RHB (*Source*: Athens Organising Committee for the Olympic Games, 2001)

Key operating principles for the AOB included (1) Delivery by ATHOC to AOB of the items included in the integrated master plan. This included pre-games plans, policies, and procedures; Games-time delivery of fit-up schedule and operational items that ATHOC was responsible for (i.e. venues, competitions, transportation, technology, accommodations, accreditations, etc.). (2) ATHOC's understanding of who is responsible for what services in regards to broadcasting so that time is not wasted debating responsibility.

Reference to its operations (multilateral and unilateral) the AOB was the primary point of contact and liaison for planning and operations concerns with ATHOC (see Figure 6.12 for AOB structure).

AOB oversaw all multilateral and unilateral requirements: co-ordinated project management for all of AOB; planned a management system for co-ordination of various on-site functions and ensured venue related information flow to all AOB departments. Furthermore, it developed a broadcast management team to oversee all operational functions at each venue; established procedural policies for Broadcast Venue Management to resolve broadcast-related issues; co-ordinated all unilateral requirements and requests at the venues (including: camera positions/platforms, commentary positions, mixed zone, announce positions, results distribution, and commentator information system); co-ordinated Broadcasters' meeting, and all venue tours/surveys for AOB and the Rights Holders; wrote and edited all AOB manuals that were distributed to the Rights Holders, including production, technical, and graphics; plans, develops, designs, and installed all broadcast facilities for the Games (including: broadcast compound, cable paths, power requirements, platform construction, lighting requirements, audio requirements, and communication systems); designed and implemented broadcast technology systems; co-ordinated design and construction of the

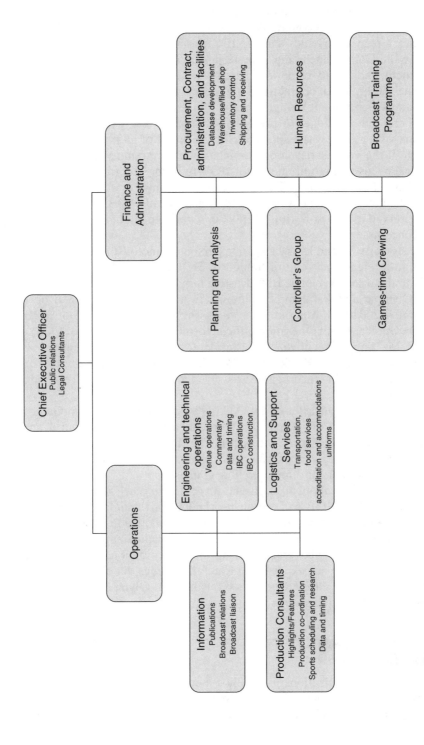

Figure 6.12 Athens 2004 AOB structure (*Source*: Athens Organising Committee for the Olympic Games, 2001)

commentary positions and commentary control rooms with ATHOC at each venue; planned all telecommunications for AOB and the Rights-Holding Broadcasters at the venues and the IBC; designed the production plan to televise the Games (including: camera positions, platform height, specialty equipment, and beauty cameras); liaised with the Sports department to co-ordinate the timing of competition and coverage; liaised with the 'Look of the Games' department to highlight the image of the Games; co-ordinated with Ceremonies/Medals to present the emotion and excitement of the Olympic experience; was responsible for the hiring of all production teams at each of the venues; developed a management system to co-ordinate all logistical needs and requirements for AOB full-time and freelance personnel; planned air and ground transportation systems for AOB personnel; established an accommodations and food plan for all AOB personnel; and finally, served as a liaison with ATHOC in regards to Rights Holders' logistical concerns.

In a similar vein and led by the same person (Manolo Romero) the BOB is a Sino-foreign joint venture funded by BOCOG and the IOC OBS, to perform the role of Olympic Broadcasting Organization (OBO) for Beijing 2008 Olympic and Paralympic Games. It was officially established on 6 September 2004 with Manolo Romero as The General Manager of BOB, and Ma Guoli as Chief Operation Officer, former Sports Director of China's CCTV. Mr Jiang Executive, Vice-President of BOCOG, was elected as Board Chairman of BOB, and the IOC Coordination Commission Chairman, Mr Hein Verbruggen was given the title of the Vice Board Chairman of BOB.

As the Host Broadcaster of the 2008 Olympic and Paralympic Games, BOB will provide ITVR signals for the broadcasters across the world, and plan, design, install, construct, and operate the IBC and the necessary broadcast facilities in other venues, and provide related services for the Rights-Holding Broadcasters during the Beijing Games.

In 2006 BOB had about 40 staffs and was going to reach 80 till the end of 2007. Before 2008, BOB will recruit nearly 300 staff compared with 4,000 during games time in 2008. BOB will use around 60 outside broadcast vans, 1,000 cameras, building an over 80,000 s.m. IBC to produce approximate 4,000 hours of live Olympic coverage. During the games billions of cumulative worldwide audience are expected to watch the games via over 200 broadcasters (Beijing Organising Committee for the 2008 Olympic Games, 2006) whose needs and requirements will be met through the work of BOB.

Allied Companies

In addition to organizations like Helios mentioned in Part Two there are several specialist agencies which assist OCOGs and the IOC Marketing Department in managing and enhancing Olympic marketing programmes.

This section lists a select few as an illustration of the type of work they contribute in the organization of the Olympic Games. Satchi and Satchi developed and produced the 'Celebrate Humanity' Olympic promotional announcements of 2004 and David Grant Special Events, a hospitality company established in 1987 that has been working with the IOC since 1996, assisted in the development and management of premier hospitality programmes for members of the Olympic Family. Its customers include the White House, Giorgio Armani, and Christian Dior.

IOC representatives are quoted in relations to their experience of the company during the Athens 2004 Games: '... your dedication, hard work, and outstanding professional staff have helped to make the Olympic Club a great success. Your decade of Olympic experience and your leadership at these Games led the success of our hospitality operation ... There is no doubt that without your know-how, we would not have been able to offer such a quality experience to our guests' (David Grant Special Events, 2007).

Similarly, Michael Payne, ex- Director of Marketing, of the IOC is quoted confirming the company's excellent performance: 'Once again you and your team have delivered beyond expectations. The Olympic Partners Club in Salt Lake was, without doubt, our most successful operation to date. With everything else that is going on at the games, its great to know that our Partner Club is in one of the most experienced set of hands in the business – just making the whole thing look simple and seamless! – Hosting the world's business, political and sporting elite is no small challenge. You continue to render a great service to the Olympic Movement by providing such quality and professional operation ...' (David Grant Special Events, 2007).

Allied commercial providers are also active in the area of ticket and hospitality packages. Jet Set Sports and CoSport formed a new partnership to develop exclusive hospitality packages for the 2010 Vancouver Olympic and Paralympic Winter Games. The companies are working with VANOC to develop and supply official hospitality packages that aim to provide spectators with 'one stop' to book exclusive packages for the 2010 Winter Games. The hospitality packages are intended to be made available in Canada and in countries where Jet Set Sports has acquired ticket-selling rights and will be developed and available for booking two years before the start of the Vancouver Games.

VANOC Chief Executive Officer John Furlong explained the role of this company as follows: The excitement and anticipation for Canadians and people around the world wanting to attend the Games in 2010 is already very high and is continuing to gain momentum.

With help from Jet Set Sports we know that those fans will receive a first-class hospitality experience. We have witnessed Jet Set first-hand at other Games and their level of service and attention to detail are remarkable.' Jet Set Sports' six-year Official Supporter partnership with VANOC provides sponsorship rights for the 2010 Winter Games and the Canadian Olympic Teams participating at the Beijing 2008, Vancouver 2010, and London 2012

Olympic and Paralympic Games. Jet Set Sports will be the exclusive provider of hospitality packages in Canada (Sports Business, 2007).

Partners

Olympic partners bring more than financial support to the Olympic Games. Their involvement through technology, expertise, products and personnel is fundamental to the actual staging of the games. Building and managing the technology for the Sydney Games was the 'largest, most complex information technology challenge in the world' according to IBM General manager, Worldwide Olympic Technology (International Olympic Committee, 2001: p. 66).

For VISA, managing a global sports sponsorship also poses particular challenge. The OCOGs change and we need to educate the OCOGs on our rights as sponsor, how we work with our members, and what the pass through rights are with various merchants. The IOC, after years of negotiations and relationship interchange, understands the nuances of our category, but that does not always mean the OCOG will (Schaaf, 2004: pp. 313–314).

Partnership with the Olympic Movement is ultimately a business investment. Olympic sponsors may have diverse reasons for investing in the Olympic Movement, but Olympic partnership is a sound business decision if sponsors meet their corporate objectives.

> We leverage our Olympic sponsorship in lost of different ways that differentiate and enhance our brand. We use it in a way that helps us build relationships with key clients and people who sell our products. We use it to motivate our people to sell products, and we use it in a way that motivates and makes our employees feel better about the company. For all those reasons and all those ways we use it – we get a return on our investment Steve Burgay, Senior Vice President, Corporate Communications, John Hancock (International Olympic Committee, 2001: p. 71).

The emergence of Olympic sponsorship as an increasingly utilized method of marketing communication represents one of the most significant marketing developments in recent decades (International Olympic Committee, 2004d). It is about brand enhancement and showcasing products, services and partnerships on the world's stage.

Furthermore, the prestige of the Olympic Games as the world's leading sports event and the related benefits to corporate sponsors are evidenced in previous Olympic sponsors. Olympic sponsorship programmes reinforce the Olympic Movement in three basic ways. They provide valuable financial resources to the Olympic Family; Olympic sponsors provide vital technical support for the organization and staging of the Olympic Games and the general operations of the Olympic Movement and they help to promote the Olympic ideals by heightening public awareness of the Olympic Games and increasing support for the Olympic athletes. All the above were considered as a great motive for Alpha Bank in order to be involved with the Olympic Sponsorship of the Athens 2004 Games as it pledged US $65 million to secure the sponsorship for the banking sector (Athens Organising Committee for the Olympic Games, 2002: p. 84)

Xerox had a similar rationale:

> We increased the valuable customer base by something like 25% over that period. We worked on various customer groups and saw the penetration of that customer group with products increased by 40%. The Chief Executive Office of AMP Ltd. Xerox has announced 20% growth in Australia in 2000 as a result of Olympic sponsorship, double the company's normal business growth in the country (International Olympic Committee (2004d: p. 77).

The Games themselves provide a global marketing platform and form one of the world's premier corporate hospitality opportunities.

> Leaders of most Fortune 500 companies travelled to Sydney in September, comprising part of the 50,000 corporate guests who were entertained by the Olympic Games. Hospitality programmes have increasingly become major components of Olympic marketing as partners use their hospitality resources to maintain or increase revenue, to strengthen customer relationships, or to reward key employees. Olympic partnership also helps to build mutually beneficial business relationships and alliances. By entering into the Olympic sponsorship family, a company opens doors to networking within the business community where previously no door had even existed, allowing growing brands a chance to place themselves in good company with national and global business leaders (International Olympic Committee, 2001: p. 80).

The sponsor hospitality village in Beijing includes provision within the Olympic Green and at competition sites for a range of sponsor hospitality opportunities. This was planned as a tiered basis with Sponsor Hospitality privileges being dependent on the level of sponsorship provided to BOCOG with all Sponsor programmes being developed on a purely cost recovery basis. The Sponsor Hospitality programme also includes the development of a Sponsor Hospitality Village for use by TOP sponsors in the form of a high-rise, luxury multi-purpose apartment building close to the main stadium. Its aim being to provide facilities for entertainment and recreation, business conferences, and exhibitions and general sponsor hospitality services during the Games period (Beijing Olympic Games Bid Committee, 2000).

The IOC offers additional support to partners through workshops, dedicated account managers, the Olympic marketing extranet, Olympic Television Archive Bureau, Olympic marketing manuals, Olympic Photographic Archive Bureau (maintained in partnership between IOC and Allsport, the Olympic Museum, Olympic Games film crews for creation of corporate or in house videos), research with leading research companies and sports marketing surveys (International Olympic Committee, 2001: pp. 82–84).

In addition to the TOP partners there are also opportunities for 28 categories of official licencees, which in the case of the Athens 2004 Games (Athens Organizing Committee for the Olympic Games, 2002) included: jewellery, perfumes, key chains and magnets, swimwear, umbrellas, sunglasses, ceramic/porcelain house ware, glassware, bags and travel goods, frames and photo albums, leather goods, outdoor toys, posters and greeting cards, pyjamas and underwear, pins, toys, publications, socks, bedding products, shoes, hats, baby clothing, sports clothing, casual wear polo shirts, towels and bathrobes, puzzles and board games, and computer accessories.

Planning and Delivering Design Parameters

Job specialization, performed horizontally and vertically varies in the life of the group of organizations delivering the Olympic Games, the Olympic Games Group (OGG). Typically it starts as low at the formative stages of the operation when there are few mainly senior staff who undertake to develop their broad areas, for example, finance, marketing, IOC and Government relations. As these areas become more established and new staff are appointed specialization increases horizontally to reflect the various levels of responsibility. On reaching the threshold of the test events specialization continues to increase and culminates during the games with the arrival of the IFs who take control in the fields of play, the incorporation of the specialized roles of the volunteer as well as the various contractors. During the games, the athletes' teams and the media join the OGG and perform their respective specialist roles of competing and media coverage. Behaviour formalization is gradually established in an OGG through the use of operating instructions, job descriptions, rules, and regulations. The Olympic knowledge reports aid this process as does the existence of the IOC games management framework discussed earlier. During the planning stages formalization is high and during the games when the various parts of the OGG need to deliver in a integrated fashion some levels of formalization are also present. This is linked to standardization of processes with the aim of regulation and predictability. High levels of behaviour formalization are also present during games times for example by the volunteers, the athletes and the IF officials who represent part of the operating core of the OGG. The accreditation of media representatives and athletes as well as the contracts the latter sign with their NOCs aid the formalization of such behaviour processes in the OGG.

166

Training in the OGG takes place before the games and is achieved through the use of formal instructional programmes to transfer skills and knowledge. Aspects of indoctrination which refers to programmes and techniques by which norms of the members of an organization are standardized are also present as OCOGs and ODAs engage in organizational communication exercises with the public at large as well as amongst its staff and voluntary force. For the IFs, the media and the athletes' teams training may have also taken place during their participation in previous games.

Unit grouping refers to the choice of the bases by which positions are grouped together into units and in the case of the OGG the grouping in OCOGs starts as functional, then becomes venue based and during the games it becomes market based as the various service recipients (NOCs, athletes, media representatives, spectators, IOC members, etc.) are attended to by defined units (unit size varying depending on the unit and the timeframe).

Planning and control systems are used to standardize outputs and are important for performance evaluation and action planning. In the OCOGs, planning is predefined to a great extent. For ODA's (or their equivalent government machinery delivering the infrastructure work) planning systems often have limited experience of anything as big as the preparation of the Olympic Games and processes there appear unique to the host country and city. The control systems for OCOGs are evidenced in the submission of progress reports, the co-ordination commission visits, and the host government's overseeing of its operations. For ODAs, the parliament represents the ultimate control mechanism. For athletes the major role of control is performed by their NOCs with whom they have signed contracts, and by the WADA that performs anti-doping tests. With reference to planning, the IOC uses the games period to regroup its network whilst also keeping a supervisory role on operations.

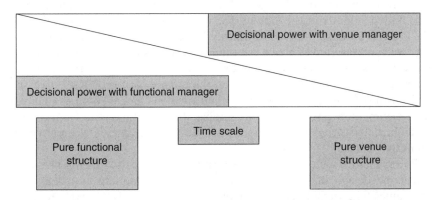

Figure 6.13 Decisional power in OCOGs (*Source*: Adapted from Mintzberg, 1979: p. 176)

Liaison devices in and among organizations refers to a series of mechanisms used to encourage mutual adjustment within and between units. In the OGG they include the establishment of liaison positions, task force standing committees, and integrating managers overlooking the work of the major OGG members.

Decentralization refers to the diffusion of decision-making power and can be either vertical or horizontal. Vertical and horizontal diffusion occurs in the planning stages and remains high even during games time when decisions need to be reached at the lowest possible level to prevent congestion in senior management echelons. During venuization (see Figure 6.13) decision power moves from the function to the venue manager as they will ultimately deliver the games from the venue.

This period is often very testing and challenging for staff who need to realign themselves to the new reality. Not only do the functional based offices need to physically be moved to the various venues, staff loose and gain power in the process, too, and this has implications on their status, remuneration, and overall involvement and satisfaction.

Situational Elements

The age and size of the OGG are clearly linked. Following successful bidding the structures that will support the games are established through the new organizations (OCOG, ODA, OBS) and as infrastructure works commence numerous contractors become involved in the undertaking. As regards the technical system used by the operating core of the OGG this includes (a) the IOC master planning framework that affects the OCOG, the IFs and the OBS and (b) the city planning mechanisms (from planning applications to the city's 'functioning' during the Olympic Games). For athletes, the media and the IFs age and size have a different dimension as they exist independently of the Games. The environment of the organizations in the OGG is understandably multifaceted given the number of organizations involved and the rate of change in their life cycle as an OGG. Following the bid's success a dynamic and complex environment surrounds the OGG. As intensity rises in negotiations between the members of the OGG, diversity and hostility feature, too, and bring their own challenges. With the Games approaching the environment maintains these features till Games time when hostility is replaced by the Games' euphoria that creates an environment that is usually friendly overall.

Power factors such as money, authority, knowledge, and media presence, affect the design of the OGG structures whilst planning and delivering the games. The outside control of the OCOG by the IOC and – to some extent – the IFs, the political agendas prevalent in the ODA, the capitalist priorities of the sponsors, the personal needs of politicians and civic leaders, the resistance of anti-Olympics groups, the athletes' messages to the world via their individual and collective behaviour are examples of the forces that vie for survival or supremacy in the Olympic 'arena'.

Co-ordinating Mechanism

The co-ordinating mechanisms that explain the fundamental ways in which organizations in the OGG co-ordinate their work vary among members of the group. For OCOGs work starts being co-ordinated by the standardization of work processes (as per planning process requirements) and during the Games, standardization of outputs (for manual workers) and skills (for white collar workers). In ODAs work is co-ordinated by work outputs as completion of various intermediate projects is necessary for subsequent ones to start and ultimately be completed before the Games or test events. The interdependencies between ODA projects is very high and co-ordination among these projects through standardization of outputs provides the glue that holds the organizations together.

Nevertheless, such a representation masks the roles of the longstanding members of the OGG; the broadcasters, the IFs, the NOCs who send the teams, the media representatives and the sponsors who take part in the event's processes and the above discussion sought to redress this imbalance of attention.

Urban Development and the Law

Papathanasopoulou (2004) argues that locating and permitting of building development projects was a problem for the Athens organizers due to the complexity and intricacy of Greek legislation. This affected land uses and the location of development projects, in particular large scale ones. Additional challenges were due to the great diffusion of responsibility among authorities for permitting building development projects at all stages: location, environmental impact assessment, and building permission. Law 2730/99 (and 2947/2001) recognized the strategic significance of the Olympic Games to the evolution of the metropolitan area of Athens and determined the location of Olympic Projects in accordance with the regional, environmental, and urban development guidelines of the master plan of Athens. This legislation also incorporated regulations about effective permitting of Olympic works and special procedures were adopted and special agencies founded in order to simplify and accelerate the issuing of permits.

The long procedure required for the acquisition of development land, both in securing the concession of public land as well as in the compulsory expropriation of private land was an additional problem. In the case of Athens, this problem was tackled by the enactment of Laws 2598/1998 and 2730/1999. In these Laws issues of compulsory acquisition and of concession of land for the construction of Olympic works – and other relevant or connected works – were settled, aiming mainly at cutting down the time of necessary procedures. A related problem was the numerous petitions made before the Council of State against the decisions of the state on environmental and town planning issues for the construction of transport projects, necessary for the organization and execution of the Olympic Games (Papathanasopoulou, 2004: p. 23).

A final legal challenge according to Papathanasopoulou (2004) was the incorporation in Greek law of the obligations resulting from the host city contract and ensuring a fruitful cooperation of public authorities at fulfilling them. The void in the Greek legal system regarding the rules and regulations prescribed by the Olympic Movement was bridged through special regulations that were incorporated in the Greek legal system (Law 2598/98) which founded an Olympic structure within the Greek public administration. In 1999 the Special Secretariat of Olympic Games was established, which eventually functioned as a support unit to the inter-ministerial Committee founded in 2000 and an executive body where Ministries were represented by their general or Special Secretaries. The emphasis on the public administration structure becomes justifiable when one realizes the overwhelming importance of public bodies in the field of Olympic works. The year 1999 was crucial to the method of development of Olympic projects. In the summer of this year the government dropped the concept of Olympic Village as a private venture developed by concessionaire and decided instead to commission the Workers' Housing Authority, a public concern enterprise, to develop and fund it as a regular project for the Authorities' beneficiaries (the largest such project ever). Gradually, a decision was taken that all Olympic projects were to be financed by public funds and constructed by public bodies as public works (the only exceptions being the Media Villages of Maroussi and Pallini). All necessary regulations to that end were incorporated in Law 2819/2000 p. 24.

Bosio (2006) describes the establishment of specialist bodies like Association 'Torino 2006' to build Turin facilities from public funds and in essence taxpayers money. He also identifies the commercial links between the FIAT Group automobile business and the vociferous objections to similar – development justified – projects such as the high-velocity train that will connect main Italian cities and ultimately offer high-speed connections to Europe, too. Bosio also highlights the development and work of those groups and movements against the Olympics drawing examples from the work of Comitato Nolimpiadi and the play fair at the Olympics, Oxfam led movement that highlights the plight of workers' rights in the sports industry.

Bertone and Degiorgis (2004) co-founders of Comitato Nolimpiadi present eight years' work of denouncing the Olympic Games in Turin. In their book they claim to analyse the organizational mechanism behind the games and reveal the commercial interests that it serves. They claim that the games present colossal financial manoeuvres in the financial benefit of the few and that the economic, social, and environmental impacts are negative.

So in the truth by State Law 285/2000 TOROC (a private organization – by contract a kind of 'local representative' of the IOC, another private, foreign organization!) has the power to head a public italian body indicating the 'Agenzia Torino 2006' what and where to build.

Baraggioli (2006) writes on the forms of governance of cultural processes in the Olympic valleys in Turin and sought to answer the questions: who should take charge of the Olympic heritage? Who can (or should) legitimately seat on the table that affronts this problem? In his analysis of cultural actors in the governance of space he maps stakeholders and their activities in Turin. Such an approach may aid researchers in identifying the reasons why certain stakeholders take centre stage whilst others remain at the periphery of activity. Understanding the organizations that make up the OGG, their missions and legal frameworks allows a better evaluation of the process of creation of the Olympic legacy positive or negative depending on whose interests are being considered.

Structure

The structure that emerges after the consideration of the organizations and agents in the OGG is similar to the divisionalized and missionary structures as defined by Mintzberg (1979). Operators of this hybrid organization can be trusted to pursue their goals, without intense central control and therefore the structure can be decentralized. Its prime co-ordination mechanism is socialization or standardization of norms and skills. The ideology of this group is a particularly significant force that give it a sense of mission. Building on the charisma of the athletes and the attractiveness of their contest, the Olympic brand remains strong and its message, deeply ideological. As mentioned earlier divisionalized structures are challenged by the forces that want them to break up in autonomous units without the need of the headquarters. In the case of the OGG the monopoly of the IOC ensures that no such threat materializes and the strong ideology gathers support for the IOC president and the IOCs members, the declared protectors of Olympism and the Olympic Games.

Conclusion

The organization of the Olympic events has been the focus of this part, outlining the bidding and planning phases involved in their delivery. The discussion identified the organizations involved in the event management process as well as the infrastructure development projects that accompany the Olympic Games in the last decades. Olympic broadcasting was considered, too in light of its significance in revenue generation for the IOC as were the continental games organized by the continental NOC associations, a host city and the country's NOC. Significant agents in the OGG also include the media organizations, the broadcaster, the athletes, the sponsors, contractors and the county's civil service and attention was given to the ways in which work is co-ordinated between the various parts, the design of the OGG and the contextual situational features that it finds itself in during the events' organization. In conclusion, the defining structural features of the OGG were identified as sharing characteristics of a missionary divisionalized structure that maintains its focus predominantly through its strong brand name and the associated Olympic ideology.

Epilogue

Having considered the parts that make the Olympic Movement and their respective roles the discussion has revealed the structure of the movement and discussed its divisionalized features. With the IOC leading the movement by virtue of its monopoly it is important not to forget that the IOC is also a chain operator of company and franchise units (the former in the case of the NOCs and the latter in the case of OCOGs that are granted permission to organize the Olympic Games) as well as the main owner of numerous subsidiaries. These and the allied entities of the sponsors add another dimension to the structure as do the public organizations that get involved in the development of the infrastructure works.

The OGG in essence is comprised by a number of organizations that are permanent to the group (IOC, IFs, NOC, Sponsors, Media, IOC preferred suppliers, OBS) and others that are periodic (ODAs, OBOs, OCOGs). The labour process analysis reveals that the IOC controls the key production mechanisms and franchises them to countries and cities that want to become part of its business. Providing that other events cannot surpass the attractiveness of the Olympic Games and their associated regenerations, the IOC will remain an important monopolistic power that can be selective on who it works with for the games delivery.

The detailed discussion on the bidding and planning processes undertaken by the various organizations reveals the complex web of interactions that take place and highlights the challenges posed by the agendas of the various parts. By standardizing Olympic Games management structures and processes to a great extent, the IOC is engaged in the macdonaldization of the event production system to maintain its quality control and brand image. Notwithstanding the strengths of standardization, isomorphic processes may also lead to decline in individuality and entrepreneurship by the local games hosts.

The issues of sustainability, autonomy, and commercialization are particularly prevalent in the Olympic structures and are likely to define the future of the movement. As the games grow in size and importance the point of social responsibility of the IOC is raised and questions are asked on whether it is doing enough to protect countries from negative side effects of its operations. Future analysts will rightly question whether planners are planning for games requirements, legacy requirements, or for capitalist gain. The IOC's attempts to capture the impact of the Olympic Games in a systematic way are steps at the right direction but as the impact evaluations are performed by an IOC franchise, the OCOG, impartiality can not be expected. If public opinion polls were to consistently suggest that the Olympic Games have increasing negative impacts, the main income source of the IOC, the broadcasters, and the sponsors can rightly be expected to withdraw their current levels of investment. This has the potential to critically halt the IOC as a chain operator and transnational corporation and it is therefore important for it to increase its profile as a socially responsible organization. Being structurally situated at the top of a divisionalized structure, the tensions for it to be replaced by autonomous units underneath are great. EU moves to streamline organizational activity in sports entities and associated calls for reform may eventually lead to some loss of autonomy by permanent members of the OGG. The issue of autonomy is a key one for the IOC that sees redefinitions in the sports market regulations as potentially threatening to its power (see Allison, 2005 for a discussion on how there could be a development of deeper nationalist voices which see SINGO power and homogenization as the enemies of local sporting culture). As Shropshire (1990; 1995) suggests the US sports industry is affected by unscrupulous, unethical, unqualified, and even criminal activity (p. 20). Professional sports leagues possess a legally protected monopolistic power that allows each league to limit the number of new franchises and use this artificially created franchise scarcity to the fullest financial advantage of the franchise owners already in the league p. 9. In a parallel view American cities are not alone in their pursuits of sports franchises as bidders for Olympic Games extent equal efforts to attract the Games to their respective city.

Paradoxically, the stronger commercial footing the IOC develops, the greater the potential for these interests to seek to remove its monopolistic power to ensure perfect market conditions for their capital growth. Athletes' groups can also be part of such a process as increasingly some see that they are treated as a commodity by sports federations and national elite sport development systems but are nevertheless not allowed market choices on where and how they develop their own market's worth.

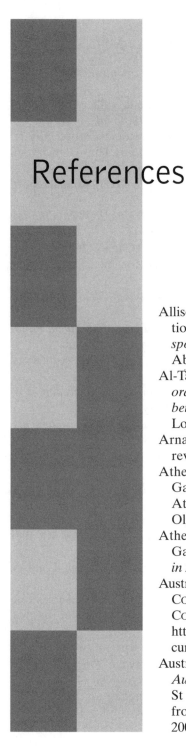

References

Allison, L. (Ed.) (2005). Afterword: More questions than answers. In *The global politics of sport: The role of global institutions in sport*. Abingdon: Routledge.

Al-Tauqi, M. (2003). *Olympic solidarity: Global order and the diffusion of modern sport between 1961 and 1980*. Unpublished Ph.D., Loughborough University.

Arnaut, J. L. (2006). Independent European sport review. Office of the UK Presidency of the EU.

Athens Organising Committee for the Olympic Games (2001). *Athens 2004: Progress report*. Athens: Athens Organising Committee for the Olympic Games.

Athens Organising Committee for the Olympic Games (2002). *Salt lake 2002. See you in Athens in 2004*. Athens: Serafim Kotrotsos.

Australian Olympic Committee (2004). CONSTITUTION OF THE AUSTRALIAN OLYMPIC COMMITTEE INCORPORATED retrieved 1/15 from http://www.olympics.com.au/files/25/constitution_current_jun06.pdf

Australian Olympic Committee (2006). *2005 Australian Olympic Committee annual report*. St Leonards: Australian Olympic Committee, from http://www.olympics.com.au/files/02/2005_AOC_AR_Webcompl180506.pdf.

Australian Olympic Foundation Limited (2006). *2005 Annual Report Australian Olympic Foundation*. St Leonards: Australian Olympic Foundation Limited.

Banner, D. & Gagne, E. (1995). *Designing effective organisations*. London: Sage.

Baraggioli, S. (2006). Le forme di governance nelle valli olimpiche. In P. Bondonio, E. Dansero, & A. Mela (Eds.), *Olimpiadi, oltre il 2006. Toriono 2006: Secondo rapporto territori olimpici*. Roma: Carocci editore.

Bedeian, A. G. (1980). *Organisations, theory and analysis*. Hinsdale: Dryden Press.

Beijing 2008 Project Construction Headquarters Office (2006). Annual report. Beijing: Beijing 2008 Headquarters' Office.

Beijing Olympic Games Bid Committee (2000). *Beijing 2008 candidature file*. Beijing: Beijing Olympic Games Bid Committee.

Beijing Organising Committee for the 2008 Olympic Games (2006). *Annual report*. Beijing: Beijing Organising Committee for the 2008 Olympic Games.

Bertone, S. & Degiorgis, L. (2004). *Il libro nero delle olimpiadi di torino 2006*. Genova: Fratelli Frilli Editori.

Bosio, R. (2006). *I giochi del potere. Gli abusi e la corruzione della multinazionale dei cinque cerchi*. Diegaro di Cesena: Marco Edizioni.

Bradach, J. L. (1998). *Franschise organizations*. Boston, Massachusetts: Harvard Business School Press.

Braverman, H. (1998). *Labor and monopoly capital: The degradation of work in the twentieth century*. New York: Monthly Review Press.

British Olympic Association (2005). *Report and financial statements*. London: British Olympic Association.

Bryman, A. (Ed.) (1988). *Doing research in organisations*. London: Routledge.

Bryman, A. (1989). *Research methods and organisation studies*. London: Unwin Hyman Ltd.

Burbank, M. J., Andranovich, G. D., & Heying, C. H. (2001). *Olympic dreams: The impact of mega-events on local politics*. London: Lynne Rienner Publishers, Inc.

Burns, T. & Stalker, G. M. (1961). *The management of innovation*. London: Tavistock.

Burrell, G. (1996). Normal science, paradigm, metaphors, discourses and genealogies of analysis. In S. R. Clegg, C. Hardy, & W. R. Nord (Eds.), *Handbook of organization studies*. London: Sage.

Carper, W. & Snizek, W. E. (1980). The nature and types of organizational taxonomies: An overview. *The Academy of Management Review, 5*(1), 65.

Chappelet, J. L. & Bayle, E. (2005). *Strategic and performance management of Olympic sport organisations*. Leeds: Human Kinetics.

Chappelet, J. L. & Theodoraki, E. (2006). Key questions for policy decisions in sport. In G. Di Cola (Ed.), *Beyond the scoreboard: Youth employment opportunities and skills development in the sports sector.* Geneva: International Labour Office.

Child, J. (1984). *Organization – A guide to problems and practice.* London: Harper and Row.

Clegg, S. R. (1990). *Modern organizations: Organization studies in the post-modern world.* London: Sage.

Clegg, S. R. & Dunkerley, D. (1980). *Organization, class and control.* London: Routledge and Kegan Paul.

Clegg, S. R. & Hardy, C. (Eds.) (1996). Organizations, organization and organizing. In *Handbook of organization studies* (p. 3). London: Sage.

Cochrane, A., Peck, J., & Tickell, A. (1996). Manchester plays games: Exploring the local politics of globalisation. *Urban Studies, 33*(8), 1336.

David Grant Special Events (2007). *Who we are.* Retrieved 1/15, 2007, from http://www.dgse.com.au/whoWeAre.asp.

Deloitte and Touche LLP (2006). *London Olympic and paralympic games.* Retrieved 1/10, 2007, from http://www.ukbudget.com/UKBudget2006/Business/Budget06_Olympics.cfm.

DiMaggio, P. J. & Powell, W. (1983). "The iron cage revisited" institutional isomorphism and collective rationality in organizational fields. *American Sociological Review, 48,* 147.

Doty, D. H., Glick, W. H., & Huber, G. P. (1993). Fit, equifinality, and organizational effectiveness: A test of two configurational theories. *The Academy of Management Journal, 36*(6), 1196–1250.

Dubi, C., Hug, P. A., & Griethuysen, P. (2003). Olympic Games management: From the candidature to the final evaluation, an integrated management approach. In *The Legacy of the Olympic Games 1984–2000.* Olympic Museum and Studies Centre. Lausanne.

Durkheim, E. (1957). *Professional ethics and civic morals.* London: Routledge and Kegan Paul.

Durkheim, E. (1984). *The division of labor in society.* London: Free.

Emery, P. R. (2001). Bidding to host a major sports event: Strategic investment or complete lottery. In C. Gratton & I. Henry (Eds.), *Sport in the city: The role of sport in economic and social regeneration.* London: Routledge.

Essex, S. & Chalkley, B. (1998). Olympic Games: Catalysts of urban change. *Leisure Studies, 17,* 187.

European Youth Olympic Festival 2007 (2007). *Technical office.* Retrieved 1/12, 2007, from http://www.jaca2007.es/ingles/oficina.htm.

Ferrand, A. & Torrigiani, L. (2005). *Marketing Olympic sport organisations.* Leeds: Human Kinetics.

Ferrel, O. C., Fraedrich, J., & Ferrel, L. (2005). *Business ethics: Ethical decision making and cases.* Boston: Houghton Mifflin.

Flyvbjerg, B. (2004). Phronetic planning research: theoretical and methodological reflections. *Planning Theory and Practice, 5*(3), 283.

Flyvbjerg, B. (2005). Design by deception: The politics of mega project approval. *Harvard Design Magazine, Spring/Summer,* 50.

Flyvbjerg, B., Bruzelius, N., & Rothengatter, W. (2003). *Megaprojects and risk: An anatomy of ambition*. Cambridge: Cambridge University Press.

Forster, J. & Pope, N. (2004). *The political economy of global sports organisations*. London: Routledge.

Foster, K. (2005). Alternative models for the regulation of global sport. In L. Allison (Ed.), *The global politics of sport: The rule of global institutions in sport*. Abingdon: Routledge.

Freeman, J. (1989). *Organizational ecology*. Cambridge, MA: Harvard University Press.

Fried, G. (2005). *Managing sport facilities*. Leeds: Human Kinetics.

Getz, D. (1991). *Festivals, special events and tourism*. New York: Van Nostrand Reinhold.

Giddens, A. (1979). *Central problems in social theory*. Berkeley: University of California Press.

Giddens, A. (1982). *Profiles and critiques in social theory*. London: Macmillan.

Gouldner, A. W. (1955). Wildcat strike: A study of an unofficial strike. London: Routledge and Kegan Paul.

Gratton, C., Shibli, S., & Coleman, R. (2005). Sport and economic regeneration in cities. *Urban Studies, 42*(5/6), 985.

Hassard, J. (1993). *Sociology and organization theory: Positivism, paradigms and postmodernity*. Cambridge: Cambridge University Press.

Hassard, J. & Pym, D. (1990). *The theory and philosophy of organizations: Critical issues and new perspectives*. London: Routledge.

Helios Partners Inc. (2006). *Our people: The helios executive team.* Retrieved 12/2, 2006, from http://heliospartners.com/people.asp.

Hofstede, G. (1980). Motivation, leadership and organization: Do American theories apply abroad? *Organizational Dynamics, 9*(Summer), 43.

Hofstede, G. (1984). The cultural relativity of the quality of life concept. *Academy of Management Review, 9*, 389.

International Olympic Committee (1999). *Olympic movement's agenda 21: Sport for sustainable development*. Lausanne: International Olympic Committee.

International Olympic Committee (2001). Marketing Report. Games of the XXVII Olympiad. Meridian Management SA for the International Olympic Committee.

International Olympic Committee (2004a). *Host city contract: Games of the XXX olympiad in 2012 working draft 19.05.2004.* Unpublished manuscript.

International Olympic Committee (2004b). *Official core terminology on Olympic and paralympic games*. Lausanne: International Olympic Committee.

International Olympic Committee (2004c). *Olympic charter*. International Olympic Committee.

International Olympic Committee (2004d). *The Olympic movement*. International Olympic Committee.

International Olympic Committee (2005a). *2006 marketing fact file*. Lausanne: International Olympic Committee.

International Olympic Committee (2005b). *Brand protection. Olympic marketing, ambush prevention and clean venues guidelines*. International Olympic Committee.

International Olympic Committee (2005c). *Candidature acceptance procedure: XXII Winter Olympic Games 2014*. Lausanne: International Olympic Committee.

International Olympic Committee (2005d). *Joint marketing programme agreement: Games of the XXX Olympiad in 2012*. International Olympic Committee.

International Olympic Committee (2006). *International Olympic Committee report 2001–2004*. Lausanne: International Olympic Committee.

International Olympic Committee (2007a). *History and role of the executive board*. Retrieved 8/10, 2006, from http://www.olympic.org/uk/organisation/ioc/executive/index_uk.asp.

International Olympic Committee (2007b). *Who belongs to the olympic movement?* Retrieved 11/2, 2006, from http://www.olympic.org/uk/organisation/movement/index_uk.asp.

International Olympic Committee and Institute of Sport and Leisure Policy, Loughborough University (2004). *Women, leadership and the Olympic movement*. Loughborough, UK: Institute of Sport and Leisure Policy, Loughborough University.

International Paralympic Committee (2003). *Spirit in motion. IPC brochure*.

International Paralympic Committee (2004). *IPC handbook*.

International Paralympic Committee (2006). *Annual report 2005*.

International Paralympic Committee. (2007). *IPC general structure*. Retrieved 10/8, 2006, from http://www.paralympic.org/release/Main_Sections_Menu/IPC/Organization/

Johnson, G. & Scholes, K. (1999). *Exploring corporate strategy: Text and cases* (5th edition). London: Prentice Hall.

Kanellis, I. (2005). *Ethnohouliganism: Expressions of the neo-Greek ideology during the Athens 2004 Olympic Games*. Athens: OKSY.

Katz, D. & Kahn, R. L. (1966). *The social psychology of organizations*. Chichester: Wiley.

Klausen, A. M. (1999). *Olympic Games as performance and public event: The case of the XVII Winter Olympic Games in Norway*. Oxford: Berghahn Books.

Knights, D. & Willmott, H. (Eds.) (1990). *Labour process theory*. Hampshire: The Macmillan Press Ltd.

Knox, K. (2004). Implications and use of information technology within events. In I. Yeoman, M. Robertson, J. Ali-Knight, S. Drummond & U. McMahon-Beattie (Eds.), *Festival and events management* (p. 97). Oxford: Elsevier.

Lawrence, R. & Lorsch, J. W. (1986). *Organization and environment: Managing differentiation and integration*. Boston, MA: Harvard Business School Press.

London 2012 Bid Committee (2005). *Political and economic climate and structure*. London: London 2012 Bid Commitee.

MacAloon, J. J. (1999). Anthropology at the Olympic Games: An overview. In A. M. Klausen (Ed.), *Olympic Games as performance and public event: The case of the XVII Winter Olympic Games in Norway*. Oxford: Berghahn Books.

Malfas (2003). An Analysis of the Organizational configurations over the life-cycle of the Sydney organizing committee for the Olympic Games, Unpublished PhD thesis, Loughborough University.

Malfas, M., Theodoraki, E., & Houlihan, B. (2004). Impacts of Olympic Games as mega events. *Journal of the Institution of Civil Engineers, 157*(ME3), 209.

Masterman, G. (2003). The event planning process: Strategies for successful legacies. *The Legacy of the Olympic Games 1984–2000,* Lausanne. Olympic Museum and Studies Centre.

Mayo, E. (1949). *The social problems of an industrial civilization with an appendix on the political problem*. London: Routledge and Kegan Paul.

McAlister, D. T., Ferrel, O. C., & Ferrel, L. (2005). *Business and society: A strategic approach to social responsibility* (2nd edition). Boston: Houghton Mifflin.

Meyer, A. D., Tsui, A. S., & Hinings, C. R. (1993). Configurational approaches to organizational analysis. *Academy of Management Journal, 36*(6), 1175.

Meyer, J. & Rowan, B. (1977). Institutionalised organizations: Formal structure as myth and ceremony. *American Journal of Sociology, 83*(2), 340.

Mintzberg, H. (1979). *The structuring of organizations*. London: Prentice Hall International.

Mintzberg, H. (1981). Organizational design, fashion or fit? *Harvard Business Review, 59*(1), 103.

Mintzberg, H. (1983). *Power in and around organizations*. Englewood Cliffs, NJ: Prentice-Hall.

Mintzberg, H. (1994). *The rise and fall of strategic planning*. London: Prentice Hall.

Mintzberg, H. & Queen, J. B. (Eds.) (1992). *The strategy process: concepts and applications*. London: Prentice Hall.

Morgan, G. (1997). *Images of organization*. London: Sage.

Olympic Delivery Authority (2006). *Management statement and financial memorandum*. London: Olympic Delivery Authority.

Olympic Foundation (2001). *The foundation 1997–2000 financial statements*. Lausanne: Olympic Foundation.

Olympic Museum (2001). *The museum 1997–2000 financial statements*. Lausanne: Olympic Museum.

Organizing Committee of the XV Pan American Games Rio 2007 (2007). *Organising committee*. Retrieved 1/15, 2007, from http://www.rio2007.org.br/pan2007/ingles/sobre_comite.asp.

Oxfam GB & International Confederation of Free Trade Unions (2004). *Play fair at the Olympics: Respect workers' rights in the sportswear industry*. Oxford: Oxfam GB.

Palaeologos, C. (1962). *Birth, establishment and development of the Olympic Games*. Second Session of the International Olympic Academy 9th–21st July, p. 131–144 Hellenic Olympic Committee. Olympia, Greece.

Palmer, R. (2006). *London's bid for the 2012 Olympic and Paralympic Games: The story of London's success*. Presentation to MEMOS VIV Executive Masters in Sports Organization Management. Rio de Janeiro.

Papathanasopoulou, V. (2004). *Briefing on the Athens 2004 Olympic Games: Finance and legal issues*. Lausanne: International Olympic Committee.

Parsons, T. (1956). Suggestions for a sociological approach to the theory of organizations. *Administrative Science Quarterly, 1*(1 June), 63.

Peters, T. & Waterman, R. (1982). *In search of excellence*. London: Harper and Row.

Pfeffer, J. (1997). *New directions for organization theory: Problems and prospects*. Oxford: Oxford University Press.

Powell, W. & DiMaggio, P. J. (1991). *The new institutionalism in organizational analysis*. Chicago: University of Chicago Press.

Pugh, D. S. & Hickson, D. J. (1976). *Organizational structure in its context: The Aston Programme 1*. Farnborough, Hants: Saxon House.

Quinn, J. B. (1977). Strategic goals: Process and politics. *Sloan Management Review, 19*(1), 21.

Reed, M. (1993). Organizations and modernity: Continuity and discontinuity in organization theory. In J. Hassard, & M. Parker (Eds.), *Postmodernism and organizations* (p. 163). London: Sage.

Reed, M. (1996). Organizational theorizing: A historically contested terrain. In S. R. Clegg, C. Hardy, & W. R. Nord (Eds.), *Handbook of organization studies*. London: Sage.

Roche, M. (1994). Mega-events and urban policy. *Annals of Tourism Research, 21*, 1.

Roche, M. (2000). *Mega-events and modernity: Olympics and expos in the growth of global culture*. London: Routledge.

Schaaf, P. (2004). *Sports Inc. 100 years of sports business*. New York: Prometheus Books.

Scott, W. R. (1992). *Organizations: Rational, natural and open systems* (3rd edition). Englewood Cliffs, NJ: Prentice Hall.

Shropshire, K. (1990). *Agents of opportunity: Sports agents and corruption in collegiate sports*. Philadelphia: University of Pennsylvania Press.

Shropshire, K. (1995). *The sports franchise game*. Philadelphia: University of Pennsylvania Press.

Slack, T. (2004). *The commercialisation of sport*. London: Frank Cass.

Sloane, T. (2001). *Operations core team*. Unpublished document. Athens Organizing Committee for the Olympic Games. Athens:

Smith, P. B. & Peterson, M. F. (1988). *Leadership, organizations and culture: An event management model*. London: Sage.

Sochi 2014 Bid Committee (2006). *Sochi 2014 candidature file, Vol. 1 Legal aspects*. Sochi: Sochi 2014 Bid Committee.

Sport and Development International Conference (2003). *The Magglingen Declaration and Recommendations*. Magglingen, Switzerland.

Sports Business (2007). *Jet set sports and CoSport provide 2010 sponsor hospitality.* Retrieved 3/22, 2007, from http://www.sportsbusiness.co.uk.

Sydney Organising Committee for the Olympic Games (1999). *Sydney 2000. 1999 Annual Report*. Sydney: Sydney Organising Committee for the Olympic Games.

The European Olympic Committees (2006). *Articles of association.* retrieved 1/17 from http://www.eurolympic.org/jahia/Jahia/engineName/filemanager/pid/13/NEW%20EOC%20STATUTES%20adoptes%208%2012%202006.pdf?actionreq=actionFileDownload&fid=17145

The Olympic Television Archive Bureau (2006). *What rights do the broadcasters retain?* Retrieved 10/5, 2007, from http://www.otab.com/faq/default.sps.

The Pan American Sports Organization (2007). *The pan American Sports Organization handbook*.

Torino 2006 (2006). *Sustainability report 2004/05*. Torino: Organising Committee for the XX Olympic Winter Games Torino 2006.

Vancouver Organizing Committee for the 2010 Olympic and Paralympic Winter Games (2006). *Annual report*. Vancouver: Vancouver Organizing Committee for the 2010 Olympic and Paralympic Winter Games.

Waitt, G. (2004). A critical examination of Sydney's 2000 Olympic Games. In I. Yeoman, M. Robertson, J. Ali-Knight, S. Drummond & U. McMahon-Beattie (Eds.), *Festival and events management* (p. 391). Oxford: Elsevier.

Wamsley, K. (2004). Laying Olympism to rest. In J. Bale & M. K. Christensen (Eds.), *Post-olympism? Questioning sport in the twenty-first century*. Oxford: BERG.

Whittington, R. (1989). *Corporate strategies in recession and recovery: Social structure and strategic choice*. London: Unwin Hyman.

Willmott, H. (1990). Beyond paradigmatic closure in organizational enquiry. In J. Hassard & D. Pym (Eds.), *The theory and philosophy of organizations*. London: Routledge.

Index